The Dynamics of
U. S. Capitalism

The Dynamics of U. S. Capitalism

Corporate Structure, Inflation,
Credit, Gold, and the Dollar

by Paul M. Sweezy
and Harry Magdoff

 New York and London

Contents

Preface

These essays were all written during the six years 1965-1971. This was a crucially important period in the development of U.S. and world capitalism during which the contradictions of the system mounted at an extraordinarily rapid rate, culminating in the collapse of the international monetary and trading arrangements so painstakingly constructed under U.S. hegemony in the immediate aftermath of the Second World War. Such a period inevitably offers splendid opportunities for observing and analyzing the true nature and working principles of the capitalist socioeconomic order; and it was largely in response to these opportunities rather than as efforts to expound a systematic body of doctrine that these essays were written. The picture which emerges from bringing them together is consequently impressionistic, but we hope that this does not mean that it is less vivid or persuasive.

In retrospect we can see that what determined the special character of the period 1965-1971 was the war in Southeast Asia. World capitalism suffered severe setbacks during and immediately after the Second World War, especially in Eastern Europe and China. But recovery began in Western Europe even before the end of the 1940s, and the next decade and a half was on the whole a period of consolidation and advance, with the United States playing the leading role and being apparently on the way to turning the whole "free world" into its imperial domain.

What put an end to this was the amazingly stubborn and successful resistance of the people of Vietnam to American

1

attempts to take over from France and establish client neo-colonial states in Indochina. As a result of this resistance U.S. military power was forced into an enormously costly stalemate which reacted on the entire structure of world capitalism. Significant sectors of the American people, particularly among the youth and the blacks, were shocked into political awareness and became the activating force of an antiwar and anti-imperialist movement which has already put serious constraints on the freedom of action of the U.S. ruling class and forced it to redouble its efforts to conceal if not modify its imperial designs. An inflationary process was unleashed in the U.S. economy which has so far defied efforts at control, persisting through the recession phase of the business cycle which set in in 1970 and compounding the material and psychological hardships of mass unemployment and job insecurity. At the same time the U.S. balance of payments, already in moderate if tolerable deficit as a result of expansionist international policies, was thrown out of kilter. The later 1960s were punctuated by a series of international monetary crises which placed an increasing and finally fatal strain on the gold-dollar standard adopted by the leading capitalist powers at the Bretton Woods conference in 1944. Within a few short years the world capitalist system, which had seemed to be so orderly and stable, was thrown into a state of turmoil unknown since the grim days of the Great Depression of the 1930s.

This is essentially a book about those years and the role played by U.S. capitalism, both as leader and as victim.* Some of the essays bear primarily on the institutions and structures which inexorably drove, and still drive, the leading capitalist power to seek undisputed domination over as large a part of the world as possible. Others are focused more on the consequences of this unbridled expansionism as it finally came into direct confrontation with forces it could no longer master.

We have not yet seen the end of this historical drama,

---

* As such it complements in the economic field our earlier book, *Vietnam: The Endless War*, by Paul M. Sweezy, Leo Huberman, and Harry Magdoff (Monthly Review Press, 1971). It should be added that three of the editorial essays in the present volume ("Foreign Investment," 1965; "Dollars and Gold," 1966; and "Gold, Dollars, and Empire," 1968) were co-authored by Leo Huberman.

far from it. The breakdown of the Bretton Woods system, officially confirmed by President Nixon on August 15, undoubtedly marks a turning point, but it does not tell us what comes next. As we write this, the capitalist world's monetary system, if indeed one may use the term at all, is in a state of total disarray. There is a remarkable consensus that if this continues, sooner or later the result is bound to be a fragmentation of the capitalist world into currency-and-trading blocs savagely fighting each other for power and profit. Where this can lead we know all too well from the experiences of two world wars: not only to terrible bloodshed and suffering but to great revolutions and massive defections from the capitalist system itself. There are those who argue that the leaders of this system, knowing the dangers, will pull back before it is too late and devise a workable substitute for the shattered structure of the last quarter century. This could take the form of a modified U.S. hegemony, accepted by the Europeans and Japanese, or of a condominium of the leading capitalist powers.

That this might happen cannot be denied. On the other hand, it also cannot be denied that such an outcome, giving the world capitalist system the prospect (though of course not the assurance) of two or three more decades of relative stability, would require the U.S. ruling class to moderate its ambitions and demands to a degree that it has so far shown no signs of being willing or able to do. A leadership that has consistently failed to understand what it was getting into in Indochina and which not only has not been able to extricate itself from that self-destructive adventure but even now is permitting the Nixon administration to plunge in deeper without the slightest prospect of achieving anything but more disaster—such a leadership can hardly be counted on to cooperate in finding viable solutions to the infinitely more complex problems which now face the world capitalist system. Unbridled expansionism seems to have bred an unbridled arrogance in those who bear the largest share of the responsibility for the future of U.S. and world capitalism. If this is indeed so, the stormy weather which we are now experiencing may be only a foretaste of what is still to come.

Whichever way events develop from here on, we hope

that these essays will help the reader to understand the forces at work and the stakes at issue. Prediction is not the proper function of social science, but understanding definitely is.

All but three of the pieces included in this volume originally appeared as unsigned editorial articles in MONTHLY REVIEW. The individual authorship and original place of publication of the others are in each case identified. Editing has been kept to the minimum necessary to eliminate errors and references which served a purpose only in the original context. Nothing of substance has been altered or added.

— P.M.S.
H.M.

New York
November 1971

Part I

Corporations, Expansion, and Stagnation

Problems of U. S. Capitalism

1965

Wave upon wave of prosperity, accompanied by ever higher levels of production and consumption, nourish the belief that the U.S. economy has found new sources of strength and that remaining weaknesses can be fairly easily overcome. The main reasons for this renewed faith are advanced in varying degrees by both radical and conservative commentators: (1) the new technology is in effect a second industrial revolution and is performing a role similar to the first industrial revolution in fostering long-range economic growth; (2) the new competition between socialism and capitalism induces extensive aid and investment in the Third World, which in turn creates new markets for advanced capitalist countries; (3) the political acceptance of the welfare state as a necessary approach to social development; and (4) the availability of an economic "tool box" which can be used to maneuver a capitalist economy so as to avoid serious crises.

Since the United States is the leading and dominant member of the capitalist world, the set of ideas that are used to explain its success is easily extended to actual or potential developments in other capitalist countries. As these ideas spread and become entrenched they often become implicit assumptions—almost axioms—for further thinking and action. In one fashion or another they have entered into the programs and practices of socialist parties and trade unions in the capitalist world, into the economic and political planning of governments

This article by Harry Magdoff originally appeared in *The Socialist Register 1965*, © 1965 by Monthly Review Press.

in the Third World, and even into some of the brave new thinking and planning of some sectors of the socialist world.

It is of course important that political programs and policies are adapted to new circumstances with the help of theory which adequately explains the changed circumstances. But the difficulty with a good deal of the thinking about the new capitalism is that it seems to be influenced not so much by critical study as by an eagerness to discover the "new" as distinct from the "old" or by the usefulness of the new ideas in serving particular political goals.

Support for this inference arises from an examination of some of the key features of recent U.S. economic developments. Among the facts of U.S. economic life which call for a more realistic appraisal of the new capitalism are the following: (1) an economy that has not been able to achieve reasonably full employment in any year since 1953; (2) an economy that but for the military effort might have from 20 to 24 million unemployed; (3) an economy which in addition to the reliance on military spending is growing increasingly dependent on injections of credit; and (4) an economy in which after twenty years of prosperity, fully a third of the young men of military age do not meet required standards of health and education.

Failure in Performance

The outstanding aspect of U.S. economic performance is that over 8 percent of the labor force is unemployed and almost 10 percent engaged in the armed forces or employed to meet military requirements. In other words, at the peak of its prosperity the civilian economy—private capital, government, and nonprofit institutions—is able to utilize only 82 percent of the labor force.[1]* One might argue that this is not a fair evaluation since the very existence of such a large military undertaking might inhibit the expansion of the civilian economy. Such an argument would be significant if there were full employment and a shortage of industrial capacity and raw materials. But this is not the case. Not only is there idle labor, but idle machinery, capacity to make more machinery, and a good

---

* Notes will be found at the end of the article.

supply of raw materials—enough to attain full employment if the economic and political institutions were able to do so.

But this is far from the whole story. The more than $55 billion spent annually on what the government agencies classify as "national defense" has a chain-reaction effect on the rest of the economy, just as other forms of investment and spending have a "multiplier" effect. It is estimated that for every $1 spent on "national defense" another $1 to $1.40 of economic product is stimulated. A crude, but conservative, calculation shows that in addition to the approximately 7.4 million people engaged in some phase of "national defense," another 6 to 9 million are employed due to the economic stimulus of defense spending.[2]

All this adds up to the rather striking conclusion noted above: some 20 to 24 million persons, out of a labor force of 78 million, are either unemployed, engaged directly or indirectly by "national defense" projects, or employed because of the economic stimulation of these projects. While the nonutilization of such magnitudes by a civilian economy would be of crisis proportions, we are not at this point engaging in the popular game of "what might have been if . . ." or "what may be if. . . ." The estimates are presented here merely to get a more realistic evaluation of the success pattern of the U.S. economy.

One observation though is needed, in this context, about the special bearing of military spending on the business cycle. Without discussing causes, the mechanics of the cycle are such that the capital goods industries are the major elements of up-and-down business swings. The postwar recessions followed this traditional pattern. Thus, in the 1957-1958 recession the production of consumer goods declined 5 percent while the production of equipment goods went down 20 percent. The special relevance of military spending in the business cycle is not so much its size as its concentration in the industries that do most of the swinging. For example, federal government spending generated the following percentages of total demand in capital goods industries: engines and turbines, 20 percent; metal-working machinery and equipment, 21 percent; electric industrial equipment and apparatus, 17 percent; machine shop products, 39 percent.[3]

Thus, military spending acts as a very convenient backstop at the strategic weak spots of the business cycle. It also acts as a special defense arm of business profits. The volatility of business profits is related to the basic overhead costs of running a business. Once sales are large enough to meet overhead costs (the break-even point), profits rise much more rapidly than further advances in sales. Conversely if sales drop sufficiently below the break-even point, losses accumulate at an increasing momentum. Mild recessions can thus turn into severe depressions if losses in key capital goods industries force a complete shutdown of many plants. However, the orders for military goods in the otherwise vulnerable industries help to pay for overhead costs, build resistance to depression losses, and inhibit the cumulative effects of recessions. In similar fashion, the strategic concentration of military procurement in metals and machinery can keep prices high and thus raise the general profit level of capital goods industries.[4]

Declining Importance of Capital Investment

The failure of the civilian economy to fully utilize the economic resources of the country is reflected in the declining role of capital investment. Thus, total investment in fixed capital (producers' durable equipment and nonresidential construction) represented 10.3 percent of the Gross National Product (the total output of goods and services) during the years 1947-1957. This percentage declined to 8.6 percent during the years 1958-1964.[5]

This is hardly the behavior of an economy that is spurred ahead by major technological changes, let alone by an industrial revolution, whether first or second. Note that the above percentages are based on total investment in plant and equipment: capital goods needed to replace worn-out equipment as well as net additions to the stock of capital. Since the replacement needs are increasing, the relative decline in net new capital (over and above replacement needs) would be larger than indicated above.

Note also that in recent years a larger percentage of the total investment has been going into office buildings, shopping centers, banks, etc., rather than in the kind of productive equipment used to make new or more products. In 1957 only 28 percent of the total expenditures for plant and equipment went into commercial enterprises (as distinguished from manufacturing, mining, transportation, and public utilities). In 1964 the proportion rose to 34 percent.[6]

Nor is this the whole story. The capital that was invested for the purpose of expanding the production of goods, after the initial postwar boom, was used in large measure to meet military needs. The evidence for this is seen in the specially large role of military demand in most of the growth industries— in those industries with an expansion rate that could only be achieved by investment in new plant and equipment. In 1958, for example, purchases by the federal government accounted for the following percentages of total demand in important growth industries: radio, television, and communication equipment, 41 percent; electronic components and accessories, 39 percent; scientific and control instruments, 30 percent; aircraft, 87 percent.[7]

The declining relative importance of capital investment, even in the face of substantial military needs, should come as no surprise if one takes into account the tendency in a capitalist economy for productive capacity to outpace effective consumer demand. Nor should the relative weakness of capital investment in the midst of significant technical changes be especially unexpected considering the decisive way the large corporations can, if they have enough power, protect their "old" capital investment when it is in their interest to do so. Evidence presented before the Subcommittee on Antitrust and Monopoly of the U.S. Senate confirmed the potential power of the large corporations and the postwar increase in such power. The 100 largest manufacturing corporations, it was shown, held close to 57 percent of the net capital assets of all manufacturing companies in 1962, as compared with close to 46 percent in 1947.[8]

One area of capital investment, on the other hand, did show a striking move forward: foreign investments by U.S. capital. The total flow of capital out of the United States in the form of direct investments added up to $6.3 billion for the combined years 1947-1955. This jumped to $15.8 billion for the years 1956-1964.[9]

The analysis of this change in relation to U.S. foreign policy and imperialist involvement is beyond the scope of this article. What is significant for the present discussion is that this upsurge in investment, along with U.S. government loans and grants to other countries, helped to support demand for U.S. production of equipment and metals.[10] These, as noted above, are the industries which are most vulnerable to cyclical decline.

Important as the high level of exports of machinery and other manufactures may be to the proper functioning of the U.S. economy, the increase of such exports—or even their maintenance—may become increasingly difficult. The trouble is not only the competition of other industrialized nations; it is concerned with the persistent negative balance of payments the United States has been experiencing in recent years.

The popular explanation of the negative balance of payments usually points to the excess of U.S. exports over imports of goods, and then pinpoints the balance-of-payments illness on military spending abroad, aid to other countries, and private forever within the present political and economic arrangements between U.S. foreign policy, its economic and political activity in the rest of the world, and its export markets. (Note, for example, that in 1963 alone, foreign affiliates of U.S. industrial companies bought at least $5 billion of U.S. goods. This represented about 23 percent of all U.S. exports of merchandise in 1963.)

Obviously the adverse balance of payments cannot go on forever within the present political and economic arrangements among nations. However, the United States may not be able to reduce its financial contributions and also maintain its export volume. Nor can the solution be sought via foreign investments. For the facts are that the United States takes in more than it sends out as a result of foreign investment: in 1954-1964, U.S. corporations sent out $16 billion for direct foreign investments; in the same years the rest of the world returned to the United States about $23 billion as dividends, interests, and branch profits resulting from direct investments.[11]

Neither the reduction of the flow of foreign investments noi an increase in foreign investments (except in the unlikely event that foreign investments continue to grow at an increasing rate) will remedy the situation. For the excess of what U.S. corporations draw out of foreign countries over what they send in is a direct result of the mathematics of such investment. In fact, this behavior is the reason corporations make foreign investments. But inevitable as this imbalance may be, it also creates other problems. When other countries reach difficulties in repaying their loans to the United States or paying out the continuous profits on U.S. investments, their recourse is to try to increase their exports to the United States and to reduce their imports from the United States. This can be a difficult pill for the United States to swallow so long as it is unable to sustain enough effective demand internally to keep its own labor force fully employed.

The Economy Grows on Credit

The initial postwar boom—say, the first eight to ten years—had real roots in the private market economy: on the one hand, the need to build up stocks of capital investment goods, housing, and consumer durable goods (cars, household equipment) which had been neglected and had deteriorated during many years of depression and war; on the other hand, the ability of the private market to finance the purchase of these goods due to the large accumulations of savings under the New Deal's wartime economic controls. The postwar boom was strengthened at first by the U.S. dominant world trade position (arising from the war devastation of other industrialized nations) and then intensified and given new life by government spending for the Korean War.

The boom fed itself for a period, bringing with it new peaks in housing, construction, capital investment, and a multitude of consumer goods. But even this boom was inadequate to provide full employment. Moreover, the capital investment stimulus began to peter out after 1957, as suggested by the data given above.

Since 1957, in the absence of a private-economy based boom, military spending stepped in as a revitalizing force. "National defense" expenditures rose continuously from $44.4 billion in 1957 to $56.8 billion a year in 1963 and in 1964. Whether this action was in response to economic need or for a "higher" political purpose is not germane to the present argument. What is important though is that this type of dynamic prop, together with foreign investment and government military and economic activity abroad, gave a significant boost to the economy and also helped to shore up the more vulnerable, the more unstable, economic sectors.

Such strong stimulation was still not enough to keep the economy at prosperity levels: what was needed, it turned out, was heavier and heavier doses of debt. Even the state and local governments could not keep up their governmental obligations and thus make their economic contribution as well without an increasing reliance on debt. During the ten years prior to 1957, state and local governments added on the average a little over $3 billion a year to their total debt load. Since 1957 these government units have been adding close to $6 billion a year.[12] The debt-creating ability of lower government organizations is quite different from that of the federal government because the states and local units do not have the power to create and regulate the supply of money and credit. Their debt-carrying capacity is ultimately limited by their revenue-raising ability, which is quite inferior to that of the federal government. To the extent that a rise in state and local government spending depends, as in recent years, increasingly on a greater proportion of debt, the inner limitations on debt expansion will inhibit expansion of this type of government activity.

While it is conceivable that the possible difficulties of lower governments' finances could be resolved by a drastic overhaul of the U.S. public finance and government structure, the same solution is not available for the private economy operating within a capitalist framework. The issue should become more apparent if we examine a few key facts. The net debt owed by private individuals and institutions (corporations, farms, and individuals) increased on the average $32 billion a year during the ten years prior to 1957. Since 1957 the average annual increase has been 50 percent higher—close to $48 bilion a year.[13] Part of this rise is attributable to a higher price level. But this is a minor element; the noteworthy change is the relative increase in debt compared with the total private (non-government) gross product, the latter also reflecting higher prices (see figures below).[14]

The danger here is not the debt itself. Credit is a useful financial instrument to help a complex economy function smoothly; it is especially useful to lubricate the mechanism of an expanding economy. Credit can serve as a handmaiden to a society in which productive wealth is accumulating, on the basis of which the economy can keep on increasing its production and investment. But it is quite another matter when a semistagnant economy keeps on increasing its debt burden. For this is an economy which can continue to maintain itself on a fairly steady keel only with ever increasing dosages of credit.

The dangers of such an eventuality are twofold. First, a weakness in the banking system that creates the credit can more readily result in a cumulative downturn of the economy. Second, to sustain an ever larger debt business eventually has to obtain larger profits to repay the debt, plus interest charges. In a semistagnant economy, larger profits cannot come from greater accumulation of capital but by reducing the share going to wages and salaries.

Year	Gross Private Product (in billions)	Net Private Debt (after repayments)	Debt as a Percentage of Gross Private Product
1945	$178.4	$139.9	78%
1950	263.8	250.9	95%
1955	363.5	402.5	111%
1960	455.3	588.4	129%
1963	526.7	752.9	143%

The potential dilemma in this event is that wage and salary earners need to increase their income steadily since they too are spending and sustaining the economy by increased use of credit. In 1960-1963 new mortgage debt on privately owned homes increased 40 percent, from $20 to $28 billion. In the same period, there was no increase in the value of new housing construction of 1- to 4-family units. Another way of looking at these figures is that during these four years $95 billion of new mortgages were added as compared with less than $72 billion of construction activity on new private homes.[15] The reasons behind this strange discrepancy are no doubt: (a) the willingness of financial institutions to lend on easier terms, which also reflect inflated, speculative values, and (b) the desire or need by consumers to keep up the feverish pace of buying, which can only be maintained by stretching debt obligations.

A similar pattern is seen in the greater dependence of the consumer durable goods market on increasing injections of consumer credit. In 1960-1963 the annual average installment credit extended to consumers amounted to 88 percent of all consumer durable goods purchased. This compares with 69 percent in 1947-1950.[16]

The net effect of all this borrowing is obviously a greater drain on consumer income. In 1951, 14 percent of consumer income went to carry their debts (amortization and interest). In 1963 the figure was 21 percent.[17] No arbitrary limit can be set on a safe maximum percentage of income for debt service. But a maximum there must be. And to the extent that there is such a maximum, there is an eventual restraint on an economy which requires ever larger doses of credit to keep moving ahead.

Roots of Persistent Unemployment

All of the special stimuli of recent U.S. economic development—military spending, foreign investment, and the spread of debt—working together have been unable to make any headway in resolving the problem of persistent unemployment. Quite the opposite: the trend of unemployment has been upward since 1953. Nor is there any evidence in sight that this trend will be reversed in the years ahead. As will be seen from the data, the problem of achieving full employment must become increasingly difficult.

The background information which can be used to appreciate the dimensions of the problem are presented in Table 1.

TABLE 1
CHANGES IN LABOR FORCE AND EMPLOYMENT

Years	Increase in Total Labor Force (*in millions*)	Employment
1930-1940	6.1	2.0
1940-1950	8.5	12.2
1950-1960	8.4	7.0
1960-1970 (projection)	12.6	—
1970-1975 (projection)	7.3	—

Source: *Economic Report of the President,* transmitted to Congress January 1964, and *Manpower Report of the President,* transmitted to Congress March 1964.

The first line of this table gives a bird's-eye view of the net effect of the Depression years on unemployment. In contrast with future decades, the rise of over 6 million in the labor force was relatively small. The labor force is measured by government agencies to determine the number of people of working age who are looking for jobs. Because of the technique used in measuring the labor force, the 6 million increase may be understated since the absence of job opportunities discouraged many from looking for work. Be that as it may, the outline of the picture is clear for the 1930-1940 decade. The 2 million net increase in jobs fell short by 4 million to meet even a conservative estimate of the number of new jobs required. This means that in 1940 there were 4 million more unemployed than in 1930.

The direction was completely reversed in the next decade as a result of war and immediate postwar needs. The growth of employment was large enough not only to provide jobs for all new workers but even to eliminate the unemployment created in the preceding decade. Hence, in 1950 unemployment was back to approximately the level in 1930.

The labor force continued to grow in the following decade by about the same amount as in 1940-1950. But in those years the growth in employment slowed down. For part of the decade, as described above, there was a strong upward lift to the economy, resulting in a drop in the official unemployment rate below 3 percent in 1953. Even this, it should be noted, was achieved with the assistance of a close to 2 million rise in the size of the armed forces. (Government estimates are based on the concept of the "civilian labor force." In this fashion the armed forces are excluded from data on labor force and unemployment.) The low "civilian" unemployment rate was short-lived, due to the subsequent slowing down in the general rate of economic growth. The net effect over the decade as a whole was the generation of more employment.

We now come to the nub of the present and future unemployment pressures. The labor force is bound to increase by more than 12.5 million in 1960-1970—an increase that is 50 percent more than in the two preceding decades. The explanation for the enlarged increase in the labor force is quite simple. Earlier growth of the labor force was influenced by the declining birth rate of the 1920s and 1930s. Birth rates were especially low during the Depression years. Consequently the increase in the labor force was relatively low in the 1950s, and especially so in the mid-'50s, when the babies born during the depth of the Depression reached working age.

Today we are beginning to get the effect of the rise in birth rates that accompanied improved economic conditions in the 1940s. But more important, the expansion of the labor force in the next five years will be even larger as a result of the so-called birth rate explosion during the early postwar years. Nor does this unusually large increase in the labor force come to an end in 1970. As can be seen from the last line of Table 1, projecting from the present population it is reasonable to expect that the labor force will grow by about 7.3 million in 1970-1975. This five-year increase is almost as large as the ten-year increase between 1950 and 1960. In other words, the labor force will grow in 1970-1975 at double the rate experienced in 1940-1960.

Some simple arithmetic can provide us with the dimensions of the problem. To attain relatively full employment by 1970, close to 15 million new jobs would have to be added by 1970 as compared with 1960: 12.6 million jobs for the net additions to the labor force (see Table 1) and about 2.2 million full-time jobs to reduce the unemployment rate to 3 percent.[18] Neither the experience of the early '60s or of the past decade justify the expectation of employment increases of such a magnitude. Only during the period of massive intervention by the government during World War II, and while benefiting from the immediate aftermath of such government intervention, did the U.S. economy prove capable of creating anything near 15 million new jobs in a decade. And even that performance of 12 million jobs would, if duplicated, leave 5.5 million unemployed at the end of 1970. In terms of current developments—it is more realistic to expect 10 million unemployed—even if the economy can avoid a major economic downturn in the interim.

This analysis highlights a special feature of the postwar U.S. economy. The period of rapid capital accumulation coincided with a period of relatively slow growth of the labor force. This has shifted—and apparently will continue for some time ahead—to the opposite: a rapid rise in the labor force accompanied by a slowdown in capital accumulation. A key phase of the latter development is clearly illustrated in Table 2.

TABLE 2
JOB GROWTH GENERATED BY PUBLIC AND PRIVATE DEMAND
(in millions)

Item	1957	1963	Increase in 1957-1963
Total nonfarm employment	52.9	57.2	4.3
Less government employees	7.6	9.6	2.0
Equals: Private nonfarm employment	45.3	47.7	2.4
Less jobs owing to government purchases from business	5.9	6.7	.8
Equals: Jobs generated independent of government spending	39.4	41.0	1.6
Less employment by nonprofit institutions	2.6	3.3	.7
Equals: Jobs generated by private demand	36.8	37.7	.9
Less adjustment for voluntary part-time employment	1.7	2.3	.6
Equals: Full-time jobs generated by private demand	35.1	35.4	.3

Note: Details may not add up to totals because of rounding off decimals. Government refers to federal, state and local. Above data do not include the self-employed.

Source: *Manpower Report of the President,* transmitted to Congress March 1964.

Starting with 1957—the year we have selected as in the nature of a turning point—and ending in 1963, 4.3 million nonfarm jobs were added. Though not large enough to prevent a rise in unemployment, this increase was nevertheless significant in size. Now where did these jobs come from? Almost two-thirds of the additional jobs (2.8 million) arose directly or indirectly by government activity. If the jobs created by non-profit institutions (hospitals, universities, etc.) are eliminated, it turns out that only 900,000 jobs were generated by private market activity. And even that is not the full story. Many of these jobs were part-time. If an adjustment is made for the latter, then only 300,000 jobs were created by the private economy after six years—most of which were years of economic upswing.[19]

The insufficiency of jobs created by private industry is only in part due to increased productivity and automation. The effect of increasing productivity is shown in Table 3. As noted

TABLE 3

PRODUCTIVITY OF PRODUCTION WORKERS IN MANUFACTURES

| Selected Years | Production Index of Manufactures (1947=100) | Production Workers Employed in Manufactures | | Output per Productive Worker (1947=100) |
		number (in thousands)	index (1947=100)	
1947	100	12,990	100	100
1953	124	14,055	108	115
1957	144	13,189	102	141
1964 (10-mo. average)	196	12,813	99	198

Source: Production indexes computed from data in *Economic Report of the President,* transmitted to Congress January 1964, and *Economic Indicators,* November 1964, U.S. Government Printing Office. Employment data—*Manpower Report of the President,* transmitted to Congress March 1964, and *Monthly Report on the Labor Force,* October 1964, U.S. Department of Labor.

there, manufacturing output almost doubled between 1957 and 1964, but the number of production workers in manufacturing remained the same. Still it is not productivity that creates the problem: it is the fact that production does not keep pace with and overtake the rise in productivity. The failure of the private economy as a job-producer is a failure—despite valiant "pump-priming" efforts—to invest enough capital and grow sufficiently to keep pace with growing productivity and a growing labor force. Nor has government activity shown the ability to cope with a growing labor force and increasing productivity except at the time of World War II.

The Disease of Poverty

The nature of the long economic boom, and its pattern of change, is well reflected in the continuous existence of large-scale poverty. For despite the important reforms introduced by the New Deal in the 1930s, the political acceptance of the "welfare state," the tremendous advance in productive capacity, and the very sizeable expansion of inner markets, no less than two-fifths of the nation still live in poverty or in a state of economic deprivation in the United States.[20]

Naturally the huge growth in the economy also brought about a drastic reduction in poverty. But what needs to be noted in terms of this analysis is the marked slowdown in recent years in the reduction of poverty. It should not be surprising to find that the pattern of change in poverty resembles the pattern of change in capital investment. The great reduction in poverty took place during the World War II era—the years of war and immediate aftermath. From the extreme of the Depression (1935-1936) to 1947 there was an average annual reduction of 4.8 percent in the total number of people living in poverty. In 1947-1953—when unemployment was relatively low, capital accumulation still relatively high, and the economy restimulated by the Korean War—the average annual rate of reduction in the number of people living in poverty dropped to 2.7 percent. And in 1953-1960—when unemployment began to mount and the maintenance of prosperity required further artificial stimulation—the rate of annual decline in poverty fell to 1.1 percent. At the latter rate of change it would take another ninety years to eliminate poverty in the United States—this is in a country that has the resources and the capacity to do so right now if the society were organized for such a purpose.

The determination of what constitutes poverty in the

wealthy United States necessarily involves certain arbitrary definitions. A discussion of these definitions would require too much space here. Suffice it to say that though the several studies on this subject made by different authorities in recent years do differ in detail, there is substantial agreement on the extent of poverty. We are using here the study made by the Conference on Economic Progress, *Poverty and Deprivation in the U.S.* (see footnote 20), which used the U.S. Department of Labor investigation of budgets of city workers' families to determine the standards of poverty. In addition, the Conference report introduced the concept of "economic deprivation" which includes people living above the stark poverty level but below what the Labor Department investigation found to be a "modest but adequate" worker's family budget.

The simple summary of the Conference report on the 1960 income situation in the United States is as follows: 34 million people in families and 4 million unattached individuals (that is, unattached economically to a family unit) lived in poverty; 37 million people in families and 2 million unattached individuals lived in deprivation. The total of 77 million comprised two-fifths of the U.S. population in 1960.

Without dwelling on the sociology of this poverty, one resultant of the persistent poverty is worth reporting on at this point. Faced with the fact that one-half of the draft registrants are rejected as unfit for military service, President Kennedy appointed a task force to study the health and education of U.S. youth. This task force found that one-third of all young men in the nation turning 18 years of age would be found unqualified if they were to be examined for induction into the armed forces. Of these, one-half would be rejected for medical reasons. The remainder would fail through inability to meet the educational standards of at least an eighth-grade level of educational attainment, and a large part of this category could not meet the educational standards of a fifth-grade level.

The President's Task Force concluded on the basis of its study: "Although many persons are disqualified for defects that probably could not be avoided in the present state of knowledge, the majority appear to be victims of inadequate education and insufficient health services."[21] The Task Force, however, did not point out that they were referring to the young men who were born and brought up during the years of their country's great wave of prosperity and historic economic achievements.

Those who believe that poverty can be eliminated within the economic and social institutions of a capitalist society see the issue of poverty as primarily a matter of social welfare. Better schooling, housing, medical attention, and more government spending to create jobs will, they maintain, break the back of poverty. What is not understood, even by the most energetic reformers, is that poverty is itself a product of prosperity. The economic system, as it operates, creates a reserve of the poor and benefits from it. In periods of rapid expansion and in periods of war, the marginal group in society is available for work and fighting. During such times the reserve of the poor may diminish, to be eventually built up again as the economy slows down, as technological change displaces workers, and when there are economic declines. Moreover, the roots of poverty are intertwined with the very functioning of the economy: the structure of industry, the methods of distribution, and the way prices and profits are formed.

The Negro Reserves

While the majority of the poor are white, the concentration of poverty among Negroes and the unique way they are used in the advanced U.S. civilization offers a valuable laboratory illustration of the operating mechanics of poverty.

Living at the lowest economic levels of the society, the Negroes are available as the ultimate reserve in times of labor shortage. In recent history the most important economic breakthrough for the Negro occurred in World War I and World War II. But as soon as the labor shortage eases, the Negroes' advance slows down or declines. The mechanics of the operation even during prosperous times are presented as one of the conclusions of a recent study:

White workers capture the newly growing fields in which labor resources are scarce, pay levels are good, prospects for advancement are bright, the technology is most advanced, and working conditions the most modern. These fields seem relatively less and less attractive to white workers, however, as the economy continues to expand and newer fields appear. Finally, the once new fields stagnate, and white workers are reluctant to enter them. Even though wages in these fields may increase rapidly, they now are low by the standards of the newer, more highly skilled occupations associated with newer technologies in rapidly expanding fields. At this point Negroes secure these jobs, which are quite attractive in comparison to what had formerly been available to them. Although working conditions and wages in the now older fields may have improved over time, they are conditioned by an older technology and customs. Moreover, newer technology is likely to result in reduced manpower needs. Thus the Negroes' newest and best opportunities often turn out to be quite vulnerable. Their gains in the operative occupations during the 1940s and 1950s are now increasingly susceptible to recent technological and market changes.[21]

The role of the Negro as a shock absorber of economic and technological dislocations shows up in agriculture as well as industry. The growth of technology on the farm, the upsurge of large industrialized farms associated with war needs, and the type of government subsidies resulted in a sharp decline in the farm population. While this meant, among other things, the removal of large numbers of tenant farmers and farm laborers, the impact fell primarily on the Negroes. Thus, the percentage of white farmers and farm laborers increased from 81 percent in 1940 to 85 percent in 1960, while the percentage of Negroes declined in the same period from 19 percent to 15 percent.[22]

In like fashion, when unemployment increases, the extent of unemployment among Negroes rises more rapidly than among whites. The official government figures on unemployment indicate a rate of unemployment among Negroes in 1963 of close to 11 percent as compared with 5 percent for whites—more than double. The spread itself has been widening as the economy slowed down—the Negro unemployment rate in 1948 was only 63 percent higher than the white rate. The same applies to unemployment among youth. In 1963 the teenage unemployment was 25.4 percent for male Negroes and 14 percent for whites, as compared with 7.1 percent and 6.3 percent in 1953.[23] Although employment opportunities increased in 1964, a special government study issued in August 1964 estimated that one-third of the Negro young people, including those who have given up looking for jobs, were without work.

The net result of the two different worlds is seen in Table 4. (The data in the last column are for nonwhites, of which over 90 percent are Negro.) The sharply contrasting patterns are suggestive of the differences between a center of empire and a colonial dependency. The analogy can be extended in many different directions. The main point is that the elimination of discrimination, even if it be more than token, would be but a minor element in any radical alteration of the income distribution of the Negro population. For it is not discrimination that causes this difference. Institutionalized discrimination contributes to particular forms of poverty among Negroes and enhances the privileges of many whites. But in the main, discrimination is the medium—in the context of U.S. economics and social history—by which a special kind of poverty and a special kind of labor reserve is maintained.

TABLE 4

1963 INCOME DISTRIBUTION OF WHITES AND NONWHITES

Annual	*Percentage of Families*	
Money Income	*White*	*Nonwhite*
Under $2,000	9.0%	25.5%
$2,000 to $3,999	15.1%	31.1%
$4,000 to $5,999	20.1%	19.6%
$6,000 to $9,999	34.3%	18.1%
$10,000 and over	21.5%	5.7%
	100.0%	100.0%

Note: These data represent only money income and do not include non-monetary income such as consumption of food raised on one's farm or the value of room and board supplied to farm and service workers.

Source: *Consumer Income*, Consumer Population Report, Series P-60, No. 43, September 20, 1964. U.S. Department of Commerce.

As in the case of white poverty, Negro poverty—more clearly seen because of its extreme character—is a function of the industrial and economic structure. Elimination of discrimination will not eliminate such major sources of poverty as unemployment, casual and intermittent jobs, and low-paid occupations. More education, more job training, and equal opportunity may only result in having better educated, better trained, and more "equal" unemployed and low-paid workers. For the sources of poverty result from the behavior of the market system itself: the structure and location of industry, methods of distribution, the price structure, and the way profits from industry and land ownership are accumulated and used. The economy functions in such a manner that it produces and reproduces poverty and economic deprivation.

The significance of this proposition is not yet well understood even by advanced groups leading the social and political struggle for freedom and equality of Negroes. This lack of understanding is no doubt due in part to the acceptance of the myths about the new capitalism and the consequent faith in what a good and wise government could accomplish.

A more careful examination of Table 4 may help to see this question in better perspective. A casual inspection of the two columns shows that from a purely statistical point of view, equality between the two groups could be achieved only if a large number of whites were pushed down the economic ladder in order to make room for nonwhites. While a society based on social justice might make a significant advance along this line, it is clear that very little, if any, progress can be made toward such an end in a society that rewards its citizens according to property ownership and work skills (where education and long training are of key importance).

Let us assume for the sake of this argument a society that is bent on reform, but reform in a practical fashion. The present distribution of incomes of whites will not be disturbed. This necessarily means that the distribution of income of the close to 5 million Negro families will not be changed. But as the economy grows and the number of Negro families increases (say, at 2 percent per year), special privileges will be given Negroes so that they get an advantage over whites for the better jobs. Hence, we will assume that new jobs and new income opportunities for Negroes will be such that 24 percent of them will result in incomes of $10,000 a year and over, instead of the 5.7 percent shown in Table 4. Only a little over 6 percent of the new jobs will result in annual income of less than $2,000, as compared with the 25.5 percent shown in Table 4. Similar drastic changes will be effected, in our assumed world, for the in-between job opportunities. The net result of all these assumptions is that it would still take a hundred years for the income distribution of Negroes to equal that of the whites.

Of course, we have merely been playing a mathematical game in the preceding paragraph in order to illuminate the severity of the problem. The historical facts are quite clear. The same Census Bureau study which produced the data shown in Table 4 also presented comparative income information for the entire postwar period. An examination of these data reveals that despite the turmoil of recent years and the talk of progress, the relative position of Negro income compared to white income has not changed. In 1948 the median income of nonwhite families was 53 percent of the median income of white families. In 1963 the percentage was still 53 percent. Any significant breakthrough in this kind of inequality and the achievement of results in the near future, and not a hundred years from now, places on the agenda the need for a new type of industrialization and a reconstruction of the physical wealth of the society. Such changes would be in direct conflict with the operations of a private market economy that creates and continuously refreshes the sources of poverty. If the goal of the society is Negro-white equality and the elimination of poverty, then the solution cannot be found in a new capitalism or through the adaptation of the Negro to the new capitalism. If the history of colonialism and the development of national independence can serve as a teacher, then we need to recognize that to achieve equality the Negro must become equal by becoming the master of his own destiny. Seen in the light of issues of this magnitude, the various proposals for even radical tinkering with the existing economic setup are akin to the romantic and utopian socialist ideas of an earlier era.

NOTES

1. The government data on unemployment show 4 million unemployed during the first half of 1964. But these are only the full-time unemployed. If one takes into account the part-time unemployed, that is, those working involuntarily part-time, the full measure of unemploy-

ment reaches 5.4 million. Added to this are 1.4 million concealed unemployed, resulting in an estimate of 6.4 million unemployed. (See *The Toll of Rising Interest Rates,* Conference on Economic Progress, Washington, D.C., August 1964.) The concept of "concealed unemployment" is used because the government measures as unemployed only those able to work and seeking work. Those who due to the lack of jobs do not actively seek jobs are thus excluded from the labor force. Thus, in the official labor force data for 1963, 98 percent of white men, ages 35 to 44, are counted in the civilian labor force, but only 95 percent of Negro men in these age groups are included. In the 45 to 54 age group, the comparable percentages are 96 percent and 91 percent; in the 55 to 64 age group, 87 percent and 83 percent. (See *Manpower Report of the President,* U.S. Government Printing Office, Washington, D.C., March 1964.)

The estimate of 7.4 million employed directly and indirectly due to military spending is made by the U.S. Arms Control and Disarmament Agency in *Economic Impacts of Disarmament,* Washington, D.C., 1962.

2. The estimate of the multiplier effect of military spending was given in the report of the U.S. Arms Control and Disarmament Agency referred to in footnote 1. The translation of the multiplier from dollar terms to employment was made by using the ratio of Gross Private Product (Gross National Product less government expenditures for employment) to nongovernment employment.

3. "Interindustry Structure of the United States, a Report on the 1958 Input-Output Study" in *Survey of Current Business,* November 1964.

4. In 1958, for example, federal government spending accounted for the following percentages of total demand in metal mining and manufacture: iron and ferro-alloy mining, 12.8 percent; nonferrous metal ores mining, 35.6 percent; primary iron and steel manufacturing, 12.5 percent; primary nonferrous metal manufacturing, 22.3 percent. Source same as in footnote 3.

5. Percentages calculated from data in *Economic Report of the President,* U.S. Government Printing Office, Washington, D.C., 1964. The data were obtained from *Economic Indicators,* November 1964, U.S. Government Printing Office.

6. *Economic Indicators,* November 1964.

7. Source same as footnote 3.

8. Testimony of Dr. John Blair before Senate Subcommittee on Antitrust and Monopoly, November 1964.

9. The data for 1947-1960 appear in *Balance of Payments, Statistical Supplement,* rev. ed., U.S. Government Printing Office, Washington, D.C., 1963. Data for years after 1960 from different issues of *Survey of Current Business.*

10. In 1958, exports accounted for the following percentages of total demand: construction, mining, and oil field machinery, 26.9 percent; metal-working machinery and equipment, 14 percent; engines and turbines, 14.8 percent; general industrial machinery and equipment, 13.4 percent. Note that exports and military procurement accounted for between 33 and 46 percent of the total demand in the following industries: engines and turbines; construction, mining, and oil field machinery; metal-working machinery and equipment; machine shop

products; radio, TV, and communication equipment; electronic components and accessories; scientific and control instruments. Source same as footnote 3.

11. Source same as footnote 9.
12. *Economic Report of the President,* 1964.
13. *Ibid.*
14. *Ibid.*
15. "The New Dimension in Mortgage Debt," Technical Paper No. 15, National Industrial Conference Board, New York, 1964.
16. *Economic Report of the President,* 1964. Not all of consumer installment credit is used for the purchase of consumer durable goods. About two-thirds of installment credit is backed specifically by paper on consumer durable goods. However, a substantial portion of the remaining credit is also used for the purchase of consumer durables as is part of the noninstallment credit which was not included in the above figures.
17. *Wall Street Journal,* June 17, 1964.
18. This calculation assumes no reduction in the size of the armed forces. The unemployment figures were adjusted to take into account part-time unemployment, but not the concealed unemployed.
19. The 1964 data classified in this fashion were not available at the time of this writing. Preliminary data indicate that employment on the private market account improved in 1964, but hardly enough to alter the main argument. If 1962 were taken as the terminal year, employment on private market account would show an absolute decline from 1957.
20. This statement and the subsequent details on poverty are from *Poverty and Deprivation in the U.S.,* Conference on Economic Progress, Washington, D.C., April 1962. The national committee of the conference includes industrialists and leaders of national trade unions and farm organizations. The research and analysis of the conference is under the direction of Leon H. Keyserling, former chairman of the President's Council of Economic Advisers.
21. Dale L. Hiestand, *Economic Growth and Employment Opportunities for Minorities,* New York and London, 1964, p. 114.
22. Calculated from data in Hiestand.
23. *Manpower Report of the President,* U.S. Government Printing Office, Washington, D.C., March 1964.

Foreign Investment

June 1965

Imperialism has many aspects, so many indeed that it is quite impossible to encompass them all in a neat definition or formula. So at a time when this hydra-headed monster is ostentatiously displaying its ugliest face in the Congo and South Vietnam, it may be useful to call attention to some of its less obvious characteristics and consequences. This may help us to avoid an oversimplified view and to keep firmly in mind the real underlying reasons for the shameful events now unfolding in Africa and Asia.

Common to most theories of imperialism, including all which claim a Marxian origin, is a stress on the central importance of foreign investment. There is no doubt that this is fully justified, but it is important to understand the phenomenon correctly and not to be deceived by certain arguments which occupy a prominent place in the arsenal of imperialism's apologists.

It is sometimes asserted, and perhaps more often just taken for granted, that foreign investment represents a transfer from one country to another of capital which might otherwise have been invested in the first country. The investing country is thus supposed to place a part of its surplus product (savings) at the disposal of the receiving country and in this way to hasten the latter's economic development. In return, the investing country receives interest or dividends, and eventually its capital is repaid, from the increased production of the receiving country. Everyone is presumed to benefit from this arrangement.

Now, such a relationship between two countries is not only possible; it actually exists in quite a few cases in the world today. For example between the Soviet Union and Cuba. The USSR has been lending money to Cuba which Cuba has been using to build up its productive capacity. These loans carry a low rate of interest (2.5 percent) and are repayable over a period of 12 years, at the end of which both the added productive capacity and its current output will be entirely at the disposal of the Cuban economy. This, however, is most emphatically not the way foreign investment works in the capitalist world: as a generalization from capitalist reality, the theory summarized above is a monstrous lie. Foreign investment has always accomplished precisely the opposite of what the theory claims—a transfer of surplus to, not from, the investing country.

The mechanics may differ from one case to another. Sometimes there is actually an initial transfer of purchasing power from the investing to the receiving country. But such is by no means always the case. The initial investment may be nothing but patents, with actual capital being raised locally. This, for example, is the way the Ford Motor Company of Canada got started. The American company took a controlling stock interest in exchange for patents, and Canadians put up money for the rest of the stock. Over the years, the enterprise was enormously expanded and the Canadian stockholders bought out—from profits earned in Canada.

Or the initial investment may consist essentially of a concession granted (usually corruptly) by the "host" country. This is obviously the basis of the tremendous foreign investments of the great international oil companies. Perhaps they sent abroad a small amount of capital some time in the distant past. If so, it was as nothing compared to the flood of profits earned by their foreign subsidiaries. These profits provided the source of all future expansion abroad as well as of a swelling tide of remittances to the parent companies in the United States and Western Europe. The orders of magnitude involved can be gathered from the following report carried by the *New York Times* of November 19th:

Probably no United States industry has fared better overseas than the oil business. Ira H. Cram, chairman of the executive committee of the Continental Oil Company noted this yesterday when he said: "During the last 40 years our country's share of the free world's oil production has fallen from 74 percent to 35 percent, but the percentage contributed by United States-based companies has only declined from about 85 percent to 71 percent." He added that United States companies had about 63 percent of the non-Communist world's proved reserves of oil.

In recent years, earnings on oil ventures abroad have brought an important return, Mr. Cram said. From 1957 to 1962, he noted, American oil companies spent $4.2 billion in foreign nations and brought home earnings of $7.6 billion. "That happens to be 51 percent of the earnings returned to the United States by all industry," he said.

What does this sucking oil and money out of the rest of the world for the benefit of giant corporations (and their stockholders) in the United States have in common with that idyllic picture which portrays foreign investment as a process of helping poorer countries to develop in exchange for a modest compensation? Obviously nothing whatever. What is involved here is a vast transfer of surplus produced abroad *to* the United States. And these multi-billion-dollar payments to the United States, far from enabling the paying countries to acquire title to the assets within their borders, go hand in hand with a steady expansion of the holdings of the American giants.

But perhaps oil is a special case? Let us see.

No one would deny that the heyday of British foreign investment was in the half century before the First World War. According to a reliable estimate, in the years 1870-1913 there was a net export of capital from Great Britain of £2.4 billion,* equivalent in those days to some 12 billion dollars having more than twice the purchasing power of today's dollar. Even by today's standards, that is a lot of foreign investment. But did it really represent a transfer of resources from Britain to the receiving countries? Evidently, the answer depends on how much income was flowing into Britain from these investments during the period in question. According to the same authority, the sum was £4.1 billion.** In other words, the flow of capital

---

* A. K. Cairncross, *Home and Foreign Investment*, 1870-1913, Cambridge, England, 1953, p. 180.
** *Ibid.*

from Britain was only about three fifths of the flow of income *to* Britain. Or to put it still another way, during the 43 years preceding the First World War Britain extracted from the rest of the world £1.7 billion more than she invested in it while at the same time steadily building up her foreign holdings. Who was "aiding" whom?

For the United States, official figures of the kind required are available for the years beginning with 1950.* In that year, total direct foreign assets of American corporations (this is by far the most important form of foreign investment) came to $11.8 billion. By 1963 this had grown to $40.6 billion, a spectacular increase of $28.8 billion, or 244 percent, in thirteen years. According to the official figures, of this increase $17.4 billion represented net export of capital from the United States. But here again we must take into account direct investment income flowing to the United States from abroad, and in the relevant period this amounted to no less than $29.4 billion. In other words: during the period 1950-1963 American corporations extracted from the rest of the world $12 billion more than they invested in it, while at the same time adding $28.8 billion to their foreign holdings.

How are such things possible?

Fundamentally, the answer is that the foreign branches and affiliates of American corporations are fantastically profitable, partly because they operate in monopolistic and rigged markets and partly because by applying more advanced American techniques they can produce at lower costs than local rivals. These profits, including large sums labeled depreciation or depletion in order to cheat the tax collector, are the source of the huge remittances to the United States, and they also provide most of the money needed for local expansion. This is indicated by a so-called sources-and-uses of funds analysis for direct foreign investments in mining, petroleum, and manufacturing which the Department of Commerce now publishes annually. During the last three years (1961-1963) foreign subsidiaries in these

---

* In the *Survey of Current Business* (published by the Department of Commerce), November 1954, and thereafter August of each year (containing an annual survey article).

fields paid out a total of $27.2 billion broken down as follows:*

Property, Plant, and Equipment......	44.1	percent
Inventories, Receivable, and		
Other Assets..................	25.9	”
Income Paid Out.................	30.0	”
Total	100.0	”

On the other side of the ledger, the sources of this same total of $27.2 billion were as follows:

Profits	42.0	percent
Depreciation and Depletion..........	26.0	”
Funds from Abroad................	18.6	”
Funds from the United States........	13.4	”
Total	100.0	”

Here the relative unimportance of funds from the United States shows up clearly: evidently most American enterprises abroad can now take care of their own financial needs, from internally generated funds and from outside local sources, while at the same time sending billions of dollars to the parent companies in the United States. The large and rapidly growing importance of the item "funds from abroad"—between 1961 and 1963, it increased by more than 50 percent—is also noteworthy. For the most part this represents borrowing from local banks and capitalists and signifies an expansion of American control beyond the limits of American ownership.

These figures on investment and income are very far from giving a complete picture of American economic penetration abroad or of the sums received by parent companies from their foreign subsidiaries. Many wholly foreign-owned companies are in one degree or another dependent on American technology and know-how, and the fact that United States investments are heavily concentrated in precisely those areas of the economies of the receiving countries where the most modern and sophisticated technologies are used lends an importance to the American sector which is much greater than the bare quantita-

---

* All figures are from Fred Cutler and Samuel Pizer, "U.S. Firms Accelerate Capital Expenditures Abroad," *Survey of Current Business,* October 1964, p. 12.

tive data can convey.

With respect to payments other than interest and dividends by subsidiaries to parent companies, the official surveys report a very rapid increase in fees for management services of various kinds and for the use of royalties, copyrights, and similar intangible property. By 1963, the total annual amount of such payments by foreign subsidiaries to companies in the United States had reached a figure of over $600 million, which was some 20 percent of direct foreign investment income. And of course there are various kinds of illegal payments which never get recorded at all—for example, those arising from manipulating prices on transactions between parent and subsidiary, a practice commonly resorted to in countries which attempt to put limits on the amount of profits which can be remitted abroad.

A Case in Point

But let us eschew further global figures and generalizations and examine in some detail a specific case of American foreign investment, the Cyprus Mines Corporation (CMC). This enterprise is both interesting and instructive for a number of reasons. In the first place, throughout most of its existence it has been quite typical of United States foreign investments in the extractive industries. Secondly, it is changing its character and approaching the pattern of the diversified multinational corporation which is increasingly dominating the field of foreign investment today. Thirdly, since the end of its operations in Cyprus seems to be in sight, we can in this case attempt at least a tentative assessment of the total impact of foreign investment on a receiving country. And finally, we can see quite clearly in this case who are the chief beneficiaries of foreign investment. To all this should be added that Cyprus is very much in the news these days and that anything which throws light on the situation and forces at work there is particularly timely.

The account which follows is based on a story which appeared in *Business Week* of October 10th, 1964 ("Hot Spot that Produces Plenty of Cold Cash," pp. 102-110.) This story does not answer all the questions we would have posed if we had been doing the research, but it answers the main ones and permits what appear to be reasonably safe inferences in the case of others.

CMC has its headquarters in Los Angeles, and until quite recently its fortunes were entirely tied to copper mining on the Mediterranean island of Cyprus. The company was born in 1912 when a prospector, backed by Col. Seeley W. Mudd, came upon the Skouriotissa mine which had been worked by the Romans and abandoned some sixteen to seventeen centuries ago. The original investment seems to have been the prospector's grubstake. Whether additional capital was provided from the United States to bring the mine into production does not appear; in any case, if the initial flow was from the United States to Cyprus it was soon reversed. The company prospered under the leadership of Col. Mudd, his son Harvey W. Mudd, and his grandson Henry T. Mudd, the present chief executive. Today, CMC is the largest employer in Cyprus with a payroll of 2,400 (the total population of the island is about 600,000); and there is no doubt that the capital for this expansion, as well as for other purposes to be discussed presently, came from the profits of the Cyprus operation.

A turning point in the history of CMC came with the opening of the Mavrovouni mine in the early 1930's. Reputed to be one of the world's richest copper ore bodies, Mavrovouni also produces commercial quantities of iron and sulphur. Shut down entirely during the Second World War, Mavrovouni, taking advantage of extraordinarily low costs (wages on Cyprus are low and ore wastage is only 12 to 15 percent compared with 95 to 99 percent in an average copper mine) and of the boom prices for metals which prevailed during the late 40's and 50's, has since become a fantastic bonanza. Postwar net profits from operations in Cyprus have amounted to about $100 million, 80 percent from Mavrovouni. Unfortunately, *Business Week* does not give a corresponding figure for remittances to the United States, but from certain facts which are reported one can infer that very nearly the whole amount of net profits must have been remitted. Liquid assets (cash and government securities) held by the parent company rose from $4.5 million in 1946 to $21 million in 1951, and this of course was in addition to dividends paid. At the present time, with the exhaustion of Mavrovouni expected in 1965, CMC is spending only about $500,000 a year on mill improvements and on preparing the long-idle Skouriotissa mine for open-strip operations. Funds for this purpose might come out of profits, but more likely would be covered by depreciation and depletion. All indications, in other words, are that CMC's policy has been to suck Mavrovouni dry and send the proceeds back home.

What has been done with these huge sums of money?

Partly they have been distributed to stockholders, enabling, among other things, the Mudd family to retain

its position as one of the keystones of philanthropy in Southern California. Harvey Mudd College in Claremont—"it was built by Mavrovouni"—occupies much of Henry Mudd's time. Other benefactions: a philosophy building at the University of Southern California, gifts to Pomona and Claremont, an engineering building at Columbia University in New York. (*Business Week*, as cited, p. 110.)

But more important, the profits from Cyprus have enabled CMC to build up an entirely new economic empire, both in the United States and abroad, which gives every sign of carrying on in the tradition of Mavrovouni, filling the coffers of CMC and providing the wherewithal for Henry Mudd and his scions after him to carry on with their good works. This new empire began to be put together in the early 1950's when Mavrovouni's profits were rising to their peak but it was already clear that the bonanza would soon be nearing exhaustion. Among CMC's new ventures, often undertaken in conjunction with other corporate giants, *Business Week* lists the following:

• An iron mining company in Peru, soon expected to be CMC's largest revenue producer.

• A copper mining company in Arizona with twice the capacity of the Cyprus mines but poorer quality and hence lower profitability.

• A Panamanian shipping company, scheduled in the near future to add to its fleet a 60,000-ton, $7.5-million ore and oil carrier.

• Timber and mill operations in Oregon and British Columbia.

- Forests in California and Alabama.
- A cement plant in Hawaii.
- Two chemical works in the Netherlands.
- A residential building company in Phoenix, Arizona.
- An iron mining company in Australia.

As it prepares to take its departure from Cyprus—the Skouriotissa mine is not expected to last beyond the early 1970's—CMC is thus being reborn as a widely diversified multinational corporation with rosy prospects for the future. What about Cyprus itself?

Like most other American corporations with large foreign investments, CMC prides itself on its progressive labor and social policies. It pays wages which are high by Cyprus standards (£1/13/- to £2 a day = $4.62 to $5.60), is the island's largest taxpayer, and "has poured millions into housing, schools, recreational facilities, a modern hospital, a program to provide milk and yogurt for children." *Business Week* quotes CMC's vice president as saying: "We could have been just an episode in the island's long history, but we're trying to create something worthwhile to leave behind." (*Ibid.*, p. 106.)

How bitterly ironical that must sound in the ears of a Cypriot familiar with the facts and not bemused by "free world" ideological mystifications! For what is it that CMC will "leave behind"? Above all 2,400 unemployed. How long will they be able to go on living in their houses, sending their children and their sick to the company-built schools and hospitals, using their recreational facilities? Presumably as long as the government of Cyprus is willing to subsidize these facilities from its reduced tax revenues, i.e., at the expense of the rest of the island's population. Will not the "beneficiaries" of CMC's largesse then angrily reflect that CMC was indeed but an "episode in the island's long history"—and in many ways the most disastrous episode in a history which has been no stranger to disasters? For imagine where Cyprus could be today if it had been able to borrow the capital to exploit Mavrovouni as a 2.5-percent 12-year loan, similar to those which Cuba has received from the Soviet Union and the other socialist countries! The loan would long since have been paid off, and the $100 million which has gone into the Mudd philanthropies and the new empire for CMC could have been used to build a viable and rapidly expanding economy. And Harvey Mudd College under another name could have become one of the great educational institutions of the Mediterranean and Middle East.

Mavrovouni is played out, and the great opportunity for Cyprus is gone. But it is still not too late to salvage something from the CMC debacle. A Cypriot government free to act in the interests of the island's people could immediately nationalize Skouriotissa, borrow on "Cuban" terms the few million dollars needed to modernize it, and retain for the island's benefit the profits of its remaining years. Did someone say compensation for CMC? No, what must be meant is compensation *from* CMC: surely if there were any justice in the world, Cyprus would be able to sue CMC for the $100 million already stolen from it.

This situation evidently throws a most revealing light on the recent history of Cyprus and its present international relations. The Left, represented primarily by the Communist Party, the largest party on the island, is very strong in Cyprus, having played a leading role in the struggle to throw off the yoke of British colonialism. A really independent government could hardly govern without its support, and would therefore inevitably take a strong anti-imperialist line. Can there be any doubt that such a government's principal targets would be the nationalization of Skouriotissa and the elimination of the British military bases (so important for the control of Britain's Middle Eastern oil empire)? Conversely, therefore, the task of the imperialist governments must be to prevent Cyprus from acquiring a really independent government.

For this the handiest instrument has been the traditional imperialist weapon of "divide and rule," with the age-old antagonism between the Turkish minority and the Greek majority as a ready-made point of insertion. This antagonism could have been alleviated, or perhaps wholly overcome, in a healthy society such as would have been possible had Cyprus been able to dispose over the wealth of Mavrovouni. But with its economic lifeblood being drained away into and through Southern California, it was easy to maneuver Cypriots into increasingly bitter fights among themselves. Hence the grant of "independence" with its provision for a Turkish minority veto backed up by intervention powers to Turkey itself; hence the incitation of Turkish Cypriots and the Ankara government (one of Washington's most loyal stooges) to resist all efforts of Archbishop Makarios's government to eliminate the veto and gain the freedom to follow a progressive nationalist policy; hence the bringing in of the UN to "mediate" the bitter communal quarrel thus brought to the stage of civil war; and hence also the sanctimonious and utterly hypocritical preachments of imperialist "statesmen" in favor of law and order, reconciliation, brotherhood, and all the other virtuous forms of behavior which imperialism has always prescribed for its hapless victims.

But enough. The lessons of Cyprus, and indeed of the whole history of foreign investment by the imperialist countries, are surely clear:

First, no country should ever under any circumstances permit foreign corporations to own and operate enterprises within its borders. Such enterprises by their very nature are not and never can be instruments of economic development; they are pumps designed to suck up the country's wealth and transfer it abroad. This principle holds not only for underdeveloped countries but also, and in a sense specially, for the advanced countries of Western Europe, Canada, and Japan where American corporations have been concentrating their foreign operations in recent years.*

Second, in countries where enterprises owned by foreign corporations already exist they should be immediately nationalized. The question of compensation is of course a political one; but the fact that in some cases it may be thought expedient to make some sort of payment (as, for example, Cuba has of-

---

* This is a subject which must be reserved for separate treatment. Here we will only say that there is considerable evidence that the capitalist classes of these economically developed countries are being pressured and bribed into conniving at and even actively assisting the American invasion: as things are going now the whole capitalist world is rapidly being incorporated into the American empire. The forces behind this trend were not properly evaluated and taken into account in our analysis of "The Split in the Capitalist World" (MR, April 1963), and it is clear that the whole subject now needs to be reconsidered.

fered to do under certain conditions) should not be allowed to obscure the fact that foreign investors have no moral claim to compensation. Quite the contrary: in 99 cases out of 100, if the eminently capitalist rule of quid pro quo is applied, it will appear that foreign investors owe large sums to the countries in which they have invested.

Third, from now on foreign capital should be accepted only as loans.

Finally, the acid test of any government or political party, the criterion by which to judge whether it is genuinely devoted to the cause of national independence and economic development, is its attitude toward foreign investment.

Economic Stagnation and Stagnation of Economics

April 1971

The *New York Times* carried a page-one, column-eight story in its issue of March 6th under the headline, "Rate of Jobless Fell in February for a 2nd Month." On the face of it this would appear to be good news: the job situation, after worsening steadily for a whole year, is apparently beginning to improve. But if one reads on, one soon discovers that this is not true at all:

The drop [in unemployment] to 5.8 percent of the labor force from 6 percent in January and 6.2 percent in December . . . occurred because of a decline in the number of people looking for work rather than a rise in the number of available jobs.

By two separate measures, the total number of jobs fell slightly in February, after allowance for normal seasonal factors. And the average work-week fell by two tenths of an hour.

So the job situation really continued to deteriorate, and this rather than a lack of need on the part of the workers accounts for the fact that fewer were looking for work. But how does such a strange paradox arise? How can there be at one and the same time fewer jobs and less unemployment?

The answer lies in the definitions and methods used to measure unemployment. Government statisticians derive their figures by surveying each month a sample of households. People in each of the households selected are asked about their employment situation in order to find out in which category each person above 16 years of age fits: employed, unemployed, or "not in the labor force." Whether a person is employed or not is a fairly clear concept. But the distinction between being unemployed and outside the labor force can be very vague. Some people are obviously outside the labor force if they are mentally or physically incapacitated for work—for example if they are in hospitals or other institutions. Others may be outside the labor force because they are retired, fully occupied with taking care of a house and small children, part of the idle rich, or just don't want to work. But what about those who do not fall into this category? How does one distinguish between those who are in the labor force and those who are outside?

Apart from various technicalities, in essence government statisticians make the distinction by asking the interviewed person whether he or she has recently looked for a job. Anyone who has actively looked for a job and is not working is counted as unemployed. On the other hand, anyone not actively looking for a job and not working is counted as outside the labor force. It is this method of measuring the "official" number of unemployed which makes possible the strange result reported in the *New York Times,* i.e., a simultaneous drop in the numbers of both employed and unemployed. For there is an inverse relation between the state of the economy and the number of job-seekers. In other words, at any given time there is a considerable number of people who need and want work if jobs are available but who do not actively seek work if jobs are scarce. The more severe the job scarcity and the longer it lasts, the greater will be the number who need jobs but do not actively seek them and the more numerous will be those considered outside the labor force.

From a common-sense point of view, it stands to reason that a person who would work if an acceptable job were available but who is not looking because he doesn't think it would do any good should be classified as unemployed. But no attempt is now made to count the number of such persons, and there is no generally agreed-upon, let alone foolproof, method of estimating. Nevertheless, an attempt must be made, and to be on the safe side it seems better to use a method more likely to underestimate than overestimate the amount of this "concealed" unemployment.

We begin with a look at data on what are called Labor Force Participation Rates, henceforth referred to simply as participation rates. The overall participation rate is the percentage of the noninstitutional population counted as in the labor force. Similarly, a participation rate for a specific part of the population, say that of black males between the ages of 25 and 34, is the percentage of black males of these ages counted as in the labor force.

Table 1 (see p. 46), which is derived from official sources,* shows the participation rates for the age, sex, and color groups indicated, i.e., the percentages not institutionalized, not in the armed forces, and actually working or looking for work on the given dates. In order to show trends it is necessary that the figures should relate to a considerable period of time; while in the interest of comprehensibility it is desirable to limit as far as possible the sheer quantity of numbers. We have therefore chosen two dates, the peak year since 1948 for the participation rate in each category, and the latest figure. The year 1948 was chosen as a cutoff date on the assumption that wartime and immediate postwar participation rates would surely be abnormal by any standard and that 1948 is therefore the earliest year that could be reasonably selected. However, there is no magic about 1948, and it seemed to us most useful to single out for each category the peak year of labor force participation since 1948 and compare it with the most recent participation rate.

In the case of males, it will be noted that the peak year for the total male labor force was 1951 and that the participation rate has declined—from 86.5 percent in 1951 to 79.1 percent at the end of 1970 for whites, and from 87.3 percent to 75.2 percent for blacks.** Elements of this decline are readily explained as due primarily to non-work-related causes. Thus the sharp decline in the participation rates for young people between the ages of 16 and 24 is obviously in large part the obverse of the vast expansion of the school and college popula-

---

* *Manpower Report of the President,* March 1970; and Bureau of Labor Statistics, *Employment and Earnings,* January 1971.
** The official category for non-whites is "Negroes and Other Races," but blacks are so far the most important proportion that no error can result from substituting "Black."

TABLE 1
CIVILIAN LABOR FORCE PARTICIPATION RATES
(percent)

Age and Color	MALE		FEMALE	
	Peak since 1948	Dec. 1970	Peak since 1948	Dec. 1970
Total (age 16 and over)				
White	86.5 (1951)	79.1	43.1 (1970)	43.7
Black	87.3 (1948)	75.2	49.8 (1969)	48.4
16 & 17				
White	52.7 (1951)	45.2	35.2 (1969)	34.3
Black	60.4 (1949)	30.5	30.4 (1951)	19.5
18 & 19				
White	76.2 (1948)	63.9	54.6 (1969)	53.4
Black	80.8 (1951)	56.9	48.7 (1967)	39.7
20-24				
White	88.4 (1951)	81.7	58.0 (1970)	58.0
Black	92.8 (1952)	82.4	58.6 (1969)	57.0
25-34				
White	97.8 (1955)	96.5	44.2 (1970)	44.2
Black	96.7 (1953)	93.3	57.8 (1969)	57.4
35-44				
White	98.3 (1955)	97.3	51.3 (1970)	51.3
Black	97.3 (1953)	92.2	60.9 (1966)	59.1
45-54				
White	96.8 (1956)	94.8	54.6 (1970)	54.6
Black	95.6 (1949)	88.3	62.3 (1964)	60.6
55-64				
White	89.6 (1948)	82.6	43.2 (1970)	43.2
Black	88.6 (1948)	78.8	49.1 (1966)	45.0
65 and over				
White	46.6 (1949)	25.4	10.6 (1960)	9.9
Black	51.4 (1949)	25.2	17.5 (1948)	12.0

tion during this period, and the even sharper decline in the participation rate for those over 65 reflects developments in the social security, retirement, and pension fields.

What is really striking in the male figures is the marked,

though of course less dramatic, decline during the past two decades of the participation rates in the so-called prime-age group from 25 to 64. In all the subgroups the peak participation rate was reached by the mid-fifties and in most cases well before that, and in every case the decline since then has been substantial. In every age subgroup, moreover, the decline has been much greater for blacks than for whites.

It is in these figures, it seems to us, that one finds the most convincing evidence of growing concealed unemployment. Why should millions of men between the ages of 25 and 64 be dropping out of the labor market unless it be because they have despaired of finding acceptable jobs? Surely it cannot be argued that a huge leisure class of ex-workers has grown up in the United States during these years, for that would contradict the evidence of our senses and moreover would oblige us to conclude that relative to their place in the total population blacks have constituted by far the largest element in this fortunate new stratum! No, the only explanation that makes sense is that jobs, especially for the unskilled and less-educated, have been getting scarcer and scarcer and that the result has been to expel millions of workers from the labor market.

In the case of women, the data on labor force participation are much less revealing. This is because both the absolute number and the percentage of women over the age of 16 in the labor force have been going steadily up since the Second World War. As recently as 1953 only 33.4 percent of the white females in this age group were in the labor force, while at the end of 1970 this had risen to 43.1 percent. For black women the comparable figures were 43.6 percent in 1953 and 48.4 percent in 1970, an increase only about half as great as for whites but still of substantial magnitude. Given these strong upward trends, the peak-year participation rates tend to coincide with or be close in time to the rates of the most recent date. Under the circumstances a comparison of the peak and latest participation rates reflects little but the upward trend itself, except for the young (16-24) and old (over 65) age groups where the same forces have been at work, though to a lesser degree, as among male workers.

This emphatically does *not* mean that no concealed unemployment exists among women. We strongly suspect, indeed, that a large part of the wide disparity between male and female participation rates is an indication of massive concealed unemployment among women, a situation which until recently has been concealed even from women themselves. It is not far-fetched to speculate that a growing awareness of the huge magnitude of concealed female unemployment is one of the main driving forces behind the women's liberation movement. But the data adduced here cannot help very much in estimating the amount of concealed female unemployment,* and this is perhaps the most important reason why we are convinced that the calculation of concealed unemployment which follows understates rather than overstates the magnitude of the problem.

The method employed is a simple one. We assume that for white males aged 20-64 the "true" participation rate at the end of 1970 was not the one actually shown but the peak rate since 1948. For white males aged 16-19 we accept the 1970 rates (though convinced that they are undoubtedly too low), but we raise the much lower black rates for these age groups to the level of the white rates. (The assumption here is that if jobs were available, at least as large a proportion of blacks would be looking for them as whites.) For black males 20 and over we use either their own peak rates or those of whites in the same age subgroups, whichever are higher. For black females aged 16-19 we assume the white rates, and for black females aged 55-64 we assume the peak rate. In summary, what we have done is the following: by using the indicated set of participation rates, we add to both the labor force and to the officially counted unemployed the estimated additional numbers who would be in the labor force if jobs were available, in order to obtain a more realistic estimate of the total volume of employment and the unemployment rate at the end of 1970.

After making certain seasonal adjustments, we find that

---

* The official figures shown in Table 1 for female blacks aged 18 and 19 present a noteworthy exception. In December 1970, only 39.7 percent of these young women are counted in the labor force, while 53.4 percent of the white women in the same age group are counted in the labor force. What this surely reflects is the fewer job opportunities for young black women.

in December 1970 there were at least 2,388,000 uncounted unemployed as compared with 5,146,000 officially counted for a total of 7,534,000. To this must be added the full-time equivalent of involuntary part-time unemployment, which comes to 556,000.* The grand total of unemployment at the end of 1970 is therefore approximately 8.1 million which is 9.4 percent of the recalculated labor force. This is 50 percent higher than the official figure of 6.2 percent. By any relevant standard this indicates a profound state of economic stagnation.

Further evidence to the same effect is provided by the huge amount of idle productive capacity which now characterizes the U.S. economy. Table 2 presents the Federal Reserve Board's index of capacity utilization in manufacturing for the decade of the 1960s and the year 1970 (*Federal Reserve Bulletin,* February 1970). It shows that by the end of 1970 well over a quarter of manufacturing capacity was idle.

TABLE 2
CAPACITY UTILIZATION IN MANUFACTURING
(percent)

1960	80.6	1967		85.3
1961	78.5	1968		84.5
1962	82.1	1969	(4th quarter)	81.7
1963	83.3	1970	(1st quarter)	79.8
1964	85.7		(2nd quarter)	78.0
1965	88.5		(3rd quarter)	76.2
1966	90.5		(4th quarter)	72.3

How does this compare with the stagnation of the 1930s, generally conceded to be the worst decade in U.S. economic history? The best year for comparisons is undoubtedly 1938 which, like 1970, was a year of recession following a long period of cyclical upswing. The official unemployment figure for 1938 was 19.0 percent, and if we make a 50 percent allowance for concealed unemployment it appears that close to 30 percent of the labor force was out of work that year. No official capacity-utilization statistics were collected in those

---

* The Department of Labor reported for December 1970: 1,382,000 employed part-time for economic reasons; that is, these workers usually worked full-time and wanted full-time jobs. Since these workers were employed on an average of 24.5 hours per week, we calculated that the lack of work was equal to the unemployment of 535,000 persons.

days, but an estimate which is doubtless sufficient as an indicator of the order of magnitude involved puts the figure at 60 percent for 1938.* Thus, as one would naturally expect, the stagnation of the present period falls far short of that of the 1930s. There was proportionately perhaps three times as much unemployment then as compared to now and a third more idle capacity.

But here of course a question arises: How much of the difference between the two periods is accounted for by the fantastic growth of the war machine and the military budget in the last three decades? To provide the answer as far as unemployment is concerned, we should compare the 1938 unemployment rate with the percentage of the labor force (including the armed forces) which is today (a) unemployed, (b) in the armed forces, (c) employed as civilians by the Defense Department, (d) employed in the production of munitions, uniforms, etc. for the armed forces, and (e) employed in producing goods and services the demand for which stems indirectly from military spending (the so-called multiplier effect). Table 3 (see p. 51) gives figures for these categories.

All in all we see no reason to doubt that the total figure of 22.3 million is a reasonably accurate reflection of reality; if anything, it errs on the conservative side. And it works out to a staggering 25.1 percent of the total labor force—not much below the expanded estimate of unemployment for 1938 given above, and somewhat higher than the highest-ever officially recorded unemployment figure of 24.9 percent in 1933.

This 25.1 percent (unemployed plus armed forces plus workers directly and indirectly dependent on military spending) may be taken as a measure of the strength of the tendency to stagnation in U.S. monopoly capitalism at the beginning of the decade of the 1970s. Not surprisingly, in view of the enormous growth of monopoly in the last quarter century, it indicates that this tendency is considerably stronger than it was in the 1930s. And also not surprisingly, we have here the source of many of the destructive forces which are literally tearing the country's social fabric to pieces. What is surprising, or at least

---

* See Baran and Sweezy, *Monopoly Capital,* pp. 237, 242.

TABLE 3

UNEMPLOYMENT AND DEFENSE-RELATED EMPLOYMENT
(December 1970)

	Millions
(a) Unemployed	8.1
(b) Armed Forces	2.9
(c) Civilian employees of Defense Department	1.2
(d) Employed in producing goods for the Defense Department	3.0
(e) Multiplier effect	7.1
Total	22.3

Sources: For (a) see above; (b) and (c) *Defense Indicators,* U.S. Department of Commerce, February 1971; (d) latest official figure
is 1968 *(Statistical Abstract 1970,* p. 253) which has been
reduced to reflect decline in defense spending since then; (e)
multiplier of 1 is the low range estimated by U.S. Arms Control and Disarmament Agency, *Economic Aspects of Disarmament,* 1962 (see Harry Magdoff, "Problems of United States
Capitalism," above, footnotes 1 and 2.

ought to be, is that this whole subject of the stagnationist tendencies of monopoly capitalism is virtually forbidden territory
to academic economists. The duly accredited members of the
economics profession not only do not study the subject, they
do not even recognize its existence.

The reason for this self-imposed blindness would seem to
be a perhaps subconscious unwillingness to face the very harsh
reality, that within the framework of the system there is absolutely no way the problem can be solved or even effectively
ameliorated. For a long time—during what C. Wright Mills
called the Great American Celebration of the 1950s and early
1960s—it seemed that cold and hot wars, in addition to making
the "free world" safe for American investment, would provide
a permanent answer. But that illusion, like much else, fell victim to the war in Vietnam. Under the impact of a soaring
military budget, the official unemployment rate (though not
concealed unemployment) improved for a few years, but only at
the cost of touching off an accelerating inflationary process
which gives every sign of long outlasting the boom which

started it. The combined effect of war and inflation was to multiply and inflame all the society's open and latent tensions and contradictions. Revolts broke out among blacks, young people, women; class struggles burst forth on the economic front after a long period of relative calm; and internationally a continuing series of astronomical balance-of-payments deficits threatens to undermine the supremacy of the dollar and with it U.S. hegemony over the capitalist world. And now a normal cyclical downturn plus a relatively minor reduction in military spending (from $78.8 billion in 1969 to $76.6 billion in 1970) have pushed the country back into the deepening stagnation typical of the late Eisenhower years from which Kennedy rearmament and the Vietnam war were supposed to have rescued it. For those with eyes to see it is now crystal clear that the whole inherently monstrous idea of salvation through war was really never anything but a cruel deception.

All of which leads straight to the conclusion which the economists are unwilling to face, that the only solution is a complete change in the economic system. Fortunately, more and more people are coming to understand this, or at least to suspect it, with the result that the economists' tacit "conspiracy of ignorance" is beginning to yield diminishing returns. How else could we explain the appearance in, of all places, the *New York Times Magazine* (Sunday, March 7) of an eminently rational and sensible analysis of the growing welfare crisis? The article, by Herbert J. Gans who is described as a professor of sociology and planning at M.I.T., begins as follows:

When the Nixon administration's Family Assistance Plan was shelved by the last Congress at the end of 1970, 15 percent of New York's population, 25 percent of Newark's population, and 6 percent of all Americans—about 12.5 million people—were on welfare, and since then their number has continued to rise faster than expected.

Further to indicate the nature of the problem, Professor Gans might have added that between the 1960 and 1970 censuses the total population of the United States rose by 13 percent while the welfare rolls shot up by no less than 94 percent. There are doubtless a number of factors at work here (the ghetto rebellions of the mid-60s certainly played a role in inducing cities to be more "generous" in dispensing welfare benefits, and the poor are clearly more aware of their rights today than they were ten years ago), but no one who has made even a cursory study of the subject doubts that the real driving force came from growing poverty related to the increase in concealed unemployment. After noting some of the proposals being made for dealing with the problem, Gans proceeds:

> None of the programs . . . can do much about the welfare problem itself. That problem is really in the heart of the American economy, which simply does not need all the unemployed looking for work at a living wage and which cannot provide for all the working poor who require higher wages to support their families. Ultimately, therefore, an end to the welfare problem requires either remaking the economy so that it provides full employment at a living wage, or altering public beliefs about welfare so that the government will provide the unneeded and underpaid with a decent income.

Which, practically speaking, is another way of saying that the welfare problem will be with us—and growing—as long as we have monopoly capitalism. For if historical experience teaches anything, surely it is that under this system power is in the hands of a class which has no intention whatever of either remaking the economy or handing over tens of billions of dollars every year to the unneeded and underpaid.

It is encouraging that academic sociologists and the *New York Times* are prepared to discuss these matters seriously and not simply in terms of the ruling-class ideology. Is it too much to hope that the economists, whose special job it ought to be, will some day catch up?

But of course this is not the really important question for socialists, whose educational task is much broader and more important that that of the academic social scientists. We have to teach literally masses of people not only the nature of the system but also that the only alternative with a chance of rescuing us from the deep trouble we're in is socialism. On our success or failure to achieve this in good time may depend the whole future of mankind. Unfortunately, this is not rhetorical exaggeration. It is a sober and sobering fact.

Militarism and Imperialism

February 1970

Peace reigns supreme in the realm of neo-classical economics. War, militarism, and the pacification of natives are treated as merely elements which disturb the harmonious equilibrium models which are to supply us with the universal truths about the allocation of scarce resources.

One of the distinguishing features of Marxist thought, on the other hand, is the conviction that economic processes must be understood as part of a social organism in which political force plays a leading role and in which war is at least as typical as peace. In this context, militarism and imperialism are seen as major determinants of the form and direction of technological change, of the allocation of resources within a country, and of the allocation of resources between countries (notably, between rich and poor countries). Accordingly, price and income relations, treated as the ultimate yardsticks of economic efficiency and social justice in neo-classical economics, are viewed, in the Marxist context, as evolutionary products of capitalist institutions in which political force and "pure" economics are intertwined. Rosa Luxemburg put the Marxist case this way:

> Bourgeois liberal theory takes into account only [one aspect of economic development]: the realm of "peaceful competition," the marvels of technology and pure commodity exchange; it separates

This is a paper delivered by Harry Magdoff at a session on "The Economics of Imperialism," at the annual meeting of the American Economic Association on December 30, 1969.

it strictly from the other aspect: the realm of capital's blustering violence which is regarded as more or less incidental to foreign policy and quite independent of the economic sphere of capital.

In reality, political power is nothing but a vehicle for the economic process. The conditions for the reproduction of capital provide the organic link between these two aspects of the accumulation of capital. The historical career of capitalism can be appreciated only by taking them together.*[1]

The facts of U.S. history provide eloquent testimony to the accuracy of this diagnosis. Thus, Professor Quincy Wright, who directed a major study of war under the auspices of Chicago University, observed in 1942: "The United States, which has, perhaps somewhat unjustifiably, prided itself on its peacefulness, has had only twenty years during its entire history when its army or navy has not been in active operation some days, somewhere."[2]

Professor Wright identifies years of peace as those in which no action of any sort occurred. A more revealing picture is obtained if we measure months of war against months of peace and bring the information up to the present. Adding up the months during which U.S. military forces were engaged in action—starting from the Revolutionary War and including wars against the Indians, punitive expeditions to Latin America and Asia, as well as major wars—we find that the United States was engaged in warlike activity during three-fourths of its history, in 1,782 of the last 2,340 months.[3] In other words, on the average, there have been three full years in which our armed forces have been engaged in action for every full year of peace. This comparison does not indicate the full extent of the use of military power by the United States to enforce its will. For example, it does not include activities such as those formerly conducted by U.S. gunboats in a "constant patrol in the Yangtze River . . . from the mouth of the river up nearly 2,000 miles into the very heart of China."[4]

It should therefore come as no surprise to discover that war-related expenditures have constituted the dominant sector of the federal budget throughout our history. Omitting the years of the Second World War and the postwar period, where

---

* Notes will be found at the end of the article.

the record is so well known, a tabulation of federal expenditures by decade, from 1800 to 1939, for army, navy, veterans' compensation and pensions, and interest on the debt—prior to the New Deal federal debt incurred was primarily a result of war spending—shows that except for one decade, at least 54 percent of federal expenditures were for military activities or preparations during the decade or to meet obligations arising from previous military activity.[5] The one exception was the decade of the great depression (1930-1939) when the percentage dropped to somewhat below 40 percent. In seven of the fourteen decades the war-related share of the federal budget was 70 percent or more.

This almost continuous preoccupation with military affairs was clearly not inspired by fears of invading barbarians. Of course, the competing colonial and commercial interests of France, England, Spain, and Russia were part of the reality in which the infant and adolescent United States had to operate. At times, self-defense had to be considered. Moreover, resolution of internal tensions, as in the Civil War, exercised a major influence on military aspects of U.S. life. All of this, however, occurred within a context of empire-building. For there has been a continuous thread in U.S. history, beginning with colonial and revolutionary days, of economic, political, and military expansionism directed towards the creation and growth of an American empire. The original expansionism, for which military investment was needed, concentrated on three main thrusts: (1) consolidation of a transcontinental nation, (2) obtaining control of the Caribbean area, and (3) achieving a major position in the Pacific Ocean.[6] It should be noted that this expansionism was not confined to what is now considered the continental territory of the United States: striving for control of the seas, as a shield and promoter of international commerce, has been an ingredient of U.S. policy from its earliest days. In fact, the struggle to incorporate the West Coast into the United States was, among other things, prompted by the desire to control Pacific Ocean ports for the Asian trade.[7]

The experience thus gained in the early stages of empire-building turned out to be most useful when the leading nations of the world entered the stage of imperialism. Several decisive and coinciding developments in the late nineteenth and early twentieth centuries mark off this new stage:

(1)   The onset of significant concentration of economic power in the hands of a relatively small number of industrial and financial giants in advanced nations. Competing interest-groups continued to exist, but now the success or failure of the advanced economies became closely identified with the prosperity of the new giant corporations whose *modus operandi* required control over international sources of supply and markets.

(2)   The decline of Great Britain's monopoly position as world trader and world banker. The burgeoning competitive industrial powers—notably, Germany, France, the United States, and Japan—pressed for a reshuffle of established trade relations and a redistribution of world markets.

(3)   Industrialization and new naval technology enabled competitive nations to build up their own naval strength to the point where Great Britain could no longer maintain unilateral control over the major sea lanes. As Quincy Wright put it in the study already referred to, "Naval inventions and the spread of industrialization had ended the *pax Britannica*."[8] Control over sea routes also involved establishing military bases where naval units could be refueled and repaired. The availability of decisive mobile military power on the one hand required acquisition of strategic foreign territory to support bases, and on the other hand provided the means for aggressive pursuit of colonial possessions.

(4)   The earliest stage of the new imperialism engendered a race by the major powers for control of available foreign real estate. According to Theodore Ropp, after 1880 "every great power except Austria-Hungary . . . became involved in . . . active, conscious colonial expansionism. . . ."[9] Of the traditional colonial powers—the Netherlands, Portugal, Spain, Britain, France, and Russia—the last four continued to add to their holdings. (Spain, after losing Cuba and the Philippines, proceeded to conquer Spanish Morocco.) And at the same time five new powers entered the race for colonial territory: Germany, Italy, Belgium, Japan, and the United States. As for

the United States, it was the Spanish-American War, of course, that placed it with both feet in the imperialist camp. And it was success in this war, plus the subsequent pacification of the Cuban and Philippine "natives," which satisfied two long-term U.S. expansionist ambitions: a leading position in the Caribbean, broadening the highway to the rest of Latin America, and a solid base in the Pacific for a greater stake in Asian business.

As far as the United States is concerned, there have been three distinct stages in the drive to empire: (1) the period when the United States was the supplier of food and raw materials to the rest of the world, when it was an importer of capital, and when maritime commercial interests were relatively very strong; (2) the period when the United States began to compete with other industrialized nations as an exporter of manufactured goods and an exporter of capital—a time when a small number of industrial and financial giants began to dominate the economic scene; and (3) the period when the United States becomes the major, dominant capitalist economy, the largest manufacturer, foreign investor, trader, the world's banker, and the dollar becomes the key international currency.

The energy and determination with which the expansionist strategy is pursued change from time to time. In the transition from one period to another, and because of internal as well as external conditions, it appears at times as if the United States is "isolationist" and uninterested in further extension of its influence and control.[10] Yet it is especially noteworthy that the drive for business opportunities on a world scale is ever present. Even when, as in New Deal days, domestic solutions were sought for crises, the development of foreign business was high on the agenda of government and private enterprise. Given the structure of the economy, the major operating levers work in such a way as to repeatedly reassert expansionism as the dominant strategy. In this perspective, the history of the years since the end of the Second World War is far from a new departure; instead it is a culmination of long-term tendencies which profited by and matured most readily in the environment created by the course of the last major war.

The postwar leap forward in empire-building and the transition of U.S. society to rampant militarism are associated with two phenomena: (1) the desire to resist and repress socialist nations and to defeat national liberation movements designed to release underdeveloped countries from dependence on the imperialist network, and (2) the extension of U.S. power to fill "vacuums" created by the decline of Western European and Japanese influence in Asia, Africa, and Latin America.

Combating the rise of socialism is of course not a new objective. The destruction of the Russian Revolution was a top priority of the imperialist powers beginning in 1917. In this connection, Thorstein Veblen's observations on the Versailles Treaty in his 1920 review of Keynes's *The Economic Consequences of the Peace* are most pertinent:

> The events of the past months go to show that the central and most binding provision of the Treaty (and of the League) is an unrecorded clause by which the governments of the Great Powers are banded together for the suppression of Soviet Russia— unrecorded unless record of it is to be found somewhere among the secret archives of the League or of the Great Powers. Apart from this unacknowledged compact there appears to be nothing in the Treaty that has any character of stability or binding force. Of course, this compact for the reduction of Soviet Russia was not written into the text of the Treaty; it may rather be said to have been the parchment upon which the text was written.[11]

The failure of the United States to join the League of Nations reflected no slackness in its efforts to contain anti-imperialist revolutions: in Russia, these efforts took the form of armed intervention and support of anti-Bolshevik forces with food and other economic supplies; in Hungary, the manipulation of food supplies to help defeat the Bela Kun government. Surely the issue at that time was not fear of aggressive Russian or Hungarian militarism. Nor can much credit be given to political or religious idealism. The relevant motive, clearly, was recovery of territory lost to free enterprise and prevention of the spread of the contagious revolutionary disease to Western Europe and the colonies. Any such spread, it was recognized, would severely affect the stability and prosperity of the remaining capitalist nations.

Capitalism as an economic system was never confined to one nation. It was born, developed, and prospered as part of a world system. Karl Marx went so far as to claim, "The specific task of bourgeois society is the establishment of a world market, at least in outline, and of production based upon this world market."[12] One might add that it has been the specific task of imperialism to fill out this outline and establish a complex international network of trade, finance, and investment. Given this network, it follows that limitation of opportunity to trade and invest in one part of the world restricts to a greater or lesser extent the freedom of action of private enterprise in other parts of the world. The dimensions of the defense of free enterprise therefore become world-wide.

The United States had long ago accepted its destiny to open and keep open the door for trade and investment in other parts of the world. The obstacles were not only the heathens who wanted to be left alone, but the preference systems established in the colonies of the older nations. The decline of political colonialism and the weakness of the other great powers thus placed upon the United States a primary responsibility for the defense of the capitalist system and at the same time afforded golden opportunities to obtain special beachheads and open doors for U.S. enterprise.

With a task of this magnitude, it is little wonder that the United States now has a larger "peacetime" war machine, covering a greater part of the globe, than has any other nation in all of past history. Imperialism necessarily involves militarism. Indeed, they are twins that have fed on each other in the past, as they do now. Yet not even at the peak of the struggle for colonies did any of the imperialist powers, or combination of powers, maintain a war machine of such size and such dispersion as does the United States today. In 1937, when the arms race in preparation for the Second World War was already under way, the per capita military expenditures of all the great powers combined—the United States, the British Empire, France, Japan, Germany, Italy, and the Soviet Union— was $25. (Germany's per capita of $58.82 was then the largest.)[13] In 1968, the per capita military expenditures of the United States alone, in 1937 prices, was $132. This was only in part due to the Vietnam War: in 1964, our most recent "peace" year, the per capita military expenditures in 1937 prices was $103.[14]

One of the reasons for this huge increase in military outlays is no doubt the greater sophistication of weaponry. (By the same token, it is the advanced airplane and missile technology which makes feasible the U.S. globe-straddling military posture.) An additional reason, of course, is the military strength of the socialist camp. I would like to suggest a third reason: that a substantial portion of the huge military machine, including that of the Western European nations, is the price being paid to maintain the imperialist network of trade and investment *in the absence of colonialism*. The achievement of political independence by former colonies has stimulated internal class struggles in the new states for economic as well as political independence. Continuing the economic dependence of these nations on the metropolitan centers within the framework of political independence calls for, among other things, the world-wide dispersion of U.S. military forces and the direct military support of the local ruling classes.

Precise information on the dispersion of U.S. forces is kept an official secret. However, retired General David M. Shoup, former head of the Marine Corps, who should be in a position to make a realistic estimate, stated in a recent article in *The Atlantic*: "We maintain more than 1,517,000 Americans in uniform overseas in 119 countries. We have 8 treaties to help defend 48 nations if they ask us to or if we choose to intervene in their affairs."[15] The main substance of U.S. overseas power, aside from its present application in Vietnam, is spread out over 429 major and 2,972 minor military bases. These bases cover 4,000 square miles in 30 foreign countries, as well as Hawaii and Alaska.[16] Backing this up, and acting as a coordinator of the lesser imperialist powers and the Third World incorporated in the imperialist network, is a massive program of military assistance. According to a recent study:

U.S. military aid . . . since 1945 has averaged more than $2 billion per year. It rose to as much as $5 billion in fiscal year

(FY) 1952 and fell to as low as $831 million in FY 1956. The number of recipient countries rose from 14 in 1950 to a peak so far of 69 in 1963. In all, some 80 countries have received a total of $50 billion in American military aid since World War II. Except for 11 hard-core communist countries and certain nations tied closely to either Britain or France, very few nations have never received military aid of one kind or another from the United States.[17]

The above factual recital by no means exhausts the international functions of U.S. militarism. Space considerations permit no more than passing reference to (a) the active promotion of commercial armament sales abroad (contributing a sizable portion of the merchandise export surplus in recent years), (b) the extensive training of foreign military personnel, and (c) the use of economic-aid funds to train local police forces for "handling mob demonstrations and counterintelligence work."[18] These are, in the main, additional instruments for maintaining adherence and loyalty of the non-socialist world to the free-enterprise system in general, and to the United States in particular.

The military forces of the politically independent underdeveloped countries frequently perform a very special function. This arises from the relative weaknesses of the competitive elite power groups: large landowners, merchants, industrialists and financiers—each with varying degrees of alliance to interest groups in the metropolitan center. When none of these ruling-class groups has the strength and resources to take the political reins in its own hands and assert its hegemony over the others, the social order is operated by means of temporary and unstable alliances. Under such circumstances, and especially when the existing order is threatened by social revolution, the military organizations become increasingly important as a focal point for the power struggle within the ruling classes and/or as the organizer of political arrangements. Space limitations do not permit a review of this special role of militarism in the underdeveloped world as, one might say, the skeletal framework of the imperialist system in the absence of colonies. It is this framework that is supported and nurtured by the practices mentioned above: military training and advisory services, the widespread military assistance programs, and the stimulus given to commercial sales of U.S. armaments.

This militarism which is working to control the rest of the world is at the same time helping to shape the nature of U.S. society. Some sense of the immensity of this impact can be obtained by noting the relevance of military spending on the employment/unemployment situation. In the first three quarters of 1969, approximately 8.3 million persons were employed as a result of the military program: 3.5 million in the armed services, 1.3 million Defense Department civilian employees, and 3.5 million engaged in producing and moving the goods purchased for the military services.[19] At the same time, there are at least 3.7 million unemployed.[20]

Consider for a moment what it would mean if 8.3 million were not engaged in military affairs. Without substitute employment, this could mean a total of over 12 million unemployed, or a 14.3 percent rate of unemployment. The last time the United States had such a rate of unemployment was 1937. The percentage of the labor force unemployed in 1931, the second full year of the Great Depression, was less than 2 points higher, 15.9 percent.[21]

So far we have not taken into account the multiplier effect. It has been estimated that for every $1 spent on national defense, another $1 to $1.40 of national product is stimulated.[22] If we accept only the lower estimate, and assume for the sake of the argument equivalent labor productivity in the military and civilian sectors, we reach a measure of unemployment in the neighborhood of 24.3 percent, in the absence of the military budget. Compare this with the unemployment rate of 24.9 percent at the depth of the Depression in 1932.

A counter-argument can, of course, be made to these broad generalizations. Unemployment insurance, for example, would to a limited extent and for a very limited time act as an offset. Conceivably, a sharp decline in military spending, if there were no financial collapse accompanying it, would reduce interest rates and thus perhaps stimulate construction and some types of state and municipal investment. A reduction in taxes would generate consumer demand. A rise in the federal social welfare program would have its effect. But it is by no means obvious that these counteractions would have anywhere near the same impact on the economy as defense spending.

Economists are to a large measure captives of the neat models they create, and they consequently ignore strategic dynamic elements which keep the economy going. For example, they tend to underestimate, if not ignore, the special effects of persistent inflation on business practices regarding inventory accumulation and investment in plant and equipment. Even more important is the almost total neglect of the influence of stock market and real estate speculation on (a) business investment decisions, and (b) the buoyancy of the especially important luxury trades. Inflation and speculation—partners of militarism—have been key triggers of our postwar prosperity, and they are too easily ignored as economists blandly transfer a block of GNP from one category to another, as if such transfers are made in the economy as simply as one keeps accounts.

The experience of the last depression still remains a challenge to economists to come up with an explanation of the way in which the economy operates in reality. For example, consider where we stood in 1939 after ten years of depression. Personal consumption expenditures had finally climbed to a new high—6 percent above 1929 in constant prices. Yet, at the same time, nonresidential fixed investment expenditures were 42 percent below the level of 1929, and residential construction was 20 percent below.[23] Despite six years of rising consumer spending, and the start of orders flowing in from France and England for rearming, the investment community was still in a state of depression, and over 17 percent of the labor force was unemployed.

In this connection, it is important to recognize that one of the major attributes of the huge military spending in the postwar years is its concentration in the producers durable field and the stimulation it gives to the demand for machinery and equipment. If we combine the spending for producers durable goods resulting from the military with private spending for the same type of goods, we find the following: 36 percent of the output of the producers durable goods industries is purchased directly or indirectly by the federal government.[24] (These data are for 1963, before the impact of the Vietnam War.) It is here, I suggest, that we find the unique role of military spending in raising and sustaining production and employment at new highs.

There are, to be sure, other impacts of defense spending that help to explain the magnitude and structure of the postwar economy: the unique role of research stimulated and financed by military and space programs; the special place of defense spending in nurturing the growth and prosperity of key giant industrial and financial enterprises; the support given by U.S. military power to acceptance of the U.S. dollar as an international currency;[25] the ease with which military orders can be fed into the economy in spurts which act as adrenalin injections to the private sector.

At the least, it can be concluded, economic theory and analysis which omit imperialism and militarism from their underlying paradigm are far removed from the reality of today's world. More realistically, it can be said that they operate to obscure the truth about the great problems and dangers of the second half of the twentieth century.

NOTES

1. Rosa Luxemburg, *The Accumulation of Capital*. New York, 1964, pp. 452-453.
2. Quincy Wright, *A Study of War*. Chicago, 1942, vol. I, p. 236.
3. Calculated from list in Lawrence Dennis, *Operational Thinking for Survival*. Colorado Springs, 1969, appendix II.
4. Office of Naval Intelligence, *The United States Navy as an Industrial Asset*. Washington, D.C., 1923, p. 4.
5. Calculated from data in *Historical Statistics of the United States, Colonial Times to 1957*. Washington, D. C., 1961, pp. 718-719.
6. Richard W. Van Alstyne, *The Rising American Empire*. Chicago, 1965.
7. *Ibid.*, chap. 5, "Manifest Destiny and Empire, 1820-1870."
8. Quincy Wright, *op cit.*, vol. I, p. 299.
9. Theodore Ropp, *War in the Modern World*. New York, 1962, p. 206.
10. The isolationism was usually more apparent than real. See William Appleman Williams, *The Tragedy of American Diplomacy*. New York, 1962, chap. 4, "The Legend of Isolationism."
11. Thorstein Veblen, "The Economic Consequences of the Peace," in *Essays in Our Changing Order*. New York, 1934, p. 464.
12. In a letter from Marx to Engels, October 8, 1858, in Karl Marx and Friedrich Engels, *Correspondence 1846-1895*. New York, 1934, p. 117.
13. Quincy Wright, *op. cit.*, pp. 670-671.
14. The data on military expenditures are the purchases of goods and services for "national defense" and "space research and technology" as used in computing Gross National Product. The 1964 and 1968 data are reported in the *Survey of Current Business*, July 1968 and July

1969. The adjustment for price changes was made by using the im-given in the *Economic Report of the President,* January 1969, Washington, D.C., 1969.

15. General David M. Shoup, "The New American Militarism," *The Atlantic,* April 1969. The figure of 119 countries seems too large. General Shoup was probably including bases on island locations, which he counted as separate countries. Our guess is that U.S. armed forces to man bases, administer military assistance, and train foreign officers are located in 70 to 80 countries.

16. *New York Times,* April 9, 1969.

17. George Thayer, *The War Business, The International Trade in Armaments.* New York, 1969, pp. 37-38. This is a summary of data presented in *Military Assistance Facts,* May 1, 1966, brought up-to-date through fiscal year 1968.

18. For (a), see *ibid.* (b), see John Dunn, *Military Aid and Military Elites: The Political Potential of American Training and Technical Assistance Programs.* Unpublished Ph.D. dissertation, Princeton University, 1961. (c), see Edwin Lieuwen, *The United States and the Challenge to Security in Latin America.* Ohio, 1966, p. 16.

19. Data on armed services and Defense Department civilian employment from *Defense Indicators* (Bureau of the Census), November 1969. The estimate of the number employed by private industry for military production is based on Richard P. Oliver's study, "The Employment Effect of Defense Expenditures," *Monthly Labor Review,* September 1967. Mr. Oliver estimated 2.972 million employed in private industry in the fiscal year ending June 30, 1967, as a result of Defense Department expenditures. We brought this estimate up to date by (1) assuming no increase in productivity or major change in the composition of production since fiscal year 1967; (2) using the expenditure data for the first three-quarters of 1969; (3) adding space research and technology and one-half of Atomic Energy Commission expenditures, both of which had been excluded in Mr. Oliver's estimates; and (4) adjusting for price increases in the last two years. The resulting figure of 3.5 million is therefore a broad estimate, but the margin of error is not such as in any way to invalidate our analysis.

20. Based on data in *Employment and Earnings* (Bureau of Labor Statistics), January to November 1969. The 3.7 million estimate represents the full-time unemployed plus the full-time equivalent of those who were working involuntarily less than a full week. This estimate does not take into account the unemployed who are not counted in the government survey.

21. Economic Report of the President, January 1969, p. 252. 1969, p. 252.

22. U.S. Arms Control and Disarmament Agency, *Economic Impacts of Disarmament,* Washington, D.C., 1962.

23. *Economic Report of the President,* January 1969, p. 228.

24. Calculated from tables in "Input-Output Structure of the U.S. Economy: 1963," *Survey of Current Business,* November 1969. The percents of direct and indirect output attributable to (a) gross private fixed capital formation and (b) federal government purchases were used. These percentages were applied to the gross output of each of the industries manufacturing durable goods. It is generally es-

timated that 85 percent of federal government purchases are for the military. The figure is probably higher for durable goods manufacturing industries alone.

25. Given the inadequate U.S. gold reserves, the U.S. dollar can serve as an international currency only as long as foreign banks are willing to keep dollar credit balances in the United States as a substitute for gold payments. It is interesting that former Under Secretary of the Treasury for Monetary Affairs Robert Roosa included the military strength of the United States as a factor in maintaining the present international monetary system: "Moreover, the political stability and enormous economic and military strength of the United States have also increased the desirability of keeping balances here rather than in any other country in the world." (Robert V. Roosa, *Monetary Reform for the World Economy*, New York, 1965, p. 9.)

The Merger Movement: A Study in Power

June 1969

During the last year or so a tremendous amount of publicity has been devoted to the corporate merger movement, but to our knowledge there has not been much serious discussion of its significance. A review of some of the outstanding facts and what they mean and do not mean may therefore be useful.

To begin with, there can be no doubt about the impressive magnitude of the movement, measured by any relevant standard. The following table is constructed from Federal Trade Commission data as reported in *Business Week* of April 19:

	1966	1967	1968
Total number of acquisitions	1,746	2,384	4,003
Number of mfg. and mining companies with more than $10 million assets acquired	101	169	192
Value of assets of acquired companies with more than $10 million assets (billion $)	4.1	8.2	12.6
Number of acquisitions made by 200 largest companies	33	67	74
Value of assets of companies acquired by 200 largest companies (billion $)	2.4	5.4	6.9

Complete data for early 1969 are not published in the article from which these figures are taken, but one statistic alone is enough to show that, far from coming to an end, the merger movement has actually accelerated in recent months. As against the $12.6 billion dollars of assets in companies with assets of $10 million or more which were gobbled up in 1968, the comparable rate of acquisition so far in 1969 has been running at about $18 billion.

As to the size of the present movement relative to earlier merger movements in U.S. history, *Fortune* magazine (February 1969, p. 80) states: "There have been merger movements in the U.S. before. One began in the 1890's and another in the 1920's; each lasted about a decade. But the current merger movement is lasting longer and is immensely bigger."

It is more difficult (and indeed may be impossible) to gauge the effects of the merger movement on the relative importance, in the economic system as a whole, of the giant corporations. The reason is that mergers (in Marxian terminology, the centralization of capital) are not the only factor operating here. In addition there is what Marx called the concentration of capital, which takes place through the growth of the separate companies rather than through their combination. The two forces—centralization and concentration—operate simultaneously and reinforce each other. Some idea of their combined effect in the postwar period can be gathered from the growth of the relative share of value added in manufacturing accounted for by the 200 largest manufacturing companies from 1947 to 1963. The figures stood at 30 percent in 1947 and rose to 37 percent in 1954 and 41 percent in 1963.*

There has certainly been a further increase in the relative importance of the giant corporations since 1963, but, for reasons just indicated, it would be wrong to attribute this entirely to the merger movement. In fact, even if there had been no mergers at all, the giants would still have grown, relative to the economy as a whole. This follows from two well-established facts: (1) On the average, the bigger a corporation is, the higher its rate of profit.** And (2) the more profitable a company is, the faster it can grow through the internal accumulation of capital. Big companies therefore normally grow faster than small ones and correspondingly take over an increasing share of the total econ-

---

* Data for 1947 and 1954 from a Senate committee report, cited in Baran and Sweezy, *Monopoly Capital,* p. 226n; and for 1963 from a special report "Corporations: Where the Game is Growth," in *Business Week,* September 30, 1967.

** On this, see the recently published study *Profits in the United States: An Introduction to a Study of Economic Concentration and Business Cycles,* by Howard S. Sherman, Cornell University Press, 1968, especially Chapter 2.

omy even without any merger activity at all. Mergers undoubtedly hasten the process, but they are by no means essential to its functioning or continuation.

In assessing the economic significance of the merger movement, a further consideration needs to be taken into account. As a capitalist economy passes from its competitive to its monopolistic stage, certain characteristic features and laws of motion come into operation: absorption of the economic surplus becomes increasingly difficult, and the system is faced ever more sharply with the alternatives of economic stagnation and mass unemployment on the one hand or mounting production for socially wasteful and destructive purposes on the other. It is by no means clear, however, that the further development of monopoly after a certain point will have a proportionate effect on the way the system works. In this connection the performance of the U.S. economy in the 1930's is particularly relevant. The length and depth of the Depression from 1929 to 1933 and the fact that the ensuing upswing came to an end in 1937 with more than 14 percent of the labor force still unemployed, suggest that the degree of monopolization reached by 1930 was already enough to dominate completely the functioning of the economy and to prevent it from achieving anything even close to full employment except through massive private and public waste. In other words the kind of viciously irrational and destructive system we have today was fully shaped as far back as forty years ago. Increasing monopolization since then has doubtless made matters worse, but not essentially different.

Let us now turn to the question of the effect of the merger movement—or, more accurately, of the growing relative importance of the giant corporations—on small business. Radicals and anti-monopoly liberals frequently assume that the increasing dominance of the giants necessarily implies the decline and fall of small business. Nothing could be further from the truth. A recent story in the *Wall Street Journal* (April 10) begins as follows:

Worried that conglomerates are gobbling up companies so fast that by the end of the century some 200 super-corporations will own all of American business?

Take heart. Far more businesses are starting out than selling out these days.

Most of the fledgling firms are small, of course, and many won't last a year, but they are being formed at the fastest clip since the years that immediately followed World War II.

Analysts estimate that between 450,000 and 500,000 new businesses will be launched this year, about 25 percent more than a half-dozen years ago. By comparison, W. T. Grimm & Co., a Chicago financial consulting firm, predicts that some 5,400 companies will go out of existence through merger or acquisition in 1969.

The government's new-business index, which measures the net growth in business formations (new businesses minus firms that discontinue operations), last December stood at the highest point since mid-1948.

The great majority of these new businesses of course are in either retailing or the service trades, but there are also many in various branches of manufacturing. And far from contradicting the interests of the giant corporations, this proliferation of small businesses serves their purposes in many ways. A detailed discussion of this problem would take us far afield, but it may be worthwhile to point out three specific ways in which the giants benefit from the existence of small businesses.

(1) Every big corporation buys thousands of items ranging all the way from huge machines to paper clips. Many of these are supplied by other big corporations, but many offer too little prospect of profit to interest the big ones and these become the domain of small business. This being the case, the giants naturally prefer that there should be an ample number of suppliers competing among themselves to ensure low prices and good quality.

(2) The markets for the products of the giants typically undergo seasonal and/or cyclical variations. This means that at any given time demand for a product can be divided into a large segment which can be looked upon as stable and reliable and a smaller segment which fluctuates and may even disappear with the vicissitudes of the market. The giants employ various strategies for dealing with this problem, depending on the nature of the product and the market; but in most cases at least one element in the strategy adopted is to allow a number of smaller companies to enter the industry and fill some part of the fluctuating demand. Benefiting from the giants' monopoly price

umbrella, these small companies may do very well when demand is strong. The other side of the coin of course is that they may be hit hard or even wiped out when demand is weak. In any case they act as a sort of stabilizer and balancer for the carefully calculating giants.

(3) Finally, much of the innovating function under monopoly capitalism is carried out not by the giants but by small firms, often specifically organized to turn out a new product or try a new method of production or distribution. And this is done not against the will of the giants but with their hearty approval. Innovating is risky. Most small outfits that try it fail, but a few hit the jackpot and it is this glittering reward that motivates a host of new hopefuls to keep at it. From the point of view of the giants all this activity serves the extremely useful purpose of showing which lines of innovation are practical and profitable, with all the risk being borne by others. Later on, the giants can move in, either buying out the successful small firm or imitating its innovation with a version of their own.

There are other business and technical reasons for the existence and spread of small enterprises in the period of monopoly capitalism, but the three described above should be enough to dispose of the unfounded notion that there is any tendency for the concentration and centralization of capital to result in the disappearance of small business. The *relative* importance of the giants grows; but as long as the system as a whole expands (and capitalism cannot live without expanding), this not only does not preclude but actually requires an *absolute* proliferation of the dwarfs.

Our analysis to this point leads to the conclusion that the current merger movement, though undoubtedly massive by historical standards, is not likely to have any profound effects on either the functioning or structure of the U.S. economy. What it means is more of the same, not anything really new. And the same goes for the much-publicized fact that the most spectacular merging activity of the last few years has been by the so-called conglomerates, i.e., companies which operate not in one market or a few related markets but in dozens or even scores of often quite unrelated markets. Two of the top five companies on *Fortune*'s latest list of the 500 largest nonfinancial corporations (General Motors which is number 1 and General Electric which is number 4) have long been conglomerates in this sense; and many, perhaps even a majority, of the others would qualify for the same designation. The real reason for the excitement about the "new" conglomerates lies elsewhere than in their newness.

For one thing, the latter-day conglomerates have been heavily promoted by all the devices of the Madison Avenue public relations industry and its Wall Street affiliates and confrères. The conglomerates—along with other corporations like IBM and Xerox which are not conglomerate or at any rate less conglomerate—have been built up as the "glamour" companies. Their masterminds are pictured as financial wizards and/or technological geniuses; their methods and operations are wrapped in an aura of magic and mystery; their potential for growth is blown up to fantastic proportions. A satirical piece in *Barron's* of February 5, 1968, purporting to give advice to the hopeful organizer of a new conglomerate, is worth quoting at considerable length both for its truth content and for its entertainment value:

Thanks for your letter telling me that you'd decided to become a conglomerate. It's about time you wised up and resolved, as they say, to flourish and make megabucks instead of knocking yourself out trying to keep the earnings of your crummy foundry from going down.

You ask how to do it. Brains, guts, funny money, a smile, and a shoeshine ought to be a sufficiency. It's really not much harder or very different from promoting one of those chain-letter games we used to play when we were kids. And don't kid yourself, it may end the same way. But you make a lot more money.

Anyway, the first thing to do is get hold of the speeches and annual reports of the real savvy swingers, who know the lingo and can make it sing. . . .

Actually, for my money, a cat out on the West Coast has the real psychedelic line—it's too bad you're not a doctor of something like he is. This doctor stuff goes over big with the security analysts. Anyway, read his stuff. He's got all the moves.

He made a speech to the San Francisco security analysts, where he talked about "advanced materials systems," "productizing R&D," and "the tools of growth: nucleation, replication, and working the synergies." He told *Business Week* the aim of his acquisition program was to provide "rivers of marketing into which we can feed the higher technology materials and products," and yaks about "the point of nucleation for a large-scale market penetration."

And this from a cat with about two-thirds of sales in defense parts, valves, actuators, structures, and metals brokerage-and-distribution. . . .

In the presentation at San Francisco, the Whittaker guys must have talked at least an hour about technology, philosophy, and the future, and hardly mentioned their present businesses except to repeat they were a growth company "in the area of advanced materials systems." Duke bought a fishing rod company . . . and convinced the analysts that he had integrated forward into materials usage. Next it will be further forward integration with a string company, and, of course, with that he's got the perfect hook for a move into oceanography—a very high-multiple area, incidentally. . . .

The point is that you have to project the right image to the analysts so they realize you're the new breed of entrepreneur. Talk about the synergy of the free-form company and its interface with change and technology. Tell them you have a windowless room full of researchers with genius IQ's scrutinizing the future so your company will be opportunity-technology oriented, so it will fashion change rather than merely respond to it like stupid old GM. . . .

If you pull off some good deals, and if the economy stays strong and your luck holds, you'll make a fortune, become a Captain of American Industry, and your stockholders will make some money too. If you pull off some bad deals or the economy goes sour at the wrong time—well, at least you ought to know enough to get out fast.

The purpose of all this fancy public-relations activity is of course to persuade Wall Street that the glamour stocks are worth a lot more than mundane balance sheets and profit-and-loss statements would seem to indicate. The desideratum is to attain, in the jargon of the stock market, the highest possible price/earnings (P/E) ratio. The stock of an old conservatively managed company which grows more or less in step with the economy as a whole (say at a rate of 4 to 5 percent a year) may sell at 10 to 15 times per-share earnings. The stock of a highly jazzed-up glamour company which has been able to show a record of rapid growth in the previous few years may, on the other hand, sell for 30 or 40 or even more times earnings. And therein lies the secret not only of the burgeoning of the latter-day conglomerates but also of the rise to wealth and prominence of a new stratum of the U.S. bourgeoisie. In order to be able to analyze this phenomenon properly, it will be useful to review some of the facts of corporate and financial life.

First, it is necessary to keep in mind as essential background the situation with respect to control of the typical giant corporation. Legally, of course, the stockholders are the owners of the corporation, and managements are simply their agents. In practice, however, the stock of most of the giants is widely dispersed among many thousands of holders, with no individual or group owning more than a small percentage of the shares. In these circumstances whatever management happens to be in power can normally remain in power and appoint its own successors.* In their famous work *The Modern Corporation and Private Property* (1932), Berle and Means found that 44 percent of the 200 largest nonfinancial corporations were management-controlled in this sense. An updating study by Robert J. Larner (published in the *American Economic Review* of September 1966) showed that by 1963 this proportion had risen to 84.5 percent. Reporting on Larner's work, *Business Week* put the following caption on a table comparing the situation in 1929 with that in 1963: "Professional managers have won ultimate control almost everywhere among the 200 largest nonfinancial corporations." Of course it is always possible for the management of such a company to be ousted by someone who succeeds in collecting proxies for a majority of the stock, and occasionally this does happen. But pulling off such a coup is very expensive and difficult: all the advantages are with the management, and under normal conditions it can go about its business without fear of attack from outsiders. Or at least that's the way it was until the new conglomerates came along. We shall return to this presently.

Next we need to know something of the way the conglomerates operate: how they grow by taking over previously independent companies and in the process generate the kind of increase in per-share earnings which is so important as a prop and booster to their P/E ratios.

---

* In many companies, incumbent managements are the lineal descendants (often in the literal family sense) of managements which were installed in an earlier period by big stockholders owning all or most of the company's stock. In this way the families of these earlier big stockholders often continue to control big corporations long after their holdings have ceased to be a significant percentage of the total stock outstanding.

We can distinguish two types of takeover: that which from the point of view of the acquired company is voluntary, and that which is involuntary. A company may want to be absorbed into another for many reasons. For example, a man may have a large part of his wealth in the form of stock in a company which he has built up in his own lifetime. If, as often happens, there is no ready market for this stock, his heirs will be in trouble when he dies. They will have a big estate tax to pay and little cash to pay it with; and if they are pushed into a forced sale of the stock, they will probably realize much less than its true value. The obvious solution is for the man in question to sell out while he is still alive and to leave his heirs cash and/or securities for which there is a ready market. And usually the most advantageous way of selling out is to get some big company to take the stock in his company in exchange for an agreed amount of its stock, the reason being that such transactions are tax-free while a sale for cash or debt securities is subject to the capital gains tax. Another common reason why one company wants to be absorbed by another is that it needs capital for expansion and lacks the absorbing company's access to banks and the money market. Or the two merging companies may both want to be part of a larger enterprise with more prestige and less vulnerability to fluctuations in particular markets. In any case, regardless of the reasons a company may have for wanting to be absorbed, the fact that it acts voluntarily greatly simplifies the whole process. Voluntary mergers have figured prominently in the growth of all the conglomerates, old and new, and doubtless will continue to do so in the future.

Involuntary takeovers present different problems, and it is with them that we are mainly concerned in what follows. The acquired company here is usually (maybe always) one whose stock is widely dispersed among a large number of stockholders, in other words a company conforming to the type which, as we have already seen, predominates among the 200 largest non-financial corporations. The usual procedure is for the acquiring company to buy up secretly anything up to 10 percent of the target company's stock. (Ownership of 10 percent or more has to be disclosed to the Securities and Exchange Commission and immediately becomes public knowledge.) The next step may be for the aggressor (call it company A) to approach the victim (company B) with arguments and inducements designed to overcome the latter's resistance. If this fails, as it often does, A then plays its trump card, a tender offer to B's stockholders. This is an offer to buy shares in B—either all that are tendered or up to a certain percentage of the total outstanding—at a price which is invariably above the current market price and may be far above the market price. Payment may be made with cash or with A's own securities or some combination of the two. Once matters have reached this stage, B's management is all but defeated. Stockholders are an unsentimental lot, interested only in making money. If someone comes along and offers them more for their stock than they can get in the market, most of them will accept. There may be some hesitation when the payment is in A's securities rather than cash, and B's management will do its best to convince stockholders that they are better off with what they have than they would be with what they are being offered. But usually this doesn't work: stockholders who think poorly of A's prospects will simply turn around and sell the securities they receive in payment (at the time of the transaction always worth more than what they give up) and buy other securities which they like better.

How does it happen that acquiring companies can afford to make such generous offers to the stockholders of target companies? Here two factors come into play: first, the arithmetic of P/E ratios and stock prices; and second, the effects of the tax laws, especially in that they treat interest paid on debt securities as a cost which is deductible in calculating net income while dividends are paid out of net income. Two highly simplified examples will serve to illustrate the principles involved.

Call the acquiring company A, the target company B, and the merged company AB. Assume the following initial situation:

	Shares outstanding	After-tax earnings	Earnings per share	P/E	Price per share
A	1,000,000	$1,000,000	$1	40	$40
B	1,000,000	$1,000,000	$1	15	$15

At this point A offers to exchange one share of its stock worth $40 on the market for two shares of B's stock worth $30, giving B's stockholders a gain of $5 a share or 33⅓ percent. But they are not the only winners. Assuming that the merged company continues to have a P/E ratio of 40, the combined result will be the following:

	Shares outstanding	After-tax earnings	Earnings per share	P/E	Price per share
AB	1,500,000	$2,000,000	$1.33	40	$53.20

What has happened is that by reducing the total number of shares outstanding from two million to one and a half million, the same amount of earnings produce an increase in earnings per share, and the same P/E ratio yields a higher price for the stock (of which A's stockholders own the same number of shares as before). Everyone, it seems, gains—except B's management which is no longer its own boss and can be kicked out at the whim of A's management. This illustration shows the supreme importance of a high P/E ratio in the merger game and explains the lengths to which its adepts will go to present to the investing and speculating community an image of a super-streamlined perpetual-growth machine. And one of the ironies of the situation is that the more successful they are, the more they can create the appearance of growth (measured by the earnings-per-share yardstick) simply by acquiring more and more companies with lower P/E ratios.

The second example, showing the tax bonanzas that mergers can produce, is adapted from a report headlined "Conglomerate Maze" which appeared on the financial page of the *New York Times* of February 27, 1969. Company A has a million shares outstanding, annual after-tax earnings of $2 million ($2 per share), pays no dividends, sells at $40 a share. Company B has 10 million shares outstanding, earnings of $30 million after taxes ($3 a share), pays a dividend of $1.50, and sells at $39 a share. A offers for each share of B's stock one debenture (an unsecured bond) with a face value of $50 and paying interest at the rate of 7½ percent ($3.75 a year). In order to make the offer more attractive, A also offers to throw in warrants good for the purchase of the merged company's shares in the future, but this does not affect the arithmetic of the immediate situation. B's stockholders thus stand to gain $11 a share in the value of their securities and $2.25 a share in their current income.

It is assumed that the earnings *before* taxes of the combined company are the same as they were before, i.e., $64 million. But earnings *after* taxes are now quite different. From the before-tax earnings of $64 million the merged company deducts interest of $37.5 million before calculating taxable income of $26.5 million. After-tax income is therefore now $13.25 million. Since the only shares now outstanding are the one million of A stock, it follows that per share earnings of A's stock have risen from $2 to $13.25. The losers this time are the U.S. treasury, to the tune of $18.75 million, and of course B's management. A has in effect acquired B by making use of B's own earning power plus generous government financing, and in the process has added handsomely to the value of A's own stock.

By now it should be clear why any conservatively managed company to which the stock market does not assign a particularly high P/E ratio and which does not have a lot of debt in its capital structure is vulnerable to takeover by one of the high-riding conglomerates which does enjoy a fancy P/E ratio and which has no scruples about going in for debt financing in a big way. And what lends special importance to this situation is simply this: *the category of vulnerable corporations includes a very large proportion of the long-established giants which are at the top of the economic and political power structure of the United States.* Discussing what it called the "conglomerate tide" in a recent issue, *Fortune* magazine had the following to say:

The tide seems virtually unstoppable; even a sharp stock-market decline, Wall Street believes, would probably stay it only for a while. An important force in the movement is the tender offer or takeover bid, in which the aggressor offers the target company's stockholders a price so irresistible that they tender him enough stock for control. Thus the stockholder, relegated by Adolf Berle and other non-contemporary economists to a limbo of impotent ownership, has found himself inadvertently practicing Stockholder Power. . . .

The targets of this aggression are some of the most upright, prudent, powerful, and self-assured corporations in the land. Self-assurance is fading. Proud old names have already been taken over, and dozens of veteran executives have been sacked. Fore-boding, frustration, and fear are epidemic in perhaps three out of five big corporate headquarters. Anguished executives who should be minding the shop are instead behaving as if they were up to some underhanded adventure, spending long hours counseling with lawyers, management consultants, proxy specialists, and public-relations men skilled in the art of forefending takeovers. (Gilbert Burck, "The Merger Movement Rides High," *Fortune,* February 1969, pp. 79-80.)

Later in the same article, the author carries the argument to its ultimate conclusion:

Sheer size of the target is no longer an obstacle to a paper takeover. A year or two ago, Wall Street jokers remarked that only General Motors and A.T.&T. were safe, but now some of the experts aren't so sure about G.M. "General Motors," argues one visionary financier, "is in many ways an ideal target. It has a low price-earnings ratio, relatively slow growth, large asset base, lots of cash, and high net worth. It is also shamefully underleveraged [i.e., low debt-to-equity ratio in its capital structure]. Like DuPont, from which it inherited its financial policies, G.M. has little debt. G.M. is thus practically a partner of the federal government, which takes more than half its gross profit. As a matter of fact, some have argued that G.M. should have borrowed billions and bought in a lot of its own stock. This would have raised earnings per share and provided leverage—would have enabled earnings per share to rise faster than earnings as a whole.

"Well, G.M. didn't take on a lot of debt. Now suppose some hero conglomerator printed up $15 billion worth of debentures and maybe another $10 billion in stock and warrants. G.M. stock, which pays $4.30, is selling at around $80. Our hero would offer, say, $125 worth of his securities, paying, say, $5 or $6, for every share of G.M. Once G.M. stockholders realized that I.O.U.'s would really be paid out of G.M.'s own pocket, with the federal government footing part of the bill, they probably would trample over one another in the rush to exchange their shares. This may sound unthinkable. But things just as unthinkable are happening all the time." (*Ibid.,* p. 161.)

At this point we must pause briefly to ask who are these high-flying conglomerators who are thus threatening the inner bastions of U.S. monopoly capitalism. And the answer is that for the most part they are "new men" who entered business after the Second World War in a quite specific way. Unlike such men as Robert McNamara, they did not go into one of the big corporations and work their way up (or if they did go into one of the big corporations, they soon left). They started their own enterprises, often getting in on the ground floor of some of the new technologies like electronics or computers, took advantage of the military-powered economic expansion which began in 1948, and naturally began to expand in proportion to the profitability of their various business ventures. In the course of this process they learned the ways of high finance and began to put together what later became the big conglomerates. Thus, for example, James Ling, the architect of Ling-Temco-Vought (number 38 on *Fortune*'s 1967 list of 500 largest industrial corporations), was a Navy electrician (no college degree) during the Second World War and started his own electrical contracting business after the war. Out of this grew a conglomerate with sales of nearly $2 billion in 1967. In some ways even more important is Litton Industries (number 44 on *Fortune*'s 1967 list) which grew from a company with $3 million sales in 1954 to over $1.5 billion in 1967. What is particularly striking about Litton is that many of the most successful operators started with Litton and, having learned the art, left to do their own conglomerating.*

For the first decade, more or less, of the conglomerate movement, most of the action took place around the periphery of the corporate establishment. A new stratum of the American bourgeoisie was taking shape outside of, but not yet in significant opposition to, what might be called the old aristocracy of wealth and power rooted in the corporate giants which had pushed to the top in the formative period of U.S. monopoly capitalism (roughly 1890-1929). But it was not to be expected that these parvenu multi-millionaires, many of them among the richest men in the country, would be forever content to remain on the outside of the corporate establishment. So, beginning a couple of years ago, they began to encroach, picking off a big company here and there and causing increasing apprehension among the others.

This process and its repercussions can be traced through three incidents: the takeovers of Wilson & Co. and Jones and Laughlin Steel Corporation by Ling-Temco-Vought, and the attempted takeover of Chemical Bank New York Trust Co. by Leasco Data Processing Equipment Corporation.

---

* For details, see "Litton: B-school for Conglomerates," *Business Week*, December 2, 1967.

On the basis of its 1967 sales of $991 million, Wilson & Co., meatpacker and producer of sporting goods, was well within the charmed circle of the 100 largest nonfinancial corporations and bigger than James Ling's entire Ling-Temco-Vought conglomerate. And yet during that year Ling, through an intricate series of maneuvers and financial coups (including a multi-million dollar loan from a European banking syndicate), succeeded in taking over Wilson and in the process jumped from number 168 to number 38 in the 500-largest list. Other acquisitions in 1967 included Greatamerica Corporation, itself a diversified company owning, among other things, Braniff Airways. And then, just about a year after swallowing Wilson, Ling pulled off his greatest coup, the takeover of Jones and Laughlin Steel Corporation. J&L is the nation's sixth largest steel producer, a long-established member of what *Business Week* (May 18, 1968) called the "tight-knit steel fraternity," and closely allied to its Pittsburgh neighbors in the Mellon empire. This was a classic case of the tender-offer technique: J&L stock was selling at about $50 a share, and L-T-V offered the stockholders a package worth about $85 a share. The result was a foregone conclusion. L-T-V will probably rank among the 20 largest industrials when J&L is included among its subsidiaries.

It was probably this incident more than anything else that caused the state of near-panic in the corporate board-rooms described in the *Fortune* article quoted above (p. 12). After all, James Ling was the very model of a bourgeois upstart. *Newsweek* (October 9, 1967) began a story about his career as follows:

It wasn't long ago that Dallas oilmen and other pillars of the Texas Establishment had an instant formula for a barrel of laughs: just mention the name of Jimmy Ling. In air-cooled private clubs 40 floors above the sun-blasted streets, the tycoons would sink into their deep, brown-cowhide chairs and poke a little fun at the rising young corporate merger artist from Hugo, Okla.

"I just won't do business with a Chinaman," one oilman would chortle. "Did you hear?" a second would ask. "He's going to take over Bell Telephone next." "What's he going to call it," a third would ask, "Ting-a-Ling?"

This fast operator, but recently a parvenu even in Texas, had now marched into Pittsburgh. What was to prevent him and others like him from storming the ultimate bastions on Wall

Street and Park Avenue? The answer was not long in coming and, as could have been predicted, it had two parts. On the one hand, the corporate establishment began to bring its enormous financial power into play; on the other hand, it called on its faithful servants in the seats of government to wake up and do their job.

Both parts of the answer were dramatically illustrated by the abortive attempt of Leasco Data Processing Equipment Corporation, a company built up by a 29-year-old financial "wizard" named Saul Steinberg, to take over the Chemical Bank of New York. Leasco operates in and around the computer industry and owns a big insurance company. Though growing rapidly, it was not large enough to be listed anywhere in *Fortune*'s 1968 directory of largest corporations (issue dated May 1, 1968). Chemical Bank (formerly Chemical Bank New York Trust Company), on the other hand, was listed as the nation's sixth largest bank with assets of $8.4 billion. In February 1969, Leasco mounted an attack on Chemical and was obviously preparing the *coup de grâce* of a generous tender offer to Chemical's stockholders. Before the end of the month, however, Steinberg was forced to admit defeat. At the time, the reports in the business press were brief and largely bare of detail. But a couple of months later the real story came out. Here are excerpts from *Business Week*'s article entitled "Why Leasco Failed to Net Chemical" in the issue of April 26th (the whole article is worth reading):

"I always knew there was an Establishment," says Saul P. Steinberg, the chubby, 29-year-old multimillionaire chairman of Leasco Data Processing Equipment Corp. "I just used to think I was part of it."

Leasco's abortive play last February for giant Chemical Bank of New York threw Steinberg against the real establishment of big, conservative money—a confrontation so jarring that Wall Street still clucks about it. In the end, says a Wall Street friend, "Saul found out there really is a back room where the big boys sit and smoke their long cigars." . . .

Chemical Bank is old, rich (sixth-biggest commercial bank in the U. S. with $9 billion in assets), and very powerful. It is a money market bank—a lender to many of the bluest of blue-chip corporations and a big dealer in U.S. government securities. On its board sit top executives of such companies as AT&T, DuPont, IBM, Sears, U.S. Steel, Olin Mathieson, Uniroyal, New York Life, and Equitable Life.

Never has so mighty a bank fallen to an outsider. To Chemical Bank, and to many of its best customers, Steinberg—young, sometimes brash, a Johnny-come-lately, and Jewish to boot—was very much an outsider. "Chemical," says a rival banker, "was afraid of losing a lot of its corporate and personal trust business if Leasco took over. Those people wouldn't sit still for a Steinberg."

The bank was apparently threatened with the loss of some business, by customers who didn't want a non-banker in a position to know so much about their financial affairs. . . .

Wall Street's choicest gossip for weeks has dealt with what happened during those 15 days [in February]—or what it thinks happened. . . . One thing that did happen was that Leasco's stock plunged from 140 to 106 in two weeks—driven down, many on Wall Street believe, as bank trust departments sold what Leasco shares they held. . . .

At least one computer-leasing customer—and perhaps more—apparently threatened to take its business elsewhere if Leasco actually made a bid for Chemical Bank. Leasco's prime investment banker, White, Weld & Co., told Steinberg on Feb. 7 that he would have to try to take over Chemical Bank without that firm's help.

Investment banker Lehman Bros. admits that it was pressured by commercial banks to not help Leasco—a ticklish situation since Lehman is a heavy borrower of bank money.

The nation's big banks, rocked by the thought of one of their number being taken over, did cluster together to create what one banker calls "a massive groundswell of opposition that was felt in Washington and Albany. The whole industry was aghast."

In Washington, Chemical Bank found support high up in the Nixon administration, in Congress, and among the financial regulators. In Albany, New York Governor Nelson Rockefeller asked for immediate legislation to shield banks in the state from takeover. A comparable bill, covering national banks, was introduced in Congress on Feb. 28 by Senator John J. Sparkman (D-Ala.), chairman of the Senate Banking and Currency Committee.

It isn't clear how much of a hand Chemical Bank had in all this. In fact, as one man on Wall Street points out, "Chemical didn't have to do very much. It had so many friends, and every one wanted to help."

As it turned out, the corporate establishment's counterattack in the Leasco-Chemical affair was only the opening salvo in a full-scale campaign to put the parvenus in their place. During the week of March 24th, the Justice Department, in what *Business Week* (March 29) called "Washington's first all-out assault on the merger-hungry giants," filed an anti-trust suit to

separate Jones and Laughlin from Ling-Temco-Vought, and at
the same time forced Ling to accept an agreement whereby,
pending the outcome of the suit, J&L would be maintained as
an organizationally independent entity, so that if the government
wins J&L can be shifted to new ownership with a minimum of
difficulty. Ling, it seems, is to be made to pay for approaching
as near as Pittsburgh to the inner sanctum.

Finally, *Fortune,* in its "Report from Washington" column
in the issue of May 1, really pulled the curtain aside and
showed what has been and is going on behind the scenes. Here
are excerpts from another piece (captioned, appropriately
enough, "It's open season on conglomerates, and established
business couldn't be happier") which deserves to be read in
full:

> Washington in recent years has shown about as much interest
> in conglomerate mergers as in the prospects of the Washington
> Senators baseball team. The Justice Department under Lyndon
> Johnson did not view conglomerates as much of a threat to com-
> petition, and the Federal Trade Commission, after blocking Procter
> & Gamble's takeover of Clorox in 1967, became passive. . . .
> Today, by contrast, antitrust and conglomerates would seem
> to rank only behind Vietnam, the ABM, and inflation in the
> capital's interest. A dozen federal investigations are under way
> into the antitrust aspects of conglomerate mergers. A slew of bills
> are before Congress to block airline and railroad mergers. Repre-
> sentative Wilbur Mills has introduced a bill to remove tax incen-
> tives to takeovers. Banking conglomerates . . . are the target of
> strict administration legislative proposals. For his part, the govern-
> ment's new trustbuster, Assistant Attorney General Richard Mc-
> Laren, has launched this spring a broad legal attack against
> mergers. Of twelve recent large conglomerate mergers, five have
> been challenged by the government.
> The result—not wholly unintended, perhaps—of these myriad
> federal moves was to knock more than $5 billion (21 percent) off
> the market value of thirteen conglomerates' shares between Jan-
> uary 27 and March 24 and, consequently, dampen their merger
> potential. . . .
> This sudden free-form, uncoordinated attack on mergers has
> surprised even such dedicated antitrust Democrats as Representa-
> tive Emmanuel Celler of New York and Senator Philip Hart of
> Michigan, who chair, respectively, the House and Senate judiciary
> subcommittees on antitrust. "I never thought that I would see the
> day when the business community would be pleading with the fed-
> eral government for an investigation of business. But that is exactly

what has resulted from the merger practices of some of our leading corporations." . . .

The events that triggered Washington into action are not hard to discern. It was not the number of mergers or the concentration ratios, but rather the threat to the established way of doing corporate business. "For years nobody paid a damn bit of attention to my antitrust hearings. But now such nice people are being swallowed up," says Senator Hart. . . .

Despite the near unanimity in the capital about the present dangers of mergers, there is in some quarters considerable support for James Ling's complaints about Washington's "conglomerate syndrome." . . . Even Senator Hart notes acidly that many of the proposals are not "referring to established conglomerates like General Electric, or R.C.A. or I.T.T. They are referring to the brand-new ones who are threatening the old-line companies." . . .

So much, then, for the attempts of the parvenu outsiders to crash the corporate establishment. They threw a scare into the big boys all right, but the latter now seem to be in the process of demonstrating that they still have what it takes to maintain a monopoly of real power in corporate America.

What lessons are the underprivileged multi-millionaires likely to derive from this experience? We don't know for sure as yet, of course. But it does seem likely that they will draw the obvious inference that economic and political power cannot be separated. If you want the one, you must aim also for the other. This consideration may lead them next time to try first of all to get control of the crucial legislative and bureaucratic agencies in Washington which could help rather than block future forays into the inner corporate circle. And for this they would need a political instrument to use against the corporate-establishment-controlled Republican and Democratic parties.

Upstart capital has always been an important source of financial support for fascist-type movements which seek to harness popular discontent and resentments to overturn existing political structures. The story recounted here of the rise and frustration of the new conglomerators may therefore have as a sequel a significant strengthening of the fascist tendencies which George Wallace's 1968 presidential campaign showed to be already well developed in certain regions of the country and strata of the population. The other side of the coin might well be that old wealth, fearful of the implications for its own power of a fascist victory, would cling more closely than ever to its tried-and-true political weapons.

But all we can say for certain at this stage is that the course of the great merger movement of the 1950's and 1960's seems certain to complicate what already promises to be a very confused and uncertain political situation in the period ahead.

Notes on the Multinational Corporation

October and November 1969

By now there exists an extensive literature on what have come increasingly to be called "multinational" corporations or companies—that is, corporations with headquarters in one country and a variety of subsidiaries in other countries.* Hardly any of it, however, is written from a Marxist point of view, a fact which, given the obvious importance of the subject, casts a revealing light on the state of Marxist social science in the United States (or anywhere else, for that matter). Our purpose in this paper is not to attempt to fill this gap in any comprehensive way but rather to raise a number of key questions and to suggest directions in which answers should be sought.

---

* Three leading examples of this literature are the following: (1) Judd Polk, et al., *U.S. Production Abroad and the Balance of Payments,* National Industrial Conference Board, New York, 1966. Polk, Economist and Acting President of the United States Council of the International Chamber of Commerce, has continued to produce studies and staff memoranda dealing with foreign investment. (2) Raymond Vernon, "Multinational Enterprise and National Sovereignty," *Harvard Business Review,* March-April 1967. Vernon is Professor of International Trade and Investment at the Harvard Business School and is heading a large-scale Ford Foundation-financed study of the subject of this paper, which is described as an "interim report." (3) Charles P. Kindleberger, *American Business Abroad: Six Lectures on Direct Investment,* Yale University Press, New Haven, 1969. Kindleberger is a professor of economics at M.I.T. whose *International Economics* is perhaps the leading academic textbook in its field. From the footnotes in *American Business Abroad* a useful bibliography can be constructed for further study.

I

First a few words about the name "multinational corporation." There is no doubt that in much of the literature this is used in a propagandistic and apologetic sense, suggesting the transcendence of national vices and rivalries and the emergence of a new institution with hopeful auguries for the future. That such connotations are nonsensical will appear as we proceed; for the moment we are concerned only with the problem of whether to abandon the name or to attempt to strip it of its apologetic aspects and make use of it for scientific ends.

The problem is by no means a new one and can hardly be said to have a uniquely "correct" solution. For example, the situation is very similar with respect to the expression "Third World" which, in its original usage, was intended to conjure up a picture of a group of countries choosing their own road to economic and social development and standing between the advanced capitalist world on the one hand and the Communist world on the other. Marxists—with the exception perhaps of the official breed in the Soviet bloc—know of course that this picture is as phony as a $9 bill, that the countries in question are really the oppressed and exploited majority of the global capitalist system, and that the only way they can achieve real economic and social development is through socialist revolution. Knowing this, should they have rejected and attempted to discredit the term "Third World," or should they have adopted it and tried to endow it with a new meaning? On the whole it seems that they have followed the second course, presumably on the assumption that the term had caught on and would be used anyway, and that the best that could be done would be to strip it of its apologetic character. And, again on the whole, it seems that this procedure has been reasonably successful. No one finds it paradoxical, for example, that Pierre Jalée should entitle his study of global imperialist exploitation *The Pillage of the Third World*: thanks largely to the work of Marxist scholars and publicists, it is more and more taken for granted that "Third World" is merely a convenient shorthand designation for that large and in many ways diverse collection of colonies, semi-colonies, and neo-colonies which form the base of the global capitalist pyramid.

It seems to us that a similar course is called for in the case of the "multinational corporation." The term is already in such wide use that it will almost certainly survive any attacks that may be launched against it. Moreover, there is no doubt about the reality of the phenomenon to which it refers. We may as well do the best we can to deprive it of its power to mislead and, as in the case of "Third World," make it into a useful term for describing and analyzing the realities of present-day capitalism.

II

First of all, then, we need to understand the precise nature and limits of the multinationality of the multinational corporation. It *is* multinational in the sense that it operates in a number of nations with the purpose of maximizing the profits not of the individual units on a nation-by-nation basis but of the group as a whole. As we shall see, from this characteristic flow some of the most important consequences of the multinational corporation; indeed we can say that it is this alone which constitutes a valid reason for using the term multinational. For in all other decisive respects we are dealing with national corporations. In particular, ownership and control are located in one nation, not dispersed throughout the corporate system. There are two exceptions to this generalization: Royal Dutch Shell and Unilever, in both of which British capital and Dutch capital genuinely share ownership and control through complex parallel headquarters structures. But these exceptions are among the oldest of multinational corporations, and the pattern has not been copied by any of the two to three hundred which have emerged in the half century since the First World War. In particular and contrary to widespread expectation, the European Common Market has not given rise to new multinationals in which ownership and control are shared in two or more countries. There have been mergers and takeovers across national boundaries, and of course many of the European giants have working arrangements with their counterparts in other countries; but we know of no new instance in which a real division of ownership and control has taken place.

Here we meet head-on one of the most persistent themes of the apologetic literature. It is true, these writers say, that up to now the multinationals have been owned and controlled in one of the advanced capitalist countries, but the *trend* is toward a genuine internationalization of both stockholding and management. In support of this contention two sets of facts are cited: the large-scale investment, amounting to many billions of dollars, by foreigners (mainly Europeans) in U.S. stocks; and the hiring by the multinationals of more and more local people at the middle- and even upper-management levels in their foreign subsidiaries. Assuming the continuation of these activities, the apologists argue that in a relatively short time the national grip on the multinational corporations will be broken and they will become, so to speak, citizens of the world rather than of any particular country.

There is no need to quarrel about the facts here, though they are considerably less massive than is sometimes asserted or implied. What is really at issue is their interpretation. As to stockholdings, the following excerpt from a story in the *New York Times* of February 22, 1968, is instructive:

Experts of the United Nations Economic Commission for Europe say there is a link between the flow of European capital into American equities and the direct investments of the big United States companies in Europe.

"Europeans," the experts say . . . , "buy the stocks of the big United States companies, which are precisely the ones that invest in Europe."

This means, in effect, that European capital joins with United States management to invest in Europe, it is asserted.

Since European stockholders, like their counterparts in the United States, normally have no influence on the composition or policies of managements, what this means is that many European capitalists, instead of investing directly in European industry, put their capital at the disposal of Americans who invest in Europe. "Internationalization" of ownership thus turns out to be one of many ways in which U.S. capital gains control over foreign capital.

As far as the hiring of local personnel to staff foreign subsidiaries is concerned, this has absolutely nothing to do with sharing control, which remains undivided in the parent company. Of course if boards of directors and top managements of parent companies began to blossom with foreigners, that would be something else which would call for serious analysis. But this has not happened. A few foreigners probably sit on the boards of some of the multinationals, but we have not run across a single case of foreigners occupying top management positions. (If there were any such cases, they would almost certainly be mightily celebrated in the apologetic literature.) What John Thackray, U.S. correspondent of the British magazine *Management Today*, has written on this subject seems, if anything, an understatement:

There are two broad classes of managers in the large international company. One is the national of the parent company, working either somewhere in the domestic operations, abroad, or at headquarters. The second is the indigenous executive manning the foreign outpost.

The existence of these two unequal classes is seldom mentioned by the persons involved; and when admitted, it is softly, softly. Corporate ideology declares that all men have equal opportunity for advancement and success—every toiling executive has the president's slide rule or the president's nameplate somewhere in the drawers of his desk.

There are good and sufficient reasons as to why there should be these two classes of executives. But their existence presents a serious impediment to the creation of a managerial structure and an executive corps in multinational companies that can be, in the fullest sense, internationalist—where the significance of a man's nationality might be no more important than the color of his tie or the style of his shoes. Because of these two classes, we may never see what would be the acid test of managerial multinationalism: an Italian as president of an American-owned multinational, for example, or a Latin American running a Dutch-owned multinational.*

None of this should be taken to imply that the existence

---

* John Thackray, "Not So Multinational, After All," *Interplay,* November 1968, p. 23. (This article forms part of a symposium under the general title "The Multinational Corporation: The Splendors and Miseries of Bigness.")

of this second and inferior "class" of executives in the multi-national company is of no importance. On the contrary these people make up a significant section of the native bourgeoisie in every country where multinationals operate. Their interests (jobs, salaries, bonuses, promotions) lie with the parent company; only to the extent that they serve it well and faithfully can they expect to advance and prosper. But, as we shall see, the interests of the parent company often contradict those of the countries in which they operate. It follows that while multinational corporations do not, as so often claimed, inter-nationalize their managements, they do *de*nationalize a section of the native bourgeoisies in the countries they penetrate. This of course weakens these native bourgeoisies and makes it that much harder for them to resist demands and pressures emanat-ing from more powerful countries.*

III

"Capital has its own nationality," says John Thackray in the article cited above. Absolutely true, provided we under-stand it correctly. The nationality of capital is not that of the nation in which it happens to be located but rather that of the people who control it. Generally speaking, this means that it is also the nationality of those who own it, but this is not neces-sarily so. If, for example, a German corporation borrows money from a French bank, the amount in question falls under the control of Germans and becomes part of German capital until the loan is repaid. It is thus possible in principle for capital of one nationality to capture and incorporate into itself capital of other nationalities.

But, you may ask, what difference does the nationality of capital make? Isn't capital, like money to which it is so closely related, perfectly homogeneous, and doesn't it function in ex-

---

* The section of the native bourgeoisie which identifies its interests with foreign companies rather than with its own class and nation is not limited to those in the direct employ of the foreign companies. It also in-cludes a variety of others such as suppliers, subcontractors, lawyers, etc., who depend on the foreign subsidiaries for the major part of their in-comes.

actly the same way regardless of the nationality of those who control it? These are difficult questions to which no brief answers can be adequate. But for our present purposes it will be enough to point out that capital, while it does have a quantitative dimension, is fundamentally not a thing or a substance but a *relation*. In the realm of abstract theory which postulates a single capitalist system organized in a large number of small competitive units, the relation in question is between the relatively small class which owns the means of production and the many times larger class which owns nothing and is therefore forced to sell its labor power. Capital is the means of buying labor power and means of production which are then combined and the product sold in such a way as to replace the value used up and to add a surplus value. This surplus value is produced by the workers and appropriated by the capitalists. The capitalists are capitalists solely because of their ownership of capital, which enables them to exploit the workers. The workers are workers (proletarians) solely because they lack capital and must therefore submit to exploitation on pain of starvation.* Ownership of capital is therefore the right to exploit workers pure and simple. All capitalists have this right, and by virtue of it their interests vis-à-vis the workers are identical. Capital, in a word, is the relation of exploitation between the owning class and the working class.

In capitalist reality things are more complicated. In particular the conception of a single capitalist system organized in a large number of small competitive units, which implies a homogeneous and undivided capitalist class, is an extreme abstraction—useful as an expository and pedagogic device and approximating the actual situation in one country (Great Britain) during one period (the middle third of the nineteenth

---

* This theme of course runs like a red thread through the entire body of Marxist literature on capitalism. Nowhere is it more powerfully expounded and illustrated than in the last part of the first volume of *Capital* entitled "The So-Called Primitive Accumulation." (*Capital*, Kerr ed., Vol. 1, Part VIII. It should be noted that the division into parts, chapters, and sections is not the same in all editions of *Capital*.) It seems to us that whoever undertakes to study *Capital* would do well to begin with this part before reading Chapter 1 on "Commodities and Money."

century), but requiring far-reaching modification to be applicable to the capitalist system as a whole or to any part of it over long periods of time.

In actual fact competition among capitalists has always been more or less massively obstructed by a variety of natural and man-made barriers—geography, political boundaries, particular conditions of demand and costs, etc. These barriers introduce inequalities into the ranks of capitalists (also into the ranks of workers, but this aspect does not concern us here). Some capitalists enjoy superior rights to exploit workers; more important from our present point of view, some capitalists are able (for example, through monopoly pricing) to transfer surplus value out of the pockets of other capitalists into their own. Under these conditions capital is no longer simply the generalized relation of exploitation between one class and another, though all of it has that quality. It is now split up, with some segments exercising greater power than others to exploit workers and/or power to exploit other capitalists. What was a simple relation between classes now becomes a complex of relations between classes and groups within classes. The conflict between classes remains fundamental, but it is now overlaid with a welter of other conflicts which at some times and in some places occupy the center of the historic stage.

For reasons which reach far back into the origins of capitalism, the deepest and most durable divisions within the global capitalist class have been along national lines. Capitalism did not come into the world fully formed, like Athena from the head of Zeus, but piecemeal and as the result of long and bitter struggle between the rising burghers of the cities and the feudal nobility. In these struggles it was usual for the bourgeoisie to ally itself with the kings or princes who were chronically fighting to assert their authority over their own feudal subordinates. In this way there emerged a series of national monarchical states. As capitalism developed within these national frameworks, the power of the bourgeoisies increased to the point where they were able to reduce the monarchs to the status of figureheads, leaving the capitalists in control not only of the economy but also of the whole state apparatus.

Each national bourgeoisie naturally made use of its control over the state to enhance the profitability of its capital—by measures designed to make it possible to squeeze more surplus value out of workers, by excluding foreigners from national markets, by appropriate taxation and expenditure policies, by forcing unequal treaties on weaker states, by conquering additional territory or annexing colonies, etc. Under these circumstances, it is impossible to speak of capital as qualitatively homogeneous: its power and profitability are functions not only of its magnitude but also of other specific characteristics among which nationality occupies an extremely important position.

One additional point in this connection. The very idea of a unit of capital divorced from any nationality—which, according to some apologetic theories, is what the multinational corporation is in the process of becoming—is a contradiction in terms. Capital is a fundamental part of a particular set of relations of production which, far from being natural and eternal, is historical and alterable. These relations of production, implying as they do the exploitation of some classes and groups by other classes and groups, were established through violent struggles and can be maintained in existence only through a sufficiently powerful apparatus of coercion, i.e., a state. Capital without a state is therefore unthinkable. But in the world as it is constituted today only nations have states: there is no such thing as a supranational state. It follows that to exist capital must have nationality. If, for example, the state of the nation to which it belonged were to collapse, capital would lose its indispensable protector. It would then either be incorporated into the capital of another nation or it would cease to be capital by coming under the jurisdiction of a revolutionary regime dedicated to the abolition of the entire set of relations of production of which capital is one part. Finally, capital of one nationality can operate in other nations only because all the capitalist classes maintain basically similar sets of relations of production and because they find it, on the whole, in their mutual interest to permit this kind of international movement of capital.

IV

As Marx showed—and it was certainly one of his most important contributions—it is of the very essence of capital to expand.* There are two basic reasons for this. First, the power and standing of the capitalist (owner or functionary of capital) is proportional to the magnitude of his capital. The way to rise in capitalist society is therefore to accumulate capital. And second, any capitalist who stands still is in danger of being wiped out. As Marx put it in a brilliant passage,

the development of capitalist production makes it constantly necessary to keep increasing the amount of capital laid out in a given industrial undertaking, and competition makes the immanent laws of capitalist production to be felt by each individual capitalist as external coercive laws. It compels him to keep constantly extending his capital, in order to preserve it, but extend it he cannot except by means of progressive accumulation. (*Capital*, Kerr ed. Vol. 1, p. 649.)

These considerations are as valid for the corporate capitalist as for the individual capitalist of an earlier period. And they are deeply embedded in the ideology of the business world where the worship of growth has attained the standing of a secular religion. "The only real security for this company or any other company," says the annual report of a major corporation which we have quoted in these pages before, "is through healthy, continuous, and vigorous growth. A company is just like a human being. When it stops growing, when it can't replenish itself through growth, then it starts to deteriorate. . . . There is no security where there is no opportunity for growth and development and continual improvement."**

In the abstract terms of Marxist economic theory, growth means that a part of the surplus value accruing to a unit of capital in one period is added to capital in the next period.

---

* See especially *Capital*, Kerr ed., Vol. 1, Part II, Chapter 4; and Part VII, Chapter 24, Section 3.

** From the 1965 annual report of Rockwell-Standard Corporation, since merged with North American Aviation to form North American Rockwell Corporation.

The larger capital now brings in a greater amount of surplus value which permits a still larger increment of growth, and so on. Marxist theory has traditionally focused on the overall consequences for the whole economy of such behavior by the individual units of capital. What has been unduly neglected are the implications of this spiral process (capital/surplus value/added capital) for what bourgeois economics calls the theory of the firm. The following highly schematic sketch may serve to indicate lines along which fruitful work can advance.

We start—as both Marx and the classical economists did—with the firm in a competitive industry. Its output is small relative to the total, and its product is more or less indistinguishable from that of all the other firms catering to the same market. Under these circumstances each firm will produce up to the point where the cost of turning out an additional unit is equal to the market price (beyond that point cost would exceed price and hence entail a reduction of profit). This is the famous equilibrium position which in textbook economics is too often treated as the end of the subject rather than the beginning.

The profitable course for the capitalist who finds himself in this position is clearly marked: he must bring down his costs and thus increase his profit margin (it is assumed that he can sell whatever he produces at the going price, so he has no sales problem). And cost reduction normally means expanding the scale of production and introducing new and improved techniques. Those who successfully follow this course prosper and grow, while those who lag behind fall by the wayside.

This process, however, cannot continue in this way indefinitely. There comes a time when the expansion in the size of the average firm, brought about by the growth of the successful ones and the elimination of the failures, alters the situation in a fundamental way. The individual firm is no longer one small producer among many, all taking the going price as a datum to which they adjust in the most profitable manner. Instead, each firm now produces a significant proportion of the industry's total supply, and each must take into account the effect of its own output on the market price. This

opens up new problems and possibilities which have been
more or less adequately studied under such headings as im-
perfect or monopolistic competition, oligopoly, and monopoly.
Here we need only point out that in addition to continuing to
seek lower production costs, the rational course for every firm
to follow is to get itself as nearly as possible into the position of
a monopolist, either individually (through differentiating its
product from those of rivals) or collectively (through acting
openly or tacitly in collusion with rivals). It follows that for
the purposes of theoretical analysis the appropriate assumption
is that the typical firm acts like a monopolist, maximizing
profits at a level of output which falls well short of the volume
at which the cost of producing an additional unit equals market
price. When this situation prevails in most of the important
industries, capitalism has entered its monopoly stage.

From our present point of view what needs to be stressed
is that in the monopoly stage, the problem of growth presents
itself to the firm in a radically different light. It is no longer
simply a question of progressively reducing costs and expanding
output of a homogeneous product. Cost reduction of course
remains as important as ever, but now the maximization of
profit requires a go-slow policy with respect to the expansion
of output. It follows that the monopolistic firm can no longer
count on being able to grow while remaining within the con-
fines of the industry of its origin and early development. Not
that expansion within the industry is entirely precluded, but it
is strictly limited by cost and demand factors which are totally
unrelated to the firm's ability and hence desire to grow, that is
to say, by its profitability. The monopolistic firm is therefore
driven by an inner compulsion to go outside of and beyond
its historical field of operations. And the strength of this compulsion is the greater the more monopolistic the firm and the
greater the amount of surplus value it disposes over and wishes
to capitalize.

Here, it seems to us, we have the fundamental explanation
of one of the decisive phenomena of recent capitalist history:
the tendency of the corporation as it gets bigger to diversify
both industrially and geographically—or, in current terminology,

the tendency to become on the one hand a conglomerate and on the other hand a multinational corporation. The great majority of the 200 largest nonfinancial corporations in the United States today—corporations which together account for close to half the country's industrial activity—have arrived at the stage of both conglomerateness and multinationality.

V

In the previous section the thesis was advanced that the self-expansion process of capital goes through two phases, the competitive and the monopolistic. In the competitive phase the individual firm grows by reducing costs, realizing larger profits, and investing in increased capacity to turn out a product which, being essentially indistinguishable from the products of its competitors, can always be sold at—or, more realistically, slightly under—the going market price. Somewhere along the line, as some firms prosper and grow and others lag behind and drop out, the average firm in an industry becomes so large that it must take account of the effect of its own production on market price. It then begins to function more and more like a monopolist for whom the problem of continued growth is radically transformed. Monopoly profits make possible even more rapid growth than in the past, but the need to maintain monopoly prices dictates a policy of slowing down and carefully regulating the expansion of productive capacity. From this conjunction of factors there results an irresistible drive on the part of the monopolistic firm to move outside of and beyond its historical field of operation, to penetrate new industries and new markets—in a word, to go conglomerate and multinational.

This is not to argue that the drive for investment abroad by monopolistic firms is stimulated solely by pressures emanating from the search for investment outlets for surplus funds. For example, capital will move to areas where it is feasible to exploit low wages and other cost advantages. And the monopoly stage adds yet another dimension. Under monopoly conditions in a given industry, it is usual to find not one but several dominant companies. It follows that when one of the leading firms invests in a foreign country, competing giants in the same industry are prompted to follow suit to make sure that they get their "proper" share of the local market. Furthermore, tariff barriers, patent rights, and other local conditions create circumstances in which the corporate giants find that they can best control the market in a foreign country through investment rather than mere exports. One of the outstanding features of the giant corporation, indeed, is that it has the means to try to control the market over a large part of the world; and, for its own security and profit, it continuously strives to do so.

It is important to understand that under monopolistic conditions the axiom according to which capital always moves from low-profit to high-profit industries and regions no longer holds. Monopoly by definition impedes the free flow of capital into protected high-profit situations; and, as we have already seen, the monopolist sitting inside these bastions is careful not to invest more than the traffic will bear, while seeking outlets elsewhere for his surplus capital. It is therefore not only possible but probably quite common for capital to move in directions opposite to those indicated by traditional economic theory.* This fact alone is enough to knock into a cocked hat that supposedly sacrosanct tenet of bourgeois thought according to which any movement of capital in search of maximum profits automatically guarantees a more efficient allocation of resources. (There are other reasons why this idea, considered as a general proposition, is fallacious, but they do not concern us here.) Unless otherwise stated, what follows relates entirely to giant corporations which have reached the monopolistic stage and are in the process of spreading into both new industries and new geographical areas. This is the actual situation of most of the giants that dominate the U.S. economy, and it is increasingly true of the large corporations of Western Europe and Japan.

The spreading process can take two forms. The initiating corporation can establish a new enterprise in the industry or country it is entering, or it can buy up an existing enterprise. We know of no empirical studies dealing with this matter, but

---

* A study of the U.S. automobile industry would provide striking confirmation of these observations. On the one hand it is one of the most highly monopolized and profitable industries in the United States, and on the other hand the Big Three which dominate it are continuous and heavy investors in other industries and abroad.

it is our impression that the preferred way is generally to buy up an existing enterprise. And there is a good reason for this. Establishing a foothold from scratch in a new field or new place can be costly and time-consuming, while buying one that already exists is quick and easy. In this connection it matters little whether the enterprise in question is doing well or badly; in fact, there is much to be said for a weak company since it can be acquired more cheaply. In any case, the parent corporation usually plans to reorganize the new subsidiary to conform to its own style and to make the most of the advantages which its superior size and strength confer upon it.

What are these advantages? It is usual to think of the large corporation thriving and growing because of its ability to take advantage of the economies of large-scale *production,* and of course there is considerable merit to this line of reasoning. But when it comes to expanding into new fields, the economies of scale may have little or nothing to do with success or failure. For one thing the technology of the new field may be entirely different from that of the base industry and may not lend itself to the development of mass-production methods. And for another, when a corporation sets up shop to produce its accustomed product abroad, it will deliberately tailor its techniques according to the size of the market rather than export its domestically developed mass-production methods.* The decisive advantages of the giant corporation lie elsewhere than in production proper. Chief among them are (not necessarily in order of importance, which will vary from case to case) the following: (1) Plenty of capital to invest and almost unlimited access to credit on favorable terms in both domestic and foreign money markets. (2) A pool of experienced managerial talent which can be deployed anywhere in the corporate empire according to need. (3) A large and effective sales apparatus which is similarly available to all units of the corporate empire. And (4) research and development facilities which can be put to work to

---

* In an important article Leo Fenster, a veteran member of the United Automobile Workers Union, has shown that for their low-volume Latin American plants the U.S. auto giants design and utilize brand new low-productivity machinery and equipment. ("The Mexican Auto Swindle," *The Nation,* June 2, 1969.)

solve all sorts of technological and marketing problems. The small independent corporation is likely to be deficient in all these respects and hence quite incapable of competing on even terms with a rival which is a subsidiary of one of the giant conglomerate multinationals. It follows that whenever one of the latter enters a new field it tends to forge ahead rapidly until it occupies a leading position along with a few other giants. At this time competitive behavior gives way to monopolistic behavior. The newly matured subsidiary begins to generate more profits than it can safely invest, with the surplus flowing back into the central pool of capital maintained by the parent company. At this time the subsidiary which began by being an outlet for surplus capital becomes a source of additional surplus capital and hence a spur for the corporation as a whole to find still new areas into which to expand—in short, to become still more conglomerate and multinational. Logically, this process should come to an end either with all major industries in all capitalist countries dominated by a few hundred giant corporations, or with the overthrow of capitalism on an international scale. At the moment we seem to be moving more rapidly toward the first denouement than the second. Judd Polk of the United States Council of the International Chamber of Commerce is responsible for the following estimates which, at least as far as orders of magnitude are concerned, seem quite reasonable:

Over the past two decades international investment and its output have been growing about twice as fast as world GNP [Gross National Product]. The effect has been to produce an internationalized sector of production that is now of a very substantial order of magnitude and is continuing to grow in relation to total world output. Already it appears that almost a quarter of all production in the market world is accounted for by the output of international companies. If we look to the end of this century, envisioning the growth of world GNP to continue at its typical pace of the 1960s, and similarly the output of international investment at its typically faster rate of the 1960s we get a picture roughly estimable as follows [table omitted]. The final figure (53 percent) shows a world economy better than half internationalized.*

* Judd Polk, "The Internationalization of Production," mimeographed, issued by the U.S. Council, International Chamber of Commerce, May 7, 1969.

By "internationalized" Polk of course means gobbled up by a relative handful of U.S., Western European, and Japanese multinational corporations.

As things are going now, this is the realistic prospect. It should be compared with some of the fairy stories of the apologetic literature which tend to give the impression, if they do not openly state, that the multinational corporations can be a great help to the underdeveloped countries in getting their own industries going under their own control. Thus, speaking of Latin America, P. N. Rosenstein-Rodan of M.I.T., by no means an extreme apologist for the big companies, envisages the gradual withdrawal of the multinationals from their Latin American subsidiaries. After pointing out some of the "main conflicts between the host country's and the foreign shareholders' point of view," he proceeds:

> They are serious but not insoluble, and with understanding can be reconciled. The general desirable pattern of future foreign equity investment is a partnership with eventual national majority holding. That amounts to an *ex ante* agreed-upon nationalization up to 51 percent of foreign enterprises. The consequent removal of tensions will improve the climate of investment to such an extent that foreign investors may change their hostile or hesitant attitude toward the new pattern and evolve a new symbiosis in learning to solve the problem of management in a minority holding.*

One might be tempted to wonder how this "new symbiosis" would help the multinational corporations to invest the vast amounts of capital which would accrue to them if 51 percent of their foreign holdings were bought out. But this would be to miss the main point, which is that the whole direction of the *actual* policy of the multinationals, as distinct from what Dr. Rosenstein-Rodan might like it to be, is to *increase,* wherever possible up to 100 percent, their holdings in their foreign subsidiaries. Even minority holdings by local capitalists are always a source of at least potential conflict of interest (suppose, to take an extreme case, the parent wants to close down all its operations in a particular country and move elsewhere); and of course majority holdings by local capitalists may mean loss

---

* Inter-American Development Bank, *Multinational Investment in the Economic Development and Integration of Latin America,* Round Table, Bogota, Colombia, April 1968, p. 78.

by the parent of the crucial element of control—control over sources of raw materials, production processes, prices, and market shares—which is of the very essence and purpose of the multinational structure of the enterprise as a whole. Even when they are *forced* to accept local partners, their aim is always to manipulate local laws and politicians in such a fashion as to maintain decisive control in their own hands, while operating under a façade of partnership. For while the innate expansive drive of capital is the motor force of monopoly corporate growth, the objectives of the process—the realization of profit and the continuous renewal of expansion—can be assured only if the maximum possible degree of control over all relevant variables is guaranteed at every step of the way. The name of the game, as they like to say in the business press, is growth (on a global scale), not retrenchment; and you can be sure that the multinationals are not going to sell out (or get out)—and thereby lose the control which is so important to them—unless or until obliged to do so by *force majeure.* In the meantime, they are buying, not selling, and they are going to do their best to see that it stays that way.*

VI

One of the implications of the foregoing analysis is perhaps worth spelling out. The more the giant monopolistic corporations conglomerate and multinationalize, the further removed their top managements become from any particular product or production process. The concerns of headquarters are increasingly purely financial, i.e., profit- and accumulation-oriented; while matters of production, technology, etc., are relegated to the division, subsidiary, and plant managers who are responsible for producing and even to a larger extent selling the corporation's many products. The situation is well reflected, for example, in the corporate structure of General Motors, the biggest of them all, which has its headquarters in New York, the financial center, its main U.S. plants in and around Detroit, popularly known as the automobile capital, and production, assembly, and sales subsidiaries in literally scores of states and

---

* On this, see Eduardo Galeano, "The De-Nationalization of Brazilian Industry," MR, December 1969.

countries all around the globe. It is doubtful if the gentlemen in New York know much more about making automobiles than most of the rest of us. But the record speaks clearly that they know a lot more about making dollars!

What this means is that the top companies in the multinational corporate empires, often pure holding companies with no operating functions whatever, are increasingly financial entities receiving and disposing over billions of dollars annually and making their decisions entirely in financial terms. (The relevant business literature is full of anecdotes and references comparing the revenues of the corporations to those of the states and nations they operate in, always tending to show the preponderance of the business entities.) They naturally have the closest relations with banks, insurance companies, and other financial institutions for whom they are by far the most important customers and business partners. As far as "control" is concerned, it is a problem which rarely arises since there are no serious conflicts of interest to interfere with a relationship of smooth cooperation, but our own guess is that, when it comes to *influence,* a General Motors or a Standard Oil can pretty well get what it wants from a Chase Manhattan or a First National City.

The multinational corporation, in brief, is the key institution of finance capital in the second half of the 20th century; and Lenin's characterization in *Imperialism* (1917) requires little modification to fit it: "The concentration of production; the monopolies arising therefrom, the merging or coalescence of the banks with industry—such is the history of the rise of finance capital and such is the content of this term."

VII

There are of course profound conflicts of interest between multinational corporations and the foreign countries in which they operate. Most of the apologetic literature attempts to play them down as either of little importance or amenable to remedial action, but none can deny their existence. Here is a fairly comprehensive list of such conflicts, cast in the form of "six major fears" felt by the foreign countries:*

(1) Fear that the international corporation will take too much and leave too little. The fear is often expressed that the big foreign corporation will take away the national resources (oil, iron ore, foodstuffs, etc.), all the profits, the most able local people (hence the brain drain), and leave only the crumbs in the form of low wages, low compared to the wages the same corporations pay at home.**

(2) Fear that the international corporation will crush local competition and quickly achieve a monopolistic dominance of the local market if not the local economy. "Who can compete with the enormous technical resources of a giant corporation whose annual sales are more than the French national budget?"

(3) Fear of becoming dependent on foreign sources for modern technology needed for national defense, and for being competitive in world markets.

(4) Fear that the international corporation's local subsidiary will be used as an instrument of foreign policy by the government of the parent company. For example, in the case of a U.S. subsidiary, fear that the U.S. government will prohibit sales to certain markets (Red China, Cuba, North Korea, North Vietnam, etc.); or that the U.S. government will prohibit the parent from sending certain technology to the subsidiary which technology would be useful locally for national defense or for other purposes; or fear that the U.S. government will prevent the U.S. parent from sending new capital to the local subsidiary, and will require the local subsidiary to remit virtually all of its earnings home, thus damaging the balance of payments of the local government.

(5) Fear that the good jobs will be given to nationals of the parent company and not to local nationals.

(6) Fear that decisions will be taken by the parent company in callous disregard for their impact on the local town, province, or even on the national economy. For example—a decision to close down a factory and put thousands of workers out of jobs.

Needless to say, none of these fears is the product of fevered imaginations; all are grounded in much bitter experience. At bottom the conflicts of interest which they reflect are related to the most fundamental characteristic of the multinational

---

* "The International Corporation and the Nation State," prepared by Business International, New York, May 1968 (mimeographed).

** A classic example of the reality underlying this fear—the rape of Cyprus by Cyprus Mines Corporation, a Los Angeles-based multinational—was analyzed in "Foreign Investment," MR, January 1965; reprinted above, pp. 31-42.

corporation, that policies for all the units in the corporate empire are formulated by a central management with a view to benefiting the whole (i.e., the parent corporation) rather than the separate parts. From the point of view of the central owners and managers, this is obviously the correct course to pursue, indeed the only possible course since there could be no other conceivable reason for putting the multinational entity together in the first place. But for the parts—and for the communities and countries in which they operate—it means that they quite literally have no interests which have to be taken into account in the formulation of their own policies. This is not the place for a catalogue of the concrete ways in which the interests of the subsidiaries, considered as separate capitalist enterprises, may be (and at one time or other actually have been) overridden by the interests of the parent. But a couple of examples, taken again from a source friendly to the multinational corporations, will indicate the kind of thing that is involved.

> Every sovereign [nation] is aware that a multinational corporate group which is able to provide export markets for the product of the host country is also capable of withholding such markets and cutting off the jobs that depend on such exports. If Nigeria should eventually become a lower cost producer of widgets than Italy, the corporate group may shift the locus of its operations out of Italy into Nigeria.
> Along similar lines, a multinational group that can provide foreign capital to the host government's economy is also thought capable of draining capital away for use elsewhere; hence the perennial accusations of "decapitalization" with which foreign investors are confronted in Latin America.*

This last paragraph points to the ultimate conflict of interest between the multinational corporation and the host country. As Paul Baran so eloquently demonstrated, the key to a country's economic development lies in the size and utilization of its surplus. We see now that to the extent that its economy is penetrated by multinational corporations, control over *both* size and utilization passes into the hands of others who are owners or functionaries of capital of a different nationality. Under these

---

* Raymond Vernon, "Multinational Enterprise and National Sovereignty," *Harvard Business Review*, March-April 1967, p. 163.

circumstances it can be said that multinational corporations are the enemy, perhaps not of *any* development in the host countries but at least of any development which conforms to the interests of any class or group within the country other than those who have been denationalized and coopted into the service of foreign capital.

VIII

The conflicts of interest between multinational corporations and the foreign countries in which they operate generate many-sided political struggles, particularly in the underdeveloped countries where the relative weight of the multinationals is greatest. Here the local bourgeoisies tend to be split and largely incapable of independent action or initiative. An important section works, directly or indirectly, for foreign capital; and much of the remainder is paralyzed by fear of social revolution. Hence the political stance of the local bourgeoisie is generally pro-imperialist and reactionary. Its rule is therefore naturally favored by the countries in which the multinationals have their headquarters. For practical purposes this means that the chief backer of local bourgeoisies in the underdeveloped countries is the United States, since the great majority of multinationals are U.S. companies. To quote Raymond Vernon again:

The overwhelming preponderance of these [multinational corporate] groups are headed by a corporate parent of U.S. nationality, and the vast majority of the parent organizations are owned principally by stockholders who are residents of the United States. If one were to list every large U.S. corporation that owns and controls producing facilities in half a dozen or more countries abroad, the roster would contain about 200 names.

To be sure, a European list of the same sort would include the familiar long-standing names of Unilever, Bowaters, Philips, Olivetti, Nestlé, Ciba, Pechiney, and a few others. But the European list would be considerably shorter, covering only 30 or so cases. And the overseas stakes of the companies on such a roster would not be as much as one fifth of the U.S. commitment.*

To complete the picture on the U.S. side, we need only remind ourselves that the government of the United States is controlled by the very same corporations which have spread

___
* *Ibid.*, p. 158.

their tentacles out to every corner of the globe. This is of course not recognized by U.S. political "science," but it is well known, if not often proclaimed, by those who are directly concerned with the business of government. This was refreshingly admitted on a recent television program by a high government official, Mr. Nicholas Johnson, a member of the Federal Communications Commission:

> I think basically you have to start with a realization that the country is principally run by big business for the rich. Maybe you have to live in Washington to know that and maybe everyone in the country knows it intuitively, I don't know, but a government of the people, by the people, and for the people, has become, I think, a government of the people, certainly, but by the corporations and for the rich.*

As actual or potential opposition to the local bourgeoisies and their U.S. backers there are various classes and strata in the underdeveloped countries: peasants and workers, petty bourgeoisie, students and intellectuals, some members of the military. Short of making a revolution, which is their ultimate threat and must sooner or later become their goal, the peasants and workers are largely excluded from the political arena, though some elements from these classes may lend support to nationalistic regimes based primarily on the petty bourgeoisie and led by intellectuals and military people. The objective of such regimes, or of those trying to form such regimes, is not to dispossess or oust the multinational corporations, which would involve a life-and-death struggle against imperialism, but to reduce their scope, to limit their freedom of action, and, by applying various economic and political pressures, to force them to operate more in the national interest than they would if left to their own devices. A good example of such a regime is the military dictatorship which seized power in Peru earlier this year. Among its first acts was the taking over of the properties of the International Petroleum Corporation, a subsidiary of Standard of New Jersey, which had been embroiled in a quarrel over taxes with Peruvian governments for more than half a century and in the process had become the chief target of Peru-

---

* Dick Cavett Show, ABC-TV, August 25, 1969.

vian nationalism.* The regime also embarked on a land reform
which impinges on the interests of another multinational, W. R.
Grace & Co. But at the same time it has made clear that it in-
tends no large-scale attacks on foreign capital, though the threat
(from foreign capital's point of view) always exists that the
situation will get out of hand and the regime, or a more radical
one that might follow it, will plunge ahead with an all-out nationalization program.

Against this background it can be seen that for the multinational corporation a world of nations is a world full of pitfalls
and dangers. Their most fundamental requirement is freedom to
do business wherever and whenever they choose, unrestrained
by any external authority. In the words of the Business International document quoted above:

> International corporations need the freedom to move capital,
> materials, technology, and technicians whenever and wherever
> needed to maximize the growth, competitive strength, and profits
> of the enterprise. They need the freedom to make decisions on
> economic grounds. It is an imperative requirement that they be
> free to respond to competition, to new opportunities and threats,
> to pressures from consumers, workers, and investors.

But nations cannot grant these sweeping freedoms without
denying their essence as nations, i.e., as collectivities with pre-
tensions to sovereignty, which means simply the right to run
their own affairs without interference from those outside the nation. Multinational corporations and nations are therefore fundamentally and irrevocably opposed to each other. The logic of
each, carried to its final conclusion, is to destroy the other. Or,
to put the point differently, the historic course of the global
capitalist system is leading to one of two outcomes: world empire or world revolution.

The *nationalism* of the countries in which the multinationals have their seats is *antinationalism* as far as the rest of
the world is concerned.** This profound antinationalism, not

---

* For the background of the IPC dispute, see Harvey O'Connor,
World Crisis in Oil, MR Press, 1962, Chapter 17 ("Peru: Standard's
Province").

** It is interesting to note that Charles Kindleberger, one of the
multinational corporations' best friends in the academic community,
actually calls himself an "antinationalist." See his *American Business
Abroad: Six Lectures on Direct Investment*, New Haven, 1969, p. 144.

surprisingly, is ideologically transmuted into the purest and most virtuous *internationalism*. Listen to Business International rhapsodize about the aims and ideals of its clients:

> Utopia for an international corporation would be world government. A world without frontiers. Absolute freedom of movement of people, goods, ideas, services, and money to and from anywhere. No armies, navies, or air forces, only local police. A single global system of patents and trademarks, of building and safety codes, of food and drug regulations. A single, global currency. A single central bank.
>
> Nation states would have the same relationship to a world government that the states of the United States have toward Washington, or the cantons of Switzerland have toward Berne [in other words, they would cease to exist as nation states]. Obviously the words "balance of payments" would be found only in history books concerning the savage days before humans learned to live peacefully on the same planet.*

"But," the authors lament, "Utopia won't come soon." And while they are less than clear, perhaps on purpose, about what that means, the same cannot be said about the main instrument of the multinational corporations in the world today, the U.S. government. For it shows by its actions, more eloquent than any words, what is considered the only possible substitute for Utopia. Actions, above all, in Vietnam but also in Cuba and Africa and South America and, yes, even in Europe. If it can't achieve a world of states on the U.S. pattern, at least it is determined to do its damndest to achieve a world of obedient satellites.

---

* *Op. cit.*

The Resurgence of Financial Control: Fact or Fancy?

November 1971

A long three-part article by Robert Fitch and Mary Oppenheimer on "Who Rules the Corporations?" in *Socialist Revolution* (vol. 1, nos. 4, 5, 6) purports to demonstrate that giant U.S. corporations are controlled by banks and other financial institutions. In order to support this thesis, Fitch and Oppenheimer (henceforth F&O) find it necessary to attack views expressed by Paul Baran and me in *Monopoly Capital.* We are labeled "Marxist managerialists" and are charged with many grave errors of omission and commission. How large this misguided group is supposed to be is not clear, since James O'Connor is the only other one specifically named as belonging to it; but it seems evident that F&O regard the three of us not as isolated cases but as representatives of a significant theoretical trend which can seriously mislead the American Left. Under the circumstances a detailed reply seems called for.

I

To begin with, F&O have misunderstood the theory put forth in *Monopoly Capital.* As a result, much of the evidence they present, to the extent that it is relevant at all, in no way refutes or contradicts the theory. This by itself would not be too serious, since putting down Baran and Sweezy is no more than incidental to their main purpose of vindicating the theory of financial control. But unfortunately in their earnest efforts

---

This article was written by Paul M. Sweezy.

to accomplish this purpose they have committed so many methodological, analytical, and even factual errors as to deprive their study of corporate behavior of whatever value it might otherwise possess.

Let me start with a passage from *Monopoly Capital* which is quoted by F&O. It purports to characterize the typical giant corporation:

(1) Control rests in the hands of management, that is to say, the board of directors plus the chief executive officers. Outside interests are often (but not always) represented on the board to facilitate the harmonization of the interests and policies of the corporation with those of customers, suppliers, bankers, etc.; but real power is held by the insiders, those who devote full time to the corporation and whose interests and careers are tied to its fortunes.

(2) Management is a self-perpetuating group. Responsibility to the body of stockholders is for all practical purposes a dead letter. . . .

(3) Each corporation aims at and normally achieves financial independence through the internal generation of funds which remain at the disposal of management. The corporation may still, as a matter of policy, borrow from or through financial institutions, but it is not normally forced to do so and hence is able to avoid the kind of subjection to financial control which was so common in the world of Big Business fifty years ago.*

It is perfectly obvious from this passage that Baran and I never had the slightest intention to deny the existence of either "outside" directors or corporate borrowing from financial institutions, from which it follows that all the evidence adduced by F&O on these points is entirely irrelevant. The question for F&O to answer is not whether bankers sit on corporate boards or whether corporations borrow from banks: of course they do. The question is whether these activities confer corporate control on banks and bankers. And here F&O have nothing to contribute but speculations, reiterated assertions, and an assortment of stories about individual cases which may or may not be relevant to the point at issue but which absolutely do not

---

* Part I, p. 87. The passage appears in *Monopoly Capital* on pp. 15-16. The omission in paragraph (2) is F&O's and has no bearing on what is here under discussion.

form a valid basis for any generalizations. I shall have to examine some of these case "studies" later on, but before we come to that, there are other questions to be considered.

The first relates to the holdings of corporate stock by bank trust departments. The Patman Committee, extensively cited by F&O, has shown that these holdings are large and highly concentrated in the hands of a few dozen of the largest big-city banks. Do they carry with them control over the corporations whose stock is held in trust in large amounts? F&O take it for granted that they do. Waxing lyrical, they declare:

> The dramatic rise in institutional shareholding during the 1960s broke down the effective separation of ownership and control on which the theory of managerialism rested. Once again ownership and control were united in the trust departments of the great Wall Street banks: Morgan Guaranty Trust, Chase Manhattan Bank, First National City Bank. It was a unity recalling the age of Morgan, when financial institutions had been able to control corporations through their lending power. (Part II, p. 68)

Such a momentous change, one would think, ought to be pretty carefully documented. But F&O offer *not one single case* of a demonstrated causal link between bank trust holdings and corporate control. In contrast, during the age of Morgan (roughly from the Civil War to the First World War) there were literally hundreds of fully documented cases of financial control over corporations. Bankers and particularly bank trust officers will of course explain this absence of evidence of control relations very simply: their business, they will tell you (and not only for the public record), is investing money for the benefit of the trust beneficiaries, a function for which trust officers are carefully trained. They not only do not control corporations; they do not even want any such responsibility which would bring all sorts of headaches and open them to expensive damage suits should losses be suffered by trust beneficiaries owing to improper actions by trustees.*

---

* In this field of trusts and fiduciaries, capitalist law defining the responsibilities of trustees to beneficiaries is both strict and on the whole strictly enforced. This is not surprising since the stratum of the population principally involved is what C. Wright Mills called the "very rich" who are well aware of their rights and never make a move without expert legal advice.

Naturally, I cannot prove that these disclaimers are sincere and reflect the actual state of affairs (the two things are by no means identical), any more than F&O can prove the opposite. Nevertheless, having informally interviewed a number of people in the trust business and taking account of the fact that they operate in huge bureaucracies under the watchful eye of customers' lawyers, courts, and bank examiners, I am inclined to discount the possibility that they are rationalizing or lying. Certainly, it is absurd in the extreme to compare the power over corporations which banks derive from their trust holdings to that of the financial tycoons of the age of Morgan. Such a comparison betrays not only a lack of knowledge of corporate history but, perhaps even more important, an absence of any feeling for what has been happening in the business world during the last century.*

Still, it must be conceded that there is one argument of a

---

* One small example will perhaps suggest what I have in mind. Everyone knows that the First National City Bank is a huge institution with scores of vice presidents, branches all over the metropolitan area, several major divisions (consumer, corporate, trust, real estate, international), and many thousands of employees. It is, in a word, a vast bureaucratic corporation in its own right, and its problems of structure, management, etc., are basically probably not too different from those of General Motors or Standard Oil. The contrast with one of its two predecessor corporations, the First National Bank, could not be more striking. Until his death in 1931, the First National was controlled in every sense by George F. Baker, Sr. who was nearly the equal of J. P. Morgan, Sr. during the latter's lifetime and inherited Morgan's mantle after his death in 1913. As late as the 1920s the First National had only five vice presidents who were also directors, occupied part of a small building at 2 Wall Street, would not accept deposits of less than a million dollars, and did no business at all with the general public. First National men sat on dozens of corporate boards, usually alongside Morgan men, and no one in Wall Street was in any doubt about their power. The changes in the business world which had taken place by the end of the Second World War, however, rendered this kind of an elite corporation-oriented bank no longer viable, and the First National was in effect swallowed up by the National City Bank which had been one of the pioneers of the new style of banking which predominates today. That a change of this kind reflects a change in the nature of the relations between banks and corporations seems obvious enough. One of the most distressing—and for me depressing—aspects of the Fitch/Oppenheimer study is that they show no awareness, not to say understanding, of the qualitative changes which have characterized the history of monopoly capitalism and of which the First National story is only one example.

structural nature put forward by F&O in favor of the thesis of financial control which makes sense. It does not suggest anything like comprehensive or permanent control, but it certainly does leave open the possibility of decisive financial intervention in cases where a corporation's management performs poorly. The traditional Wall Street rule, F&O point out, has been "if you don't like management, sell." But, they go on, the growth of large institutional investments may make it practically impossible to apply the rule in some cases. And here they quote David Rockefeller as follows:

I suspect that such investors will become more demanding of management as time moves on—that, as holdings expand, institutions, as well as individuals, will feel obliged to take more active interest in seeing that corporations do indeed have good management. That will be true especially if their holdings become so large that they cannot readily or quickly liquidate their investments, as is now their practice when they become dissatisfied with the management of a corporation in which they hold shares. (Part II, p. 62)

Let us assume, for the sake of the argument, that this situation is on the way to becoming general, i.e., that in the typical case institutional investors are, or soon will be, ready and able to intervene in order to assure what David Rockefeller calls "good management." The question is, what does he mean by the term? F&O do not ask the question, perhaps because to do so would raise serious doubts about the kind of implicit or explicit assumptions concerning the motives of financial institutions that are sprinkled throughout their essay. But whatever their answer might be, I for one have no doubt that for David Rockefeller and the vast majority of his financial colleagues, a "good management" is one which has a good record of earning profits and expanding its company's profit-making base. This, it should be noted, is typical *capitalist* behavior (as analyzed by Marx in *Capital*), and it is what gives to capitalism its unique historical character as a value-expansion process (*Verwertungsprozess*).

If I am right about this, the implications are interesting. Financial control in this sense is certainly an argument against bourgeois "managerialism," as exemplified for example by Galbraith, according to which present-day corporate managers are no longer interested in maximizing profits. But for the kind of "managerialism" which Baran and O'Connor and I are supposed to represent, what may be called the David Rockefeller argument brings nothing but support, the stronger the more seriously the argument is taken. For what we are saying is simply that in monopoly capitalism the giant corporation is the basic unit of capital and that it operates according to the classical/Marxian principles of profit maximization and capital accumulation. Obviously, to the extent that financial watchdogs oversee this process and hold managements to the straight-and-narrow path of making and expanding profits for the corporation, and indirectly for its stockholders and creditors, our position is by that much strengthened.

I am not implying that the concentration of trust holdings in a handful of huge banks raises no substantial questions. One in particular—and it is an aspect of the problem about which Representative Patman is specially exercised—is the question of the availability to bank trust departments of confidential information on corporate affairs acquired by the same banks' lending departments and representatives on corporate boards of directors. There is no doubt, and the banks themselves do not deny it, that the normal relations between banks and corporations provide the former with vastly more inside information than is available to the average investor. If this information is turned over to trust departments and used by them in managing their clients' portfolios, it is obvious that the cards are stacked in favor of one set of investors at the expense of others. A case in point was provided by the Penn Central bankruptcy. According to a story in *Business Week* of July 24, 1971:

A Patman committee aide, Benet D. Gellman, found that Chase Manhattan and several other large banks with loans outstanding to the corporation had unloaded huge amounts of stock just prior to its collapse. The Chase sold 436,000 Penn Central shares out of its trust accounts in one week.

Patman was quick to note that Stuart Saunders, then Penn Central's board chairman, was also a director of the Chase. He charged further that the selling patterns of Penn Central stock strongly suggested that several banks, in selling portions of their stock, had acted in concert so as not to touch off too much downward price reaction.

The banks' answer to such charges is of course a pious denial. *Business Week* quotes David Rockefeller, chairman of Chase, as follows:

The trust and fiduciary investment functions of our bank are performed by departments that are wholly separate and distinct from our commercial lending activities, said Rockefeller. To assure the proper use and control of information received by the bank in its several capacities, there is no flow, or incidental communication of inside information, from commercial departments or divisions of the bank to the fiduciary investment department or to the pension or personal trust divisions of the trust departments.

Anyone familiar with the way business works will, of course, discount statements like this at very close to 100 percent. Here Patman wins hands down. But it is certainly no new discovery that the financial markets are stacked in favor of the big guy and against the little guy, nor is there any reason to believe that the particular twist given to this stacking process by the growth of bank trust holdings has had or will have any fundamental effects on the functioning of monopoly capitalism.

We shall return later to F&O's handling of the Penn Central bankruptcy.

II

Apart from basic questions of theory, I find it impossible to discuss "Who Rules the Corporations?" in a logical or systematic way. F&O jump about from subject to subject, from hypothesis to fact and vice versa, from assertion to case study, in a most bewildering way. For example, at the beginning of Part II they raise the question of the significance of trust holdings by banks and quote David Rockefeller as above. They next cite certain cases where financial institutions (not necessarily trust departments of banks) have had difficulty disposing of large blocks of stock. We now have the hypothesis to be tested or proved or at least illustrated: the trust holdings of banks are a source of corporate control. Here is the way F&O make the transition from hypothesis to "evidence":

Faced with such potential losses it is not surprising that the institutional investor may decide to intervene in corporate affairs. During the sixties, for example, financial institutions took an active role in the merger movement. (Part II, p. 63)

Off and running, F&O now proceed to treat us to several pages of anecdotes mostly culled from the pages of *Fortune* and the *Wall Street Journal* about how various types of financial institutions (banks, investment bankers, mutual funds) were involved in the merger movement of recent years, all of which add up to exactly nothing except that a large part of the business of financial institutions is dealing with corporations in one way or another. Hardly a surprising discovery, to be sure. And indeed as F&O conclude this section (entitled "Do Financial Institutions Exercise Their Stock Voting Power?"), they come pretty close to conceding that it is all much ado about nothing: "That financial institutions do not always exercise Stockholder Power [they have in fact not proved that they ever do] is no proof of their indifference or impotence. It may mean that management is performing to their satisfaction." Here again, as in the quotation from David Rockefeller, the question of "good management" is raised. What do financial institutions want from corporate managements? But once again F&O decline the implied invitation to provide an answer. Wisely, I think, for if they were to give the straightforward answer that financial institutions expect profitable performance from managements, they would be fatally undermining many of the arguments they so laboriously put together later in the essay.

This example of methodological muddle is by no means unique: on the contrary it is typical, as I think careful readers, once alerted, will have no difficulty convincing themselves. My aim in the rest of this critique is to dispose of various specific arguments and theories which might mislead a reader who has little prior acquaintance with the field of corporate behavior and finance, and approaches the Fitch/Oppenheimer study with the perfectly reasonable hope of gaining useful information and knowledge.

Dividend Payouts. F&O make much of a supposed interest of financial institutions in increasing the proportion of corporate profits paid out as dividends to stockholders. The alleged reasons are, first, that raising the payout rate is a "sure-fire" way of boosting the price of a company's stock; and, second, that the more profits are paid out as dividends the less money is left for investment, thus forcing the company to borrow more from the banks. Neither of these arguments, alone or in combination, has the slightest claim to general validity. There are circumstances in which raising the dividend rate will lead to a fall in stock price—for example, if investors and speculators judge that the effect will be to deplete a company's cash below foreseeable needs and thus to jeopardize its solvency. The problem is complicated and no simple formula can possibly cover all cases. And by the same token the main interest of banks is often to limit or reduce dividends rather than raise them, the purpose being to make sure that companies have enough money to service already existing loans. It is, I am sorry to say, all too characteristic of F&O's methods that elsewhere in their essay, when it serves their immediate purpose, they provide ample evidence for this concern of the banks. The discussion of dividend payout rates occurs in Part III, especially pp. 39-40, where the banks' interest in corporate liquidity is not even mentioned. On p. 82 of Part II, on the other hand, they present a table entitled "Long-term Lenders' Conditions" which lists conditions to which *Fortune's* top fifty companies have agreed in order to obtain long-term loans (these are called "restrictive covenants" and are a normal feature of loan agreements). In twenty-four of these fifty cases, the *only* condition noted is "dividends restricted," and in two others dividend limitation is listed as one of two conditions. The banks' enthusiasm for raising dividend payout rates seems, to put it mildly, less than overwhelming!

Even more peculiar is a piece of statistical "evidence" offered by F&O in connection with their argument that finance capital exercises pressure for higher payout rates. On p. 39 of Part III they present a table entitled "Corporate Dividend Payouts by Asset Size: 1960-1970." This shows that in every year there is a close correlation between asset size and payout rate: the larger the company the higher the payout rate. While the conclusion is not stated in so many words, it is clearly implied that this reflects the "fact" that the power of finance capital is similarly correlated with corporation size. Strangely enough, however, F&O fail to note—or, if that seems unlikely, at any rate fail to point out to the reader—that in every asset category there occurs a dramatic and continuous *decline* in the payout rate during the decade of the 1960s, presumably precisely the period when finance capital was moving from one triumph to another. For example, in the largest size category (assets over $1 billion) the payout rate in 1960 was 70.8 percent, and in 1970 it was 55.5 percent. Do the financiers lack the power attributed to them by F&O? Or the goals? Or both? The most plausible answer, I think, is both.

Before we leave this subject, let me cite one more example of how F&O handle "evidence." Because Baran and I maintain that "the making and accumulation of profits hold as dominant a position today as they ever did," F&O flatly assert: "According to Baran and Sweezy, the development of monopoly has no effect on capital accumulation at all." (Part III, p. 37) When I first read this, I rubbed my eyes in amazement. How could anyone really read *Monopoly Capital* without recognizing that the effect of monopoly on the accumulation of capital is what the book is all about?* But never mind, what Baran and Sweezy did in *Monopoly Capital* is one thing and what F&O are interested in demonstrating is something else. They want to show that the rate of capital accumulation has declined in the last hundred years or so and that this is due to the growing power of finance capital.

The first thing to note is that F&O *define* the rate of accumulation as the proportion of profits reinvested which, for a corporation, is simply the inverse of the dividend payout rate. One could of course set up a highly simplified model of capitalism in which the only form of accumulation is the reinvestment of profits by firms. But this is far from being the case in capitalist reality, where accumulation takes a number of other forms as well—savings by dividend-receivers and others with relatively high incomes, so-called forced savings due to price inflation, investment of speculative profits, etc. It is totally inappropriate, not to use a stronger term, to attempt to interpret,

---

* See, for example, pp. 81-88 and chapter 8.

as F&O here do, an actual historical process in terms of a concept which could have meaning only in the context of an abstract theoretical analysis. Let us ignore this, however, and see how good a case F&O can make with their own private definition of accumulation.

We have already seen (p. 121) that according to their own figures, the dividend payout rate has decreased sharply in the last decade, which means that in their sense the rate of accumulation has to the same extent *gone up*. But how about the last century? Here the problem would be to gather comparable figures for the nineteenth century. Of course no one has done it, and owing to lack of raw data no one could do it except in a highly speculative and impressionistic way. But this does not daunt our authors:

> The heroic anality of eighteenth- and nineteenth-century entrepreneurs, saving their profits and retaining them in the business, is a frequently told tale of economic history. Rates of accumulation were *obviously* very high. Just how high we are told less often. And aggregate figures for the various branches of industry are probably impossible to state with *complete* accuracy. (Part III, p. 38. Emphasis added.)

Next F&O cite what the author of a "widely used text" said about "one well-rooted British textile firm," to which they add that "other available records" show that "especially in the early stages of successful entrepreneurship, profit retention actually approached one hundred percent. And some businesses were even more strenuous in their demands for profit retention." Secure in the knowledge that these over-one-hundred-percenters must push the average up, F&O confidently continue: "So despite the gaps in existing historical records, *it seems safe to conclude* that early capitalist entrepreneurs accumulated at least half of their profits, and very likely considerably more." (Emphasis added.)

The reader, dazzled by this display of scientific economic history, is now ready for the clincher, which must obviously be proof that the "modern counterparts" of these early accumulators are indeed a different kettle of fish. But, alas, he is in for a sad disappointment. "We can get a fairly precise idea of the present rate of accumulation," we are informed, "by exam-

124 *The Dynamics of U.S. Capitalism*

ining dividend payout ratios." (They have in fact *defined* the accumulation rate as the inverse of the payout ratio.) There follows the discussion of payout rates analyzed above. But what is carefully omitted is the "completely accurate" fact that, according to F&O's own figures, the unweighted average payout rate in 1970 was 42.3 percent. This corresponds to a Fitch/Oppenheimer accumulation rate of 57.7 percent, which would seem to fit comfortably into the formula of "at least half of their profits, and very likely considerably more."

Faced with workmanship like this, one is hard put to know whether to laugh or weep.

Depreciation. Baran and I are accused of committing what F&O consider to be the egregious error of assuming that depreciation is a source of internal funds which has played a large part in liberating the managements of giant corporations from the kind of subservience to finance capital which characterized the age of Morgan. Not so, they say: "Depreciation is a cost of fixed assets—a cost, not a gain. Depreciation can no more be used to finance expansion than other deductions from revenues, provision for bad debts, fire loss, etc. The only internal funds that can be used for expansion are retained earnings." (Part II, p. 69n) All perfectly true in elementary accounting theory. But for better or worse we are talking about corporation finance, and in this realm matters stand very differently.

In the first place, no one knows even in theory what the "true" amount of depreciation is, so that in practice it is almost always what the tax authorities allow.* And since tax authorities in a monopoly capitalist society are notoriously servants of the leading echelons of the capitalist class, this means that characteristically a big hunk of what ought to be classified as profits and taxed accordingly is actually called depreciation and entirely escapes taxation. In practice, therefore, F&O's dictum that depreciation cannot be used to finance expansion is wrong: it often is used for precisely that purpose.

In the second place, and even more important, what is at

---

* The reasons for the theoretical indeterminacy of depreciation as a cost in a dynamic monopoly capitalist economy are explained in *Monopoly Capital,* pp. 99-104; but the subject, like much else in the real world of monopoly capitalism, is apparently not one that interests F&O.

issue here is not expansion as such but the availability of cash, the lack of which forces dependence on banks and in extreme cases means bankruptcy. And in this respect a dollar labeled depreciation has exactly the same significance as a dollar labeled after-tax profits: they both can be used for any corporate purpose and neither is in any way tied to replacing worn-out or obsolete assets. From the point of view of corporate managements, large and small, the key concept is not depreciation or retained earnings but *cash flow*. It is theoretically perfectly possible for a company with a relatively large amount of fixed assets, and hence a robust cash flow on depreciation account, to quit one line of business entirely and enter another more profitable line without ever retaining a penny of profits or borrowing a nickel from the banks. To be sure, this is not likely to happen in this extreme form, but it is important to understand how and why it could happen. The company with a strong cash-flow position is *never* forced to go hat-in-hand to the banks. The shoe is more likely to be on the other foot: such a company, whenever it wants to raise additional capital, say for a major acquisition or an ambitious foreign expansion program, can pick and choose among possible lenders, playing one off against the other and in the final analysis imposing its own terms on the financiers. And this is precisely the situation of General Motors, Jersey Standard, General Electric, IBM, and many of the other corporate giants which dominate the U.S. economy. Here we can see with crystal clarity how silly it is to equate, as F&O do, external financing with financial control. Logically, it could just as well be taken as an indication of corporate control over the banks and other financial institutions.

Who Controls Whom? I am not suggesting that control of the banks by the big corporations is the normal state of affairs. I do not know—any more than F&O do—enough about what goes on in the boardrooms and executive offices of the big business world to make such an assertion or even hypothesis, and the gentlemen directly involved are not likely to fill us in on the missing information. But it is interesting and salutary to note that a *prima facie* case for the theory of corporate control over the banks can be constructed on the same kind of data that F&O use to "prove" the opposite. Furthermore, F&O know it as well as I do, as shown by two little footnotes which they seem to have been anxious to make as unobtrusive as possible.

The first of these footnotes, on p. 99 of Part I, is addressed to unnamed persons "who argue that interlocks between banks and corporations could just as easily prove the corporations' control of the banks as vice versa." According to F&O, these people should consider bank stockholdings. Well, we have considered bank stockholdings (i.e., the holdings of the banks' trust departments) and have seen no reason to assume that they are used as instruments of control. What about the interlocks? Taken by themselves, it is certainly true that they could "just as easily prove the corporations' control of the banks as vice versa"—or rather, taken by themselves, they don't prove anything. Since F&O obviously know this, one cannot but wonder why they bother to put so much stress on interlocks.

The second footnote (Part II, p. 77) casually remarks that "some [again unnamed] managerial economists have maintained that corporations control the banks and not vice versa because the corporations, through their deposits, are net lenders to banks." I am not one of the "managerial economists" referred to here since I must admit that I had not previously thought of this argument. Nor do I believe that, taken by itself, it carries much weight: global figures are frequently of little use in revealing relations of cause-and-effect or domination-and-subordination. What we would need to know is where the balance of power lies in the open or tacit bargaining between giant corporations and giant banks over who places deposits where and who borrows from whom, and there seems to be no way in which this question could be empirically decided. Perhaps the safest hypothesis is that both sides hold strong cards and that their mutual lending and borrowing operations provide no basis for assuming that either controls the other.

At the same time, however, one should not overlook that from the point of view of the slapstick methodology employed by F&O, the argument in question is a powerful one *against* their main thesis of financial control. That they have relegated it to a three-line footnote does not speak well for their sense of scientific integrity.

Reciprocity. F&O devote a lengthy section of their essay to what they call "Financial Control and the Rise of Reciprocity" (Part III, pp. 77-92). "Reciprocity" is the business term applied to the widespread practice of corporations' simultaneously buying from and selling to each other. General Motors needs business machines and IBM needs automobiles and trucks; their mutual requirements therefore lay the basis for mutually profitable deals. As suggested by their use of the expression "the *rise* of reciprocity," F&O are under the impression that there is something recent about the practice. They also believe, among other things, that reciprocity is tied to financial control, that it contradicts all theories which assume corporate maximizing behavior, and that "managerialists" like Baran and Sweezy—who are presumably unaware of the practice—are unable to take account of it in their theories and are hence refuted by its very existence.

Here, as in many other places, F&O reveal their ignorance of U.S. economic history. Reciprocity became notorious in this country during the nineteenth century when it was universally practiced by the railroads and their suppliers and customers. When it is remembered that during the second half of the nineteenth century, investment in railroads exceeded that of all other industries combined, it will be appreciated that nothing could be more out-of-focus than to view reciprocity as a recent development. Nor could it be argued that reciprocity declined during the early decades of the twentieth century, to experience a resurgence in the post-Second World War period. The Interstate Commerce Commission published a multi-volume report during the 1920s proving that reciprocity was as prevalent among the railroads then as it had been in the earlier period, and throughout its history the Federal Trade Commission (founded in 1914) has been more or less continuously engaged in a largely futile effort to curb the practice.

As for Baran and Sweezy's neglect of reciprocity, I must ask the reader to bear with me while I quote a passage from *Monopoly Capital* (p. 50):

The attitude of live-and-let-live which characterizes Big Business . . . derives from the magnitude of the corporation's investment and from the calculating rationality of its management. By and large, this attitude is reserved for other big corporations and does not extend to the smaller businessman. For example, the big three automobile companies behave toward one another in a way that Schumpeter appropriately called "corespective," while their behavior to the scores of thousands of dealers who sell their products to the public is notoriously overbearing and dictatorial. The reason, of course, is that each of the big ones recognizes the strength and retaliatory power of the other big ones and as a matter of deliberately calculated policy avoids provoking them. But corespective behavior is by no means limited to competitors. If one big corporation is not a competitor of another, it is quite likely to be either a customer or a supplier; *and in this realm of corporate relations the sovereign principle is reciprocity,* which enjoins corespective behavior as surely as competition does. (Emphasis added.)

It should perhaps be added, what is clear from the context in the book, that the "competition" referred to is monopolistic or oligopolistic competition, not the pure competition of traditional economic theory.

F&O might perhaps argue that Baran and Sweezy are inconsistent in admitting the ubiquity of reciprocity and at the same time insisting that corporations act to maximize profits. But this is only because they *assume* that corporations are typically controlled by financiers who also control other corporations and that there is no way these outside controllers can act to achieve simultaneous maximum profits for all of them. "That is," F&O explain, "marginalists deal with the issue of oligopoly by ignoring one simple fact of economic life: that a director who represents two corporations cannot possibly maximize profits for both corporations." (Part III, p. 79) They then go on to drive their point home in typical Fitch/Oppenheimer fashion:

Take, for example, the case of Mr. John A. Mayer, Jr., chairman of the board of the Mellon National Bank. Mayer sits on four boards of giant industrial corporations: General Motors, Heinz, Armco Steel, and Alcoa. All four do business with each other. . . . Even with the best possible intentions, how can Mayer simultaneously maximize profits for all the corporations he serves as a director? If he tries to get bargain steel for GM, he isn't maximizing for Armco, and vice versa. Simultaneous maximization on intercorporate sales is an impossibility for a man who represents both companies. If this point is grasped, academic microeconomics becomes entirely untenable.

The trouble with this argument is that it ignores a "simple fact of economic life," namely, that Mr. Mayer's primary responsibility is to maximize the profits of the Mellon National Bank, and there is no *a priori* reason why this should be incompatible with all four of the other companies' acting to maximize *their* profits.

This does not mean, of course, that GM, Alcoa, Armco, and Heinz may not indulge in all sorts of reciprocal deals with each other. It only means that if they do enter into such deals, each corporation is going to be doing the best it can for itself and not simply carrying out the orders of some financier who pulls the strings for all of them. On the other hand, the fact that Mr. Mayer sits on all four boards is by no means enough to assure that these corporations will select each other as reciprocity partners. GM, for example, might find it more profitable to do a deal with U.S. Steel than with Armco. It all depends on the specific circumstances, which may or may not include consideration of common banking ties.

It is interesting that what concrete evidence F&O introduce on actual, as distinct from possible, reciprocity relations fails to support their thesis that "the networks of reciprocity in corporate America appear to parallel, and to be created by, networks of financial control." (Part III, p. 78) They cite Congressional hearings to show that tight reciprocity relations exist between rubber and oil companies. From the point of view of a rival oil company which was anxious to break into this arrangement, the line-up was as follows:

CUSTOMER	SUPPLIER
B. F. Goodrich	Gulf
U.S. Rubber	Texaco
Firestone	Shell
Goodyear	Sun and Sinclair

I am writing this without access to corporate manuals, but I am quite willing to take it for granted that F&O carefully examined these pairs of companies for interlocks, banking ties, etc. And by the same token I conclude that the fact that they mention none reflects an absence of such relations rather than incompetence on the part of the authors.

On the next page, however, F&O finally come up with

their "proof," which is characteristically introduced by the sentence: "Consider the history of the relationships between Du-Pont, General Motors, and U.S. Rubber (now Uniroyal)." No one familiar with the subject doubts that these three companies were, and perhaps still are, under the common control of the DuPont family, or that they have engaged in extensive reciprocity dealings.* The focus of F&O's attention is the situation which existed prior to 1962 when, by U.S. Rubber's own admission, it was selling tires to GM practically at cost, thus in effect transferring profits from one corporation in which DuPont ownership was around 10 percent to another in which it was nearly 25 percent. The trouble is that this *is* part of the history, not the present status, of the relationships we are asked to consider. Since 1962, partly as a result of an antitrust suit forcing DuPont to divest itself of GM stock but probably also because of a change in DuPont managerial strategy, the situation has radically changed. Once again, F&O relegate to a three-line footnote (Part III, p. 90) facts which contradict their thesis: "Since the divestiture Uniroyal's share in GM tire purchases has dropped to 42 percent [which is less than GM's share of the automobile market]. However, Vila [president of Uniroyal] says that the company now makes a profit on its GM tire sales."

The upshot is that this bit of DuPont history brings support not for the Fitch/Oppenheimer thesis of outside/financial control but for the position adopted by Baran and Sweezy in *Monopoly Capital*. After sketching changes in the typical behavior of the various Standard Oil companies in the half century or so following the break-up under the Sherman Act of the original company in 1911, we wrote:

It is possible that the old Standard companies may still be subject to Rockefeller influence, perhaps even control: publicly available information is not conclusive one way or the other. But if they are, one can only infer that the Rockefellers have decided that the best way to promote their interests is to allow, or perhaps

---

* F&O's attempt to link DuPont control to banker control takes the form of designating the controlling power as "DuPont-Wilmington Trust." This is nothing but a cute trick: Wilmington Trust is in reality nothing but a DuPont house bank playing absolutely no independent role in the whole complex.

encourage, each of the companies to promote its interests. In these circumstances the issue of Rockefeller control becomes irrelevant to the behavior of the companies or the *modus operandi* of the system of which they form constituent parts. . . .

This does not of course mean that each giant corporation operates in isolation, that there are no alliances and alignments, no agreements and groupings. On the contrary, these forms of action—like their opposites, competition and struggle—are of the very essence of monopoly capitalism. All that we are asserting is that the relevant line-ups are determined not by ties to outside control centers but by the rational calculations of inside managements. In the oil industry, for example, Standard companies are as ready and willing to ally themselves with or fight against non-Standard companies as with or against other Standard companies. It all depends where the maximum profit lies. (*Monopoly Capital*, pp. 19-20)

The DuPont case could have been cited in support of precisely this position. Ironical that F&O, despite their opposite intentions, should make the point for us.

After they get done delivering themselves of sweeping generalizations and denouncing all existing brands of economics, F&O have an endearing way of coming down to earth and confessing, a little shamefacedly perhaps, that we needn't take them too seriously after all. The conclusion of their section on reciprocity is an excellent example. "It may be objected," they write, "that government litigation, such as that carried out against DuPont, now prevents outside financial interests from exercising control over sales and purchases." I wouldn't make this particular objection, since I doubt that—except in a few special cases—government litigation has played much of a role in this regard. But I can go along with the conclusion they draw from it: "In other words, reciprocity linkages aren't determined by stockholdings, directorships, and ties to outside financial institutions." The preceding fourteen pages were of course based on the assumption that this is indeed precisely the way reciprocity linkages are determined. Now, however, F&O in effect admit that all the seeming "evidence" they have offered has little or no bearing on the question:

Such a possibility [that reciprocity relations are determined in some other way] requires empirical investigation into intercorporate relations, investigating whether the traditional market factors of price, quality, and service do, in fact, determine market shares. [Why assume that this is the only alternative possibility?] But in the meantime, the pervasive influence of financial institutions and other outside groups on intercorporate relations seems to provide a basis for further investigation. (Part III, p. 91)

So we end up with a plea for "further investigation." Splendid! This is one of the few things in the whole Fitch/Oppenheimer essay with which I can wholeheartedly agree.

The Mode of Capital Accumulation. F&O have a long section (31 pages) entitled "The Mode of Capital Accumulation," defined as "the way in which profits are ploughed back and redeployed." (Part III, p. 47) This is another one of those private Fitch/Oppenheimer concepts—I do not remember ever having run across it in the Marxian literature—which provides the launching pad for what struck me, after several readings, as a strange jumble of seemingly carefully researched facts along with largely unrelated and sometimes quite nonsensical speculations and pronouncements. In the very first paragraph of the section, for example, we read: "Acceleration of the rate of accumulation broke up guild production and changed relations between masters and journeymen into relations between capitalists and proletarians. The increase in the rate of accumulation of the material forces of production created new relations of production." We have already seen above (pp. 10-12) how F&O define the rate of *capital* accumulation, to which they now add the undefined notion of the "rate of accumulation of the material forces of production." These rates, which in some unexplained way must have existed in precapitalist as well as in capitalist society and which are presumed to have been increasing, are now credited with bringing about a social transformation. This is sheer mystification of the real historical process in which what Marx called primary accumulation played the decisive role. Only *after* the social transformation had taken place does it make sense to speak of a rate of accumulation and even then not in F&O's historically distorted sense.

There are many other passages which seem to me to be similarly erroneous or confused, but analyzing them would serve no useful purpose. I would, however, like to try to disentangle what I take to be F&O's major theoretical argument. If I have misunderstood them, I shall be glad to be corrected.

The key passage is the following:

> In the capital transfer process, a corporation operating in a low-profit industry takes its surplus value and recycles it into a corporation operating in another industry with a higher rate of profit. Capital is thus reconstituted. It serves a new social purpose, creating different commodities or services. Its potential for self-expansion is based on a different human need. This cross-industrial transfer distinguishes it from "classical" accumulation, in which surplus value was converted into capital by the entrepreneur, but the capital remained within the same firm.
> This new mode of capital accumulation is typical of the mature monopolies. . . . (Part III, p. 49)

According to this view, classical accumulation—which I suppose means accumulation in the period of competitive capitalism—took place entirely within firms each of which was committed to a particular line of production. Only later, in the period of monopoly capitalism, did a "new mode of capital accumulation" emerge which allows capital to be transferred from one line of production to another. This transfer process is presided over by financiers who manipulate it in various ways, frequently starving some lines of production (railroads, utilities), force-feeding others (computers, photocopiers, etc.), and of course taking the cream off the top for themselves. From the transfer process, which as we have seen is itself supposed to be a "new mode of accumulation," there thus emerge two other new modes of accumulation: the accumulation of loan capital and the accumulation of speculative capital. These new modes of accumulation have "an advanced socialized form" but "a thoroughly decadent and destructive content." (Part III, p. 75) They "amount to a primitive and socially reactionary form of *planning* within capitalism itself." (p. 77) According to F&O, "The next step in the socialization of the investment process must be the transformation of its social relations: the elimination of the financial oligarchy and its replacement by committees of workers operating under the control of popular assemblies." (*Ibid.*)

The programmatic hint in this last sentence raises interesting questions with which, however, I cannot attempt to deal in the present context. What I would like to call attention to is F&O's peculiar conception of "classical accumulation." If there is no transfer process, if every firm stays in the line of business it happens to be in, and if all accumulation takes place through ploughing back profits within firms, then the whole competitive mechanism—which is central to classical, Marxian, and neoclassical economics alike—goes by the board. For how else than through capital flows from less to more profitable industries is an average rate of profit formed and supply adjusted to demand at prices equal to values or prices of production? Can F&O really be so ignorant of the history of economic thought that they are unaware of all this? Or, knowing it, have they deliberately set up a straw man ("classical accumulation") as a point of departure which enables them to hail as "new" (some of) the methods by which the transfer process is carried out? To put it mildly, neither assumption is very flattering.

This is not the occasion to discuss historical changes in the forms of capital accumulation and the role of banks and other financial institutions therein. Suffice it to say that from the earliest days of capitalism, accumulation has *always* encompassed many forms other than the direct ploughing back of profits—which, incidentally, has acquired more, not less, importance in the era of giant corporations than it had in the "classical" period—and that banks and other financial institutions have *always* played an indispensable role in mobilizing capital and channeling it into the most profitable lines of activity. This role of the financiers has naturally carried with it influence and sometimes control over industrial enterprises, but only in the formative period of monopoly capitalism—roughly the half century after 1870—was financial control the regular and normal condition in the world of big business. Since the Second World War the giant corporations have generally been strong enough to stand on their own feet and relate to the financiers as at least equal, and often more than equal, partners.*

Do any of the many real facts cited by F&O contradict this theoretical perspective? I do not think so. As throughout their

---

* Here, as throughout this critique, I am following F&O in confining attention to the United States. Modifications would be necessary in the case of other advanced capitalist countries.

essay, F&O in the section under examination *assume* financial control and then "explain" all sorts of things in terms of the presumed motives of the financiers. In the absence of proof of financial control and given F&O's lack of real knowledge of financiers' motives, such explanations are unfortunately worthless. I will cite only one of several possible examples. Discussing the way financial management allegedly prevents utilities like American Telephone and Consolidated Edison from foreseeing and meeting rising future demand for their services, F&O write:

> AT&T's directors *could* float enough bonds to take care of New York Telephone and all its other ailing subsidiaries. But it is highly unlikely that they will do so, for AT&T and its subsidiaries already account for about a quarter of *all* the corporate bonds sold in the United States. And AT&T's directors are the men who control the bond market at both ends. To let AT&T unleash all the bonds it needs on the American bond market would send prices down faster and farther than such market-makers as Morgan, Stanley; Dillon, Read; and First Boston could care to see. Nor would those AT&T directors who represent the largest *holders* of AT&T debt—insurance companies like Metropolitan, Prudential, and Equitable—care to see the prices of these bonds fall. (Part III, p. 66)

This is simply a series of *non sequiturs*. The proportion that AT&T bonds constitute of all corporate bonds is irrelevant. If AT&T needs to sell bonds to raise capital, it can always do so on terms that are about as good as any other corporation can obtain. In this connection it is necessary to bear in mind something of which F&O are apparently ignorant, i.e., that regulatory agencies always permit utilities to charge prices which cover interest payments before the calculation of net profits: in the case of AT&T, which is the biggest of all regulated monopolies, this means that the corporation's bonds carry something very close to a government guarantee. Under these circumstances, banks and insurance companies would not want to sell (or buy) more AT&T bonds only if they were uninterested in selling (or buying) any more high-grade corporate bonds. But of course this is ridiculous, as F&O would have to agree, since one of their main contentions is that these financiers are always pushing the corporations to issue more bonds.

As to F&O's seeing in their alleged "new modes of accumulation" signs of "socialization" of the investment process and embryonic forms of "planning," I can only say that this strikes me as the most arrant nonsense. There is plenty of very real socialization of *production* (not investment) in the modern factory, and more than embryonic planning within the giant corporation itself and in the Pentagon; and these are of course harbingers of the socialized and planned economy to come.* But to find evidence of socialization and planning in the miserable speculative shenanigans which take place in parts of the financial superstructure of the corporate economy—and it is from this area that F&O derive most of their "evidence"—seems to me to betray a woeful lack of that sense of proportion and historical perspective which is so crucial to the fruitful practice of political economy.

The Typical and the Untypical. This brings me to what in the final analysis has to be one of the most damning criticisms of the whole Fitch/Oppenheimer performance. They do not understand the necessity, for scientific purposes, of grasping and focusing on what is typical and ignoring or relegating to a secondary position what is untypical. Instead, they seize upon any facts (or "facts") that lend support, or seem to lend support, to their preconceived ideas, without ever bothering to ask whether the phenomena they are dealing with are typical or untypical.

How else, for example, could one explain using the case of Howard Hughes (Part II, pp. 86-91) to illustrate *any* generalization about the U.S. economy? ("The Hughes case," F&O conclude, "is a spectacular example of the dominant role external finance demands to play in the corporate world.") Hughes, to put it crudely, is a billionaire nut who makes great copy for the popular magazines precisely because he operates outside all the norms of the system.

But even more revealing of F&O's failure to grasp even the first elements of scientific method is their answer to an absolutely correct observation by James O'Connor. "The picture

---

* This does not imply that socialist planning takes the same form as the planning of giant corporations and the Pentagon. Winter's harbingers of spring are by no means the same as spring.

of a few finance capitalists," O'Connor wrote (in MONTHLY REVIEW, December 1968, p. 32), "manipulating stock, acquiring huge overnight profits, and frantically putting together and taking apart industrial empires with an eye to immediate financial gain is simply not consistent with what is known about managerial decision-making in the vast majority of large corporations today."

To this F&O reply: "But 'immediate financial gain' is exactly what the conglomerate 'movement' was all about, and exactly what the railroad and utility 'diversification' efforts are aimed at achieving." (Part II, p. 114) In relation to railroad and utility diversification this is almost certainly not true: long-run rather than immediate gain is the only aim that makes sense. But this is not the point. O'Connor made a statement about "the vast majority of large corporations today," in other words, about *typical* corporate behavior. From F&O's answer one can only conclude that they either do not know what this means or do not understand its decisive importance for the subject under examination.

Penn Central. According to F&O, "The Penn Central illustrates . . . the untrammeled dominance of finance capital in the stage of corporate senescence." (Part II, p. 105) The evidence for this is at first sight rather impressive. "Overall, before the bankruptcy in April 1970 [actually it was in June 1970], the fourteen [Penn Central] board members included eleven men with fourteen interlocks with twelve commercial banks. The twenty-three-member board of the Penn Central Transportation Co., which manages the railroad, had nineteen interlocks with fourteen commercial banks." (p. 107) Furthermore, the big banks held large amounts of Penn Central debt: First National City Bank—$387 million, Morgan Guaranty—$91 million, Chemical Bank—$20 million, Chase Manhattan—$8 million. (table 5, p. 110) All in all, it would appear that here at any rate is a case in which F&O are justified in claiming that the banks had "an unassailable position." (p. 109) And the way they used this position indicates to F&O that "they seemed anxious to make off with everything but the tracks themselves." (p. 114)

And yet if we look at what actually happened at Penn

Central, we get quite a different picture. The banks, for all their apparent power, got not "everything but the tracks" but bad debts and huge financial losses. In a story on bank loan losses, *Business Week* (June 28, 1971) wrote:

> New York stock dealer M. A. Schapiro & Co. estimates that loan losses in 1970, mostly because of the Penn Central debacle, were the heaviest for any single year since the 1930s. The ten members of the New York Clearing House Assn. ran aggregate net loan charge-offs of $191.5 million. And the *New York Times* made an interesting document public this week: an internal message to senior officers from Chairman Walter Wriston of First National City Bank of New York. Citibank was the Penn Central's lead bank and, in the message, Wriston concedes that the bank last year had to revise "our net loss estimate upwards to $47.7 million, or more than four times as much as originally anticipated."

None of the possible advantages derived by the banks from their relationship to Penn Central—which, from F&O's account, were not very impressive anyway—could possibly have compensated for such enormous loan losses.

What is the explanation? That the banks, though firmly in control, were too stupid to protect their own interests? Perhaps there is an element of truth in this. But there is a much more plausible explanation, namely, that the banks were hoodwinked by a crooked management into approving and pouring money into what was dressed up as a profitable diversification program but was in fact a series of investment fiascos, from at least some of which top Penn Central management people personally profited. Let me quote again from *Business Week*'s report on bank loan losses:

> Looking back at Penn Central now, Woodruff [executive vice-president of Manufacturers Hanover Trust Co.] feels: "We were awed by its size. We should have had more information about the company. But I've heard that Penn Central financial people were adroit in avoiding giving information."
>
> Some government banking officials put it more bluntly: Penn Central's financial data were "fabricated, and bank credit groups just didn't pick it up until too late."
>
> Some bankers have a "there, but for the grace of God, go I" feeling about Penn Central. Says a senior executive of one of New York's six largest banks, "We had a less difficult time than others

did because a real smart young vice-president here spotted trouble. We gave them no unsecured loans, even though 'Gorman"—Penn Central's last chairman—"was a member of our board."

Banks and other investors have of course been swindled and victimized in similar ways throughout capitalist history, and no doubt will continue to be in the future. For my part, I would not want to draw any heavy lessons from the episode. But if I were in F&O's shoes, I would be more than reluctant to cite it as an illustration of "untrammeled dominance of finance capital."

Baran and Sweezy on Profits. My purpose has been to criticize F&O's essay, not to defend Baran and Sweezy. But I cannot let them get away with blatant misrepresentation. On page 75 of Part II, they write:

Of course, for managerialists, corporations never lose money. The surplus keeps rising, along with the real wages of the working class. This is the heart of the matter. The unarticulated premise of Sweezy and Baran's account of corporate finance is the *invulnerability of monopoly profits.* Internal funds are sufficient because the flow of profits grows ever wider and unchecked. But profits **do** fluctuate, and the business cycle does exist. . . .
Beginning in 1965, managerialism notwithstanding, United States profits fell. . . . (Emphasis in original.)

The statement is absurd and shows either that F&O cannot understand a theoretical argument or, if they did understand it, that they have shamelessly distorted it. The thesis of *Monopoly Capital* is that there is a *tendency* for surplus to rise but that monopoly capitalism fails

to provide the consumption and investment outlets required for the absorption of a rising surplus and hence for the smooth working of the system. Since surplus which cannot be absorbed will not be produced, it follows that the *normal* state of the monopoly capitalist economy is stagnation. With a given stock of capital and a given cost and price structure, the system's operating rate cannot rise above the point at which the amount of surplus produced can find the necessary outlets. And this means chronic underutilization of available human and material resources. . . . Left to itself —that is to say, in the absence of counteracting forces which are no part of what may be called the "elementary logic" of the system—monopoly capitalism would sink deeper and deeper into a bog of chronic depression. (*Monopoly Capital,* p. 108.)

In various other parts of the book, especially chapter 8 ("On the History of Monopoly Capitalism"), this theory is applied to the analysis of all or parts of the last hundred years or so of U.S. history, and nowhere is there anything which could conceivably be interpreted to mean what F&O say in the above-quoted passage. And, to cap it off, the statement that beginning in 1965 U.S. profits fell is simply not true. Here are the relevant official statistics (*Economic Report of the President,* 1971, p. 282):

CORPORATE PROFITS (BEFORE TAXES) AND
INVENTORY VALUATION ADJUSTMENT
(billions of dollars)

	All Industries	*Manufacturing*
1960	49.9	24.4
1961	50.3	23.3
1962	55.7	26.6
1963	58.9	28.8
1964	66.3	32.7
1965	76.1	39.3
1966	82.4	42.6
1967	78.7	38.7
1968	85.4	42.4
1969	85.8	41.8
1970	77.4	34.1

It will be seen that total profits increased sharply in both 1965 and 1966, and for the whole period 1960-1970 went up by 55 percent despite the cyclical decline of 1970. The other decline of the decade, in 1967, was also of a cyclical nature. And yet a few pages after the passage quoted above, F&O can blandly assert: "As we have seen, when profits turned down in 1965, corporations began to rely increasingly on external finance."* (Part II, p. 93) It should not be necessary to remind them that when one finds misstatements of "facts" about which one has knowledge, one is not inclined to have much confidence in an author's reliability in other areas.

---

* This statement should also be evaluated in the light of F&O's own figures (see p. 122 above) showing that the dividend payout rate sharply declined during the 1960s. With profits rising and payout rates failing, it is clear that corporations have never before been so amply provided with internal funds.

III

In conclusion, I should like to return briefly to the question which F&O pose at the outset: Who *does* rule the corporations?

The best short answer, I think, is that *monopoly capital* rules the corporations, *including not only industrials and utilities but also banks and other profit-making financial institutions.* I do not mean this in any metaphysical sense: the corporations are of course run by people, not by abstractions. But the people are of no interest in themselves. As Marx said in the Preface to the first edition of Volume I of *Capital,* "Here individuals are dealt with only insofar as they are the personifications of economic categories, embodiments of particular class relations and class interests." The question is what economic categories, what class relations, what class interests do the people who run the corporations personify and embody?

F&O want us to believe that there is a basic split within the capitalist class between the industrial sector and the financial sector, that the two have different and conflicting interests, and that it is the financial sector which holds the upper hand and imposes its will on the industrial sector. This thesis is implicit throughout the whole essay and is stated explicitly in the following passage (Part III, p. 46):

Radicals . . . like to explain the manifold irrationalities of capitalism by observing that it is profits, not production, that turn the gears of modern industry. But this formulation too has now become inadequate. Just as production and sales are no longer ends in themselves [who, beside bourgeois managerialists, ever said they were?], neither are industrial profits—at least for the stratum of the bourgeoisie that controls the giant corporation. Just as production must contribute to sales and sales to industrial profits, so too industrial profits must contribute to the appropriation of financial profits by the corporate oligarchs. Specifically they must contribute to the appreciation of common stock values; to increasing flows of dividends; to larger commissions for investment bankers; and to larger interest payments accruing to commercial bankers. The key point here is that the pursuit of financial profits can be partially dissociated from the pursuit of industrial profit.

Though they do not say it in so many words, it is clear from the examples they cite and the way they interpret them that F&O believe not only that the pursuit of financial profit is distinct from the pursuit of industrial profit—this indeed is self-evident—but that in pursuing their special interests the financiers regularly act in a way to reduce the long-run profit-making potential of the underlying industrial system. This amounts to saying that the rulers of the corporations do not personify the economic category of capital as such and do not embody the class interests and class relations of the bourgeoisie against the proletariat. Their primary concern is not to maximize the total pool of surplus value but rather to maximize the amount of surplus value accruing to them even if this means reducing the total pool. In other words those who control the corporations, according to F&O, do not represent the capitalist class as a whole but a particular segment of the capitalist class which has its own special interests and acts as a debilitating parasite on the entire society. According to this theory, finance capital is not only the enemy of the proletariat. It is also, and in a more immediate sense, the enemy of industrial capital. This follows from the circumstance that finance capital is supposed to enlarge its take not by increasing the exploitation of the working class but by milking industrial capital. F&O are thus positing the existence of a basically antagonistic contradiction within the ruling class.

It is important to understand that what is at issue here is not merely struggles among contending groups and factions of the ruling class over the division of surplus value. Such struggles, many of which take place in the financial sphere, have always existed under capitalism and always will exist as long as the system survives. But Marxian theory has never treated them as a manifestation of antagonistic contradictions: as against the rest of society, the capitalists form a unified class which intuitively understands that its primary interest lies in maximum possible exploitation of the working class. Compared to this, the struggle over the division of the spoils is a secondary concern.

F&O, whether they recognize it or not, are proposing a fundamental revision of this central tenet of Marxian theory. If they were right—and this is at bottom a factual, not a theoretical, question—the implications not only for economic analysis but also, and perhaps even more important, for political strategy would be far-reaching indeed. But they are *not* right. The vast majority of large corporations, and this includes banks and insurance companies as well as industrials, are run by people whose primary aim is the maximization of the profits of the companies to which they are principally attached. This ensures that the policies they adopt will, apart from mistakes and miscalculations, operate to increase the pool of surplus value, which is precisely the common interest binding the capitalists, despite all their internecine quarrels and conflicts, together into a single and basically unified ruling class. This is what I mean when I say that monopoly capital rules the corporations: *monopoly capital is the economic category personified by the individuals who happen to sit in the executive suites and boardrooms of America's giant corporations.*

The question naturally arises as to whether this view contradicts the Leninist thesis of the dominance of finance capital in the imperialist stage of capitalism. I do not think so. The truth is that today's giant conglomerate-multinational corporations—and most of them have both characteristics—are essentially financial, not production, units. In the typical case, these financial units both own and control dozens or even scores of diverse producing subsidiaries, all operated in such a way as to maximize the profits of the group as a whole.

This constellation, I submit, corresponds perfectly to Lenin's concept of finance capital, by which he meant the *coalescence* of industrial and financial interests which emerges in the stage of monopoly capitalism. In the United States this coalescence reaches its apex precisely in the concentration of power in the hands of a few hundred giant corporations. It is this concentration of economic power which makes possible not only a more effective exploitation of labor but also the development and application of more advanced technology and a closer cooperation with the state in the profitable utilization of economic and social resources. It also makes possible the appropriation of a larger share of surplus value from other competitive or less-monopolized economic sectors: small competitors, other weaker industries, suppliers of machinery, retail and wholesale trade, etc. In addition, monopoly capital squeezes whatever it can from the ever-fluctuating stock, bond, and real estate markets, and by utilizing the savings that accumulate throughout the economic system via banks, insurance companies, and other financial intermediaries. It follows that giant corporations in manufacturing, extraction of natural resources, public utilities, and provision of services are not, and cannot be, purely "industrial" in a world of mixed monopoly. They become, and are able to operate as, monopolies only by exercising as much *control* as they can possibly muster in order to extract for themselves as much of the social surplus as is feasible. To possess themselves of the necessary control, the giant corporations must operate in a wide diversity of areas and through many channels—in the capital and money markets as well as in industrial markets. And it is this which provides the basis for the kind of coalescence of industry and finance which is of the very essence of monopoly capital.

Since such coalescence assumes concrete forms in the course of struggles among greedy centers of power, each seeking greater control and maximum profits for itself, the particular forms of the coalescence vary over time, as between different countries, and from one area of the economy to another. The strategy of each power center must take full account of the maintenance of the value of already-accumulated capital, the avoidance or minimization of risk, and the probable countermeasures of rival giants. The dividing lines between intensive competition and various partnership arrangements among the various capitalist units and groups are in no sense hard and fast. Thus a General Motors will be lavish in spending for advertising and promotion, thus sharing its surplus with TV, radio, and the printed media. It will also willingly share some of its profits with commercial and investment bankers, but at the same time reserve for itself a huge financial plum in the form of a credit company to finance installment sales of its products.*

---

* If F&O were right that GM and the other automobile companies are under the control of banks, it would be completely incomprehensible why they should be permitted to retain enormous (and enormously profitable) subsidiaries (General Motors Acceptance Corporation, etc.) to finance automobile purchases, a business in which they compete directly with the banks.

What must never be lost sight of, in discussions of the various ways in which the giants share and struggle over the surplus, is that the source and size of what is being shared and struggled over lies in the labor-and-production process. Capitalists in all branches of the economy understand this well enough, even if their academic ideologists do not. And if by chance in their greed they ignore this first principle of capitalist existence, sagging commodity and financial markets soon bring them back to their senses. In the final analysis, it is this production and reproduction by daily life of an awareness of where the golden eggs come from which, willy nilly, welds the capitalists together into one great single interest group.

Part II

Inflation, Credit, Gold, and the Dollar

Dollars and Gold

December 1966

In the early years after the Second World War the center-piece of the world monetary puzzle was a persistent surplus in the United States balance of payments (looked at from the point of view of the rest of the world, this was the famous "dollar shortage" of those days). In recent years the center-piece has been a no less persistent United States deficit. In other words, this country as a whole has been, and is now, spending abroad more money than it has been taking in from abroad. The difference, at least in the first instance, takes the form of increased dollar holdings by foreign central banks and governments. But if the latter choose to do so, they can turn these dollar holdings in for gold (since by law the United States monetary authorities are bound to sell gold to foreigners at the rate of one ounce for every $35 presented). On the other hand, if they think the dollar is "as good as gold," they can keep the dollars and earn interest on them (to that extent the dollar is *better* than gold).

As a matter of fact, the foreign central banks and governments have been doing both, buying gold and building up their dollar holdings. Obviously this cannot go on forever if only because sooner or later the United States gold stock would be exhausted. But it is usually argued that long before that hap-

---

In slightly longer form, this article comprised a preface to the December 1966 issue of MR, which was largely devoted to the monetary problems and crises of the world · capitalist system. The David Michaels article referred to at several points is "The Growing Financial Crisis in the Capitalist World."

This piece originally appeared under the title "Weak Reeds and Class Enemies."

pened, the assumption that the dollar is as good as gold would be undermined and there would take place a rush to cash in dollars. At this point the United States would be forced to abandon the gold standard (i.e., stop selling gold to foreigners for dollars), just as Great Britain, then the world's leading financial center, was forced to abandon the gold standard in 1931. The result, it is feared, would be a world-wide financial crisis similar to that which occurred 35 years ago and did so much to deepen and prolong the Great Depression of the 1930's.

On this view the United States balance-of-payments deficit is a powerful time bomb ticking away in the financial engine room of the world capitalist system. Unless the bomb is defused in good time, a shattering explosion is inevitable, with possibly disastrous consequences for the future viability of the system.

But how is the defusing to take place? This is obviously the crucial question.

At first glance the answer seems simple: the United States has got to stop acting like a profligate spendthrift. Instead of showering paper dollars all over the place, and in the process undermining confidence in its ability to redeem them in gold, which is still the only universally acceptable form of money, the United States must resolve to live within its means—to spend abroad no more than it takes in from abroad. The only way to deal with the deficit, in other words, is to eliminate it. Once this has been done, all doubts about the soundness of the dollar and its free convertibility into gold will be dissipated, and the primacy of New York as the capitalist world's financial center will be assured.

To judge from its actions, however, the American capitalist class does not accept this diagnosis and cure. The country has been running the deficit ever since 1950; nearly 40 percent of the gold stock held at that time has been lost; and foreign dollar holdings are substantially in excess of the remaining gold stock. For the last decade at least, there has been no lack of warnings and cries of alarm from many quarters, and yet no really serious action to reduce the deficit has been undertaken or even initiated. Nor, as David Michaels shows in his article below, is there any indication that such action is contemplated or likely now or in the visible future. How are we to account for this seeming anomaly? Is it a case of blindness? Or impotence? Or does the American capitalist class perhaps think there is some way of solving the problem other than by eliminating the deficit?

Let us try to see the problem as it appears to a clearheaded representative of this class. To begin with he will emphatically reject the analogy between the United States and a spendthrift individual. Such a person goes into debt until his creditors no longer trust him, and then he is forced into bankruptcy: he lives beyond his means and in the end has nothing but debts to show for it. Our capitalist will insist that nothing like that is involved in the case before us. To be sure, the United States has been going into debt to the extent of the foreigners' increased dollar holdings, but at the same time the United States has been using a large part of the dollars spent abroad not on ephemeral luxuries but to construct or purchase valuable capital assets. The proper analogy, he will say, is not with a spendthrift individual but with a banking institution.

A bank collects money by accepting deposits and then proceeds to invest in various kinds of income-producing assets (loans to individuals, corporate notes and bonds, etc.). It has to keep a cash reserve at all times to meet the needs of its depositors. But this reserve is never more than a small proportion of total deposits: it is always true that if all depositors demanded cash simultaneously, as they have a right to do, the bank would be unable to pay them off and would have to close its doors. In normal times, however, and if the bank has followed prudent investment policies, the assets can be sold or otherwise turned into cash (e.g., loans can be called), and depositors could therefore be paid off in full after some delay. Knowing this, they demand cash only to meet their normal personal and business requirements, and the bank is thus enabled to continue performing its useful and profitable function as an intermediary between those who have more money than they need and those who need more money than they have.

Our capitalist friend will tell us that the financial relations of the United States and the rest of the world (and more especially Europe) are similar to those of a bank and its customers. The holders of dollars are like depositors. They can of course demand cash (gold) any time they want to, although, as in the case of the bank, everyone knows that if they were all to do so at the same time there would not be enough to go around. But this does not mean that there are no valuable assets to offset the dollar liabilities. Again as in the case of the bank, the United States has invested in various kinds of income-producing assets (branch plants, stocks and bonds of foreign corporations, etc.). If necessary, these assets could be sold for foreign currencies, the foreign currencies thus acquired could be cashed in for gold, and the gold could be used to pay off the dollar "depositors."

Now a sound bank naturally has to maintain—as a matter of business practice and in most countries also as a matter of law—an ample margin of cash plus investments over deposits. Is the United States in this sense a sound international "bank"? In other words, are its short-term obligations to foreigners amply exceeded by its gold plus its longer-term foreign investments? Here are the latest figures as reported in the *Survey of Current Business* of September 1966 (Table 14, p. 40). They relate to 1965. "Short-term assets and U.S. Government obligations" held by foreigners (these are what we have been referring to as dollar holdings) amounted to $32.5 billion. At the same time the United States gold stock was $13.8 billion, or only 42 percent of dollar claims which could be presented for payment on short notice. It is this gap which is usually pointed to with alarm by those who fear for the safety of the dollar. However, the picture looks rather different if we add that United States long-term private foreign investments amounted to $70.8 billion and United States government credits and claims on foreigners to $25.1 billion. If we add up the assets (gold + private long-term investments + government credits and claims = $109.7 billion) and subtract the short-term liabilities ($32.5 billion), we see that the United States "bank" had a safety margin of $77.2 billion, which amounts to no less than 238 percent of the foreign dollar holdings.

Our capitalist will point to these statistics as proof positive that the dollar, far from being a weak currency, is in an immensely strong position. There is no more reason, he will say, for foreign holders of dollars to demand gold than there would be, for example, for depositors in the Chase Manhattan or the First National City to withdraw their deposits in banknotes. Either form of action would be irrational and irresponsible.

Our friend is likely to go even further and argue that foreigners should be grateful to the United States for running a deficit. Everybody agrees that gold production has not been sufficient in recent years to provide the world with what it needs in the way of monetary reserves. But as long as it is also accepted that the dollar is "as good as gold," these monetary reserves can be supplemented by dollars; and this in fact is what has been happening, thanks to the continuing United States deficits which have been providing a steady flow of dollars into the monetary reserves of foreign central banks and governments. This arrangement, according to our friend, is an eminently sensible one and should be recognized as such and made a permanent part of the international monetary mechanism. It would be unsound only if the United States failed to increase its foreign assets as fast as its short-run dollar obligations. But this is no danger: the United States has actually been increasing its foreign assets *faster* than its short-term dollar obligations, and there is no logical barrier to the indefinite continuation of this process.

What our friend does not say, but must surely think, is that from the United States point of view this arrangement has the added and by no means incidental advantage that it greatly facilitates, and indeed makes a shining international virtue out of, the rapid and thorough penetration of foreign economies by American capital. For that is precisely what the massive build-up of United States foreign assets means.

Against this background it is not hard to understand why the American capitalist class, despite increasingly shrill warnings and alarms, shows no signs of moving toward the elimination of the balance-of-payments deficit. To do so would be to put a brake on American economic expansion abroad and at the same time to cripple what it considers to be a well-functioning and perfectly sound international capitalist monetary system. Far better to persuade the foreign holders of dollars to forget about acquiring more gold, accept the present system, and devote their energies to making it work better.

But, as noted earlier, these "unreasonable" foreigners have been acting otherwise. They—and this applies particularly to France but also to other Western European countries—have been cashing in a considerable part of their dollar holdings for gold; and as things now look, they seem likely to continue doing so, perhaps on an expanding scale, in the period ahead. The reasons are undoubtedly varied and may, as some Americans think, contain a large admixture of "outdated" economic thinking—gold fetishism, irrational fear for the safety of the dollar, and so on. But, as David Michaels shows in his article, from the point of view of rival capitalist classes, there is a very strong and entirely rational reason for their behavior. By refusing to accept the dollars created by the United States deficit and instead threatening to exhaust the Americans' gold reserve, they can hope to *force* the United States to eliminate the deficit. This in turn would check the American penetration of their economies and enable them to avoid the fate, which now seems to threaten them, of being gradually turned into full-fledged neo-colonies of the United States. From *this* standpoint, what the Americans regard as the special virtues of the present international monetary system—that it facilitates the expansion of American capital and thus in effect strengthens the dollar as a reserve currency—appear as its greatest evils.

We thus see that behind all the complexities and mysteries of the monetary system lie the real issues of interest and power. The Americans obviously are not going to be able to *persuade* the Europeans to change their policies. The question is whether the Europeans can *force* the Americans to change theirs.

David Michaels is undoubtedly right to emphasize the global importance of this conflict. Whether he is also right that the Europeans hold most of the trump cards and that any conceivable outcome "seems certain [to] involve an enormous economic setback for the United States" is much more doubtful. We will not stop to analyze the particular solution which he seems to think is most likely to be adopted—a simultaneous devaluation of all currencies in terms of gold. He explains in some detail how it would work and in the process helps to elucidate the *modus operandi* of the present international monetary mechanism. The question we would like to raise is one which Michaels fails to consider: Is it not possible that the relative strength of the two sides is such that the United States capitalist class, rather than being pushed to the wall, will be able to force an "American" solution on its European rivals? That this possibility is envisaged on the American side is indicated in no uncertain terms in an article which Michaels cites (Emile Despres, Charles P. Kindleberger, Walter S. Salant, "The Dollar and World Liquidity," *The Economist*, February 5, 1966). (It is characteristic that this article, which expresses the American imperialist view in its most nationalistic and aggressive form, should have been written by three economists who have long records as liberals reaching back to New Deal days. People like this can see through the humbug of economic orthodoxy but have so little historical understanding that they have no qualms about putting their talents at the service of the most powerful and ruthless exploiting class of all time.) After arguing that Europeans would be well advised to swallow whatever dollars the United States chooses to feed them, the authors continue:

But if, nevertheless, Europe unwisely chooses to convert dollars into gold, the United States could restore a true reserve-currency system, even without European cooperation. . . . The decision would call for cool heads in the United States. The real problem is to build a strong international monetary mechanism resting on credit, with gold occupying, at most, a subordinate position. Because the dollar is in a special position as a world currency, the United States can bring about this change through its own action. Several ways in which it can do so have been proposed, including widening the margin around parity at which it buys and sells gold, reducing the price at which it buys gold, and otherwise depriving gold of its present unlimited convertibility into dollars. The United States would have to allow its gold stock to run down as low as European monetary authorities chose to take it. If they took it all, which is unlikely, the United States would have no alternative but to allow the dollar to depreciate until the capital flow came to a halt, or, much more likely, until the European countries decided to stop the depreciation by holding the dollars they were unwilling to hold before. If this outcome constituted a serious possibility, it seems evident that European countries would cease conversion of dollars into gold well short of the last few billions.

Translated into blunter language, this says to the European capitalists: Don't think you can bluff us! If you want to take all the gold, go ahead. We'll cut the dollar loose from gold, and in the world of today you'll soon find that you need the United States and the dollar more than you need gold. You know this in your hearts; and when you discover that your bluff isn't going to work, you'll call it off and join us in devising an arrangement which recognizes the supremacy of the dollar and at the same time safeguards your interests as junior partners in the world capitalist system.

Is the United States prepared to go so far? No one knows, and for the present at least a more pertinent question is whether the Europeans really intend to put the matter to a test. David Michaels thinks so. "Since the European capitalist class has a long history and memory of being 'top dog,' and now has great financial power," he writes, "we believe it must and will soon make a stand and fight." Without further backing, the argument is not very convincing. The British capitalist class has an even longer history and presumably just as good a memory of being top dog, and yet it has accepted the role of docile satellite with no noticeable resistance. It is true that the Europeans have greater financial strength than the British, but this is based on short-term dollar holdings and not, as in the American case, on massive financial *and* technological penetration of practically the entire capitalist world. It is not at all clear that in a showdown the purely financial strength of the Europeans would be able to confront effectively the much more broadly and solidly based economic strength of the Americans. For this reason alone, it seems to us, one must be skeptical about the depth and seriousness of the European will to "stand and fight."

In this connection, something can be learned from Claude Cadart's "France Between China and the U.S." (MR, December 1966). Cadart does not doubt the authentic character of de Gaulle's independent anti-American foreign policy, and he argues effectively that it derives a good deal of its support from the corporate and bureaucratic sections of the French ruling class. Cadart also notes, however, that in France, as in other European countries, there is a pro-American wing of the bourgeoisie; and he believes that de Gaulle has been able to go as far as he has in his anti-Americanism only because his policy enjoys genuine popularity among the masses. This is a situation full of actual and potential contradictions. If persisted in, the policy will almost certainly lead to increasing trouble with the United States, and this may be expected to polarize the French bourgeoisie even further. To gain the support needed for a real battle against the colossus of the capitalist world, de Gaulle would be obliged to solidify his support in the working class. But the further he went along that road the more he would alienate the big capitalists. The intensification of the crisis on the international level would thus in all probability lead to an ever deeper crisis at home. In a showdown, there can be little doubt that de Gaulle would side with his own class against the workers, even if that meant calling off the struggle against the Americans.

Similar considerations, only on a much larger scale, apply to any serious conflict between the United States and European capitalists in general. If the latter were really to inflict what David Michaels calls "an enormous economic setback" on the United States, it is quite likely that the true beneficiaries would be not European capitalists but the world revolution and the socialist countries. And that, we may be sure, is an outcome which even the most nationalistic of European bourgeoisies will shun as conscientiously as the devil shuns holy water.

The moral of this story, if there may be said to be one, is that socialists and revolutionaries can never count on capitalists to fight their battles for them. The defeats which have been inflicted on United States imperialism in the period since the Second World War—most notably in China and Cuba and Vietnam—have all been the work of the revolutionary people, not of any kind of capitalists. Sooner or later the same will have to be true of Europe—and of the United States too.

Gold, Dollars, and Empire

February 1968

People had been saying for a long time that the pound would have to be devalued, and on November 18th it happened. Britain, presumably under heavy United States pressure, had used up much of its gold and foreign exchange reserves and had gone deep into debt trying to keep the pound at $2.80. But it was all in vain. Persistent balance-of-payments deficits plus inept and ineffective governmental policies convinced international capital that the pound could not be saved, and against this conviction the British government was powerless.

Was the dollar next?

A lot of people with money thought so. In the weeks immediately after the fall of the pound, hoarders and speculators bought hundreds of millions of dollars worth of gold, most of which had to be supplied by the United States Treasury. Though it will not be known until late January or February exactly how much gold the United States lost in this greatest of all "gold rushes," the indications are that the figure will be very large. According to a Treasury announcement of January 3, as summarized by Edwin L. Dale Jr. in the next day's *New York Times*, "total [gold] transfers from the Treasury stock to the Stabilization Fund [through which transactions with foreign countries are handled] in 1967 amounted to $1,175,000,000, of which $925 million was subsequent to the devaluation of the pound." This reduces the Treasury stock to $11.95 billion, down about 8 percent for the year.

This gold was of course bought at the official price of $35 an ounce, and what motivated the purchases was the expectation that the price would have to go up. In simple supply-and-demand terms, the reasoning behind this expectation is as follows: In every year but one since 1949, the United States has paid out to foreigners more than it has received from foreigners. As a consequence foreign governments and central banks and capitalists have accumulated the tremendous sum of 31.2 billion United States dollars for which they can demand gold any time they want to. What's more, the continuing deficit in the United States balance of payments, which was sharply up in 1967 to between $3.5 and $4 billion (Johnson's New Year's press conference), is steadily adding to this preponderance of potential demand over actual supply. Sooner or later, the reasoning goes, whatever inhibitions are keeping these foreigners from rushing to cash in their dollars will give way and the actual demand will greatly exceed the actual supply. The United States will then either have to raise the price of gold (devalue the dollar) or stop selling gold (go off the gold standard) which would presumably also result in a rise in the price of gold. Hence the smart thing is to buy gold now and wait for the rise.

The United States government for its part has insisted all along that it is determined to maintain the value of the dollar at the rate of $35 per ounce of gold. So two questions arise: (1) What is the likelihood that it can succeed? And (2) what are the probable consequences if it fails?

Can the Dollar Be Saved?

To begin with we have to distinguish between the short-run and the long-run prospects. Having survived the wave of speculative gold-buying which followed the devaluation of the pound, the dollar may actually be stronger for a while. This is because holding gold is expensive;* and many speculators, seeing that they are not going to make a big killing in a hurry, are likely to sell gold, thus tending to replenish the United States Treasury stock.

---

* We quote from a dispatch from London in the *Wall Street Journal* of January 3rd: " 'It is now costing a gold hoarder about 10½ percent a year in insurance, storage charges and such to hold gold,' says one banker here. 'When you couple that with the fact that an investor can put his money to work and get a 7 percent return without any trouble, it is apparent that the gold hoarder is over 17 percent behind for every year that he has his money in gold bars.' "

But any strengthening of the dollar from this source will of course be purely temporary. In the longer run what matters is the behavior of the United States balance of payments. It was failure to cure a persistent balance-of-payments deficit which eventually toppled the pound, and there is no doubt that the same cause can have the same effect in the case of the dollar. What, then, is the explanation of the United States deficit, and what is the prospect of its elimination?

The answer to the first part of this question is clear enough and can be summed up in one word: imperialism. Senator Jacob Javits, in a press conference in New York on January 4th, practically said as much:

He traced the country's payments difficulties to expenditures in the defense of Europe and Asia and help to the underdeveloped nations. The war in Vietnam, he said, caused at least 40 percent of the expected deficit for 1967. (*New York Times*, January 5, 1968.)

"Defense of Europe and Asia" (against Europeans and Asians, of course) involves maintaining armed forces all over the world. Quantitatively, according to a Washington dispatch by Edwin L. Dale Jr. in the *New York Times* of January 5th, "the cost of maintaining troops abroad, including those in Vietnam, results in a dollar outflow of more than $4 billion." It is not so easy to put a price tag on "help to the underdeveloped nations," since a multiplicity of programs, both military and civilian, come under the heading. But an idea of the order of magnitude involved can be gathered from the fact that during the first half of 1967 the balance-of-payments item labelled "U.S. Government grants and capital, net" was running at an annual rate of $4.3 billion. (Council of Economic Advisers, *Economic Indicators*, December 1967, p. 25.) The cost to the United States balance of payments of policing and shoring up the American Empire, alias the "Free World," can thus be put at something over $8 billion.* This is enough to eat up all the dollars earned through the United States exporting more

---

* The *total* cost is of course much greater since the bulk of military spending, even that caused by a war in Southeast Asia, takes place within the United States itself and hence does not enter into the balance of payments.

goods than it imports (the favorable merchandise balance was running at an annual rate of $4.4 billion in the third quarter of 1967), and to account for the entire 1967 deficit, which, as already noted, Johnson estimated at between $3.5 and $4 billion in his New Year's press conference.

It is against this background that we must evaluate the Johnson administration's program "to bring our balance of payments to—or close to—equilibrium in the year ahead," announced on New Year's Day. And the verdict must be that the program is a hodge-podge which does not even touch the heart of the matter and seems most unlikely to succeed in its stated objective.

Not that it may not be possible to trim as much as a billion dollars from the outflow of private capital to foreign countries, with special emphasis on Western Europe. The European economy is in a state of recession at present, and a slowdown of United States investment there would probably occur in the normal course of events. Furthermore, many giant United States corporations are in a position to continue expanding abroad even without the help of dollars from the home office: their size and profitability enable them to compete successfully for capital in the local money markets. Nor is there any reason why the government can't reduce the rate of tourist spending outside the Western Hemisphere, provided of course that Congress will cooperate by passing the necessary legislation. Here, however, the balance-of-payments savings are less certain since foreign countries may well retaliate by discouraging their tourists from coming to the United States. For the rest, the Johnson program is mostly an expression of hopes of what may be saved if other countries feel like helping the United States out of its difficulties. They can, for example, change their method of taxation in such a way as to stimulate American exports; or they can buy more military hardware in the United States; or they can invest more money in United States securities; or they, meaning in this case primarily the West Germans, can pay all or most of the costs of the American troops which occupy their territory. But none of these ideas is particularly new, and to judge from past experience none is very promising. No wonder the *Wall Street Journal's* man in Washington (Richard F. Janssen) opened his lead story on the payments program with the following pessimistic appraisal:

> Will the government's desperate new drive against the run-away balance-of-payments deficit be enough to save the dollar?
>
> Despite the initial outpouring of optimism from Johnson administration officials, there's a strong undercurrent of doubt among knowledgeable analysts here that the ambitious effort announced on New Year's Day can succeed in its basic aims. "Frankly, I don't see it working," declares one seasoned analyst.
>
> And if the dollar drain does not almost cease, some strategists candidly confess, the U.S. and the world could well be facing a genuine financial crisis in about a year. Should President Johnson's package of controls prove much less than fully effective, "come back next New Year's for the devaluation announcement," says one insider only half in jest. (*Wall Street Journal*, January 3, 1968.)

It is of course hardly surprising that a remedy which fails to touch the root of the problem has little chance of succeeding. For, as we have already emphasized, the reason for the persistent deficit is the high cost of empire; and in this respect the Johnson administration, true to its nature and its record, has not the slightest thought of retrenching. In the words of the statement issued to the press on New Year's Day: "We cannot forego our essential commitments abroad, on which America's security and survival depend." What is meant of course is America's security and survival as boss and exploiter of a world-wide empire.

At this point it is perhaps worthwhile to digress for a moment to deal with a question which may arise in some readers' minds. If the empire costs so much, who needs it? Answer: those who benefit from it—the giant multinational corporations which reap billions of dollars in profits from their global operations. Even in purely balance-of-payments terms, the take of the giants is enormous: during 1966 the flow of dollars to the United States as income plus fees and royalties from direct foreign corporate investments was $5.1 billion. And this takes no account of the additional billions which are paid out or reinvested abroad, or the profits of the $30-billion export business, or the profits of supplying arms and munitions to America's $70-billion military establishment. Nor must it be forgotten that while the benefits of empire accrue to a few hundred giant corporations, the costs are shared by all the taxpayers. The empire is expensive, no doubt about that; but from the point of view of its beneficiaries, who also happen to be in control of the United States government, every dollar spent in holding it together and protecting it against its enemies is a dollar well spent.

Under these circumstances what the Johnson administration ought to be asking itself is not whether it can *eliminate* the deficit by a few superficial controls and regulations, but rather whether it can realistically hope to keep the deficit from *increasing* in the period ahead. In other words, is it not likely that the cost of empire, like the cost of living, is on the way up?

The answer seems to us to be obviously in the affirmative. Last month in these pages we analyzed the situation in Southeast Asia and came to the inescapable conclusion that the trend there is toward a wider war. The United States military wants it, and there is unfortunately no real evidence that the corporate establishment is prepared to oppose the military in any serious way. No one can predict now how far the escalation will go, but the costs of the war seem almost certain to go on rising for the foreseeable future. If Johnson has any plans for coping with this prospect, he has been altogether successful in keeping them secret.

And then there is the threat of more Vietnams, in Asia itself or in Africa or in Latin America—or maybe even in some tortured country of Europe like Greece or Portugal. When and where are obviously unknowns, but if anything seems certain in this uncertain universe it is that the historically near future will witness great revolutionary struggles in many parts of the world and that the United States will do all in its power to suppress them. In the face of this prospect, to dream of eliminating the deficit in the United States balance of payments is about as realistic as to believe in the liberal utopia of a return to free competition.

Finally, not only are the costs of counter-revolutionary wars likely to go up but also the costs of trying to prevent them. That, in essence, is what help to the underdeveloped countries is all about. And as the impoverished countries of the "third world" sink deeper and deeper into the morass of underdevelopment—as they must, given their rapid increase of population and their rotten colonial and neocolonial economies and social structures—their frightened oligarchies will increasingly appeal to the mother country for food to feed the starving and guns to shoot the rebellious. The Congress may balk, as it did in 1967 by cutting the "foreign aid" appropriation, but the result will only be to hasten the coming of more Vietnams.

The realistic prospect is thus an expanding, not a contracting, deficit in the months and years ahead. And this in turn means that the likelihood that the dollar can be saved—in the sense of remaining freely exchangeable for gold at $35 an ounce—is very small indeed.

From the Gold Standard to the Dollar Standard?

When the United States goes off gold, the chances are that other countries still remaining on the gold standard will follow suit and a regime of fluctuation exchange rates will ensue. This is nothing new, at least not in principle; in fact, it has long been advocated by a respectable school of monetary theorists. Attempts may be made to revive the gold standard at a new parity—say, $70 an ounce with other currencies being correspondingly revalued*—but it is hard to see how general agreement could be reached and it is more likely that gold will finally lose its role as the indispensable flywheel in the "free world's" monetary mechanism. This is, after all, a logical historical step since, as Schumpeter put it, "an automatic gold currency is part and parcel of a laissez-faire and free-trade economy.** It is, to be sure, a long time since the gold standard could be said to operate "automatically," but still that it has continued to exist at all is testimony to the fact that up to now an international economy containing at least half-way independent national capitalist units has remained in operation. What now appears to be happening is that the United States is moving to stake out a claim to full dominance over the entire capitalist world, and in this context the gold standard—but-

---

* For an analysis of what this might mean, see the article "The Growing Financial Crisis in the Capitalist World," by David Michaels, MR, December 1966. Two other articles in that issue of MR, one by the editors and one by Jacob Morris, should also be helpful in understanding the present international monetary situation.

** Quoted by Jacob Morris in "Marx as a Monetary Theorist," *Science & Society*, Fall 1967, p. 406. This article also helps to clarify the role of gold under capitalism, as well as Marx's monetary theories.

tressing, however feebly, what is left of the independence of a country like France—is simply an obstacle to be got rid of. This murder of the gold standard will apparently take place not deliberately and in cold blood but after a suitable show of trying to save its life and under the seeming *force majeure* of a financial crisis and run on the dollar.

After the gold standard, what?

From the point of view of United States imperialism, there can naturally be the only one answer: the dollar standard. The subordinate units of the empire will be expected to hold their reserves in dollars, perhaps somewhat disguised by a label provided by the International Monetary Fund, and to accept additional dollars as the United States chooses to pay them out in the form of balance-of-payments deficits. Imperialism's monetary theorists consider this to be an excellent arrangement on two counts. First, the "free world's" need for an expanding currency base, at present threatened by a shrinking supply of monetary gold, will be fully and flexibly met.* And second, the United States will be able to continue running the deficits which, as we have already seen, are part of the indispensable costs of empire.

The "only" question is whether the other nations of the capitalist world will go along, accepting their role as neocolonies of the United States and tacitly agreeing to bear a share, through holding increasing numbers of surplus dollars, of the costs of keeping the empire together.

Many, apparently including Great Britain, have already made their decision: they will do whatever they are told to do. But France and the Common Market still present a big question mark. At the moment, to be sure, even de Gaulle seems more inclined to talk independence than to act it. But one has to reckon with the possibility that the situation will change quite drastically in the next year or so. If the United States, as now seems likely, plunges ahead into an ever-expanding war on the Asian mainland, its strength and bargaining power in the rest

---

* The shrinkage of the supply of monetary gold comes from an increased demand for industrial and hoarding purposes on the one hand and a stable or perhaps even declining rate of production of new gold on the other.

of the world will steadily ebb. And under these circumstances, it is not far-fetched to assume that not only France but the Common Market as a whole might elect to fight United States imperialism rather than join it. In monetary terms this would mean establishing a rival currency block into which as many client states as possible would be drawn. Tariff and trade wars would again become the order of the day, as during the 1930's. And the Europeans would probably be tempted to try to make rather far-reaching tactical alliances with the socialist countries.

We are not predicting that this will happen, still less what the outcome of such renewed inter-imperialist rivalry might be. But it does seem to be a development well worth watching for as the dynamics of the present infinitely complex international situation unfold in the months and years ahead.

Notes on Inflation and the Dollar

March 1970

It has long been known that in a monopoly capitalist economy inflation is possible without any excess of aggregate effective demand over productive potential. It is enough that demand should increase sharply in one or more important sectors of the economy, permitting monopolistic corporations in these sectors to raise prices and reap higher profits. Other sectors of the economy, even if characterized by excess capacity, have no reason to lower prices to offset the higher prices in what may be called the dynamic sectors, so that we already have an explanation of an increase in the average level of prices. But this is not the end of the matter. The increased activity in the dynamic sectors means increased demand for labor, materials, and equipment. Prices of these factors of production therefore rise, and the raises naturally tend to spread in the form of higher costs to the other sectors. Capitalists in these other sectors then raise their prices to compensate for the higher costs, and another upward push is imparted to the general price level. As price increases spread out from their starting point like ripples in a pond, they affect more and more sectors of the economy, public as well as private, obliging everyone to try to protect himself as best he can by raising the price of *his* goods or services. This whole process tends to take on a self-perpetuating character once it has been set in motion. In particular the subsiding of the increase in demand in the original dynamic sectors, though it is likely to initiate a recession in production, is by no means enough to stop the price inflation; and any new important shift in sectoral demand can give it a new impetus. To bring inflation to an end in a monopolistic economy may therefore not be possible without a prolonged period of stagnation in which excess capacity and unemployment become general throughout the system.*

The foregoing explanation of the inflationary process seems to fit recent U.S. experience quite well. During the last two decades there have been three marked inflationary episodes—that associated with the Korean War, that of 1956-1958, and that of the 1960s which moved into high gear in 1965 and is still going strong. At no time during this whole period has the economy been under real strain as it was, for example, during the Second World War. Whereas in 1944 unemployment reached an all-time low of 1.2 percent of the labor force, only once during the fifties and sixties did the rate dip below 3 percent, reaching 2.9 percent in 1953. And data on utilization of capacity indicate that, overall, the American economy has normally been provided with a comfortable cushion of idle capacity during these years. That there is no direct correlation between inflation and the fullness of utilization of human and material resources is sufficiently demonstrated by the facts that at the time of writing consumer prices are rising at a rate of about 7 percent a year (at or near the peak for the entire two decades) while unemployment is almost 4 percent of the labor force and capacity utilization has dipped under 80 percent for the first time since 1958.

The Korean War brought with it a large increase in both military spending and investment in plant and equipment. These were clearly the dynamic sectors responsible for the inflation of the early 1950s. The 1956-1958 episode was different: there was no war then and, as Charles Schultze convincingly showed in the work referred to above, the milder inflation of those years was initiated by a boom in capital goods spending. The latest inflation, beginning in earnest in 1965, repeats in essentials the pattern of the Korean War period. Comparing 1964,

---

* The pioneer study of this kind of inflation, still well worth careful study after ten years, was Charles L. Schultze, *Recent Inflation in the United States,* Study Paper no. 1, materials prepared in connection with the Study of Employment, Growth, and Price Levels for consideration of the Joint Economic Committee, Congress of the United States, September 1959.

the last year before the Americanization of the Vietnam War, with 1969, we get the following picture (billions of dollars):

	1964	1969	Increase
Military Outlays	50.0	79.3	58.6%
Plant & Equipment	47.6	75.3	58.2%

It is of course a coincidence, though a remarkable one, that military spending and plant-and-equipment spending increased by almost exactly the same percentage. But in any case we are left in no doubt that these have been the dynamic sectors during this latest bout of inflation. Nor is there any reason to question that as between the two it was the military which played the triggering role.

Let us now look more closely at the present situation. We have already noted that inflation is proceeding at a brisk pace, while there is plenty of slack in the economy. In fact the amount of slack is rapidly increasing as we move into what many Establishment economists and pundits are calling the country's first recession in a decade.

Most observers seem to hold the view that this recession was brought on by the tight-money policies adopted by the Nixon administration when it came to power a year ago. Tight money, so the argument runs, pushes up interest rates and this in turn discourages certain kinds of spending, resulting in cutbacks of production, layoffs, and a general slowing down of economic activity. No doubt it works out that way in some circumstances, but it is questionable if this mechanism has been of crucial importance in the present case. Rising interest rates are a normal accompaniment of inflation:* the trend has been

---

* The reason for this is not far to seek. Suppose the price level is rising at a rate of 10 percent a year. A person lending money at 10 percent interest would have 10 percent more money at the end of the year but exactly the same amount of real purchasing power as he had at the beginning. Under these circumstances it is obvious that no one would lend money: it would be better to buy real assets, trying to select those whose prices are rising faster than the price level as a whole. It follows that lending will take place only at a rate of interest exceeding 10 percent. Applying this reasoning to the United States, we see that real rates of interest—i.e., rates which are adjusted for price changes— are not particularly high. With prices rising at 5 to 6 percent a year, interest rates in the 8 to 10 percent range, such as have recently prevailed for high-grade debt instruments, translate into a *real* interest rate in the

upward since 1965 and would probably have continued through 1969 regardless of the government's monetary policies. What brought on the present recession is therefore not tight money, though it may have made a contribution to the extent that it drove interest rates higher than they would otherwise have gone. The responsible factor was rather a leveling off followed by the beginnings of an actual decline in military spending. Here are some excerpts from an article in *Business Week* of January 24th commenting on the woes of the aerospace industry, the heart of the military-industrial complex:

> After living through their poorest business year in a decade, U.S. aerospace companies face what could be an instant, bone-crunching replay. . . .
> President Nixon has committed himself to a $5-billion reduction in defense spending for the 12 months beginning July 1, following a $4-billion cut during the current fiscal year. . . .
> At the National Aeronautics and Space Administration, another big source of aerospace contracts, an additional $150-million cut for fiscal year 1971 was reported this week, reducing its budget to about $3.35 billion. NASA's budget for the current fiscal year is $3.7 billion, down $200 million from the previous year. . . .
> Whatever comes in fiscal 1971, the industry cannot wish away the continuing impact of cutbacks already made in the last six months of 1969, *when defense contracting started a marked downward* drift. From July through September, the latest quarter for which statistics are available, contracts fell to $8.6 billion from $10.9 billion a year earlier. At the same time, aircraft contracts dropped to $1.6 billion from $2.1 billion a year earlier. (Italics added.)

The italicized clause is particularly significant, since it is changes in the volume of contracts let which foreshadow future changes in spending and, in an apt phrase of *Business Week*'s writer, send "shockwaves from the big contractors to their sub-contractors." That the sector of the economy where the infla-

___

neighborhood of 4 percent, which was about the yield on such instruments in the period just before the rate of inflation began to pick up in 1965. One thing needs to be added, however: if and when the rate of inflation slows down or halts, long-term borrowers who contracted debts at high money rates which seemed reasonable in the light of rising prices suddenly find that the real rate they are paying has gone up on them. In this way there is created an increasingly strong vested interest in the continuation of inflation.

tion started should also be the one which initiated the recession in production is in accord with the theory set forth above. Also in accord with the theory is that, once well under way as it now is, inflation can easily survive such a recession and propagate itself for a long time to come.

What else will happen, in addition to the continuation of inflation, is impossible to predict. Perhaps the Establishment economists are right who foresee a relatively brief recession followed by an upturn, moderate growth, and gradually receding inflation. And then again, maybe they aren't. The uncertainties of the situation are clearly indicated by *Fortune* magazine in the "Business Roundup" section of its February issue:

> It is clear that the Fed [Federal Reserve system] is going to have to do something . . . , and do it soon, to facilitate a transition from lagging real demand to modestly rising demand without a major recession. To accomplish this without refueling inflation is the very delicate task that Chairman William McChesney Martin is handing over to his successor, Arthur F. Burns.

The trouble is that no one knows how to perform this "very delicate task"; and if Mr. Burns and his colleagues fail to find the secret in good time, it may well be that whatever they decide to do will contribute to more inflation or deeper recession or both at the same time. In looking ahead, it would even be wrong to exclude the possibility of a financial crisis and a real depression. In nearly ten years of expansion under the impact of the military buildup begun by Kennedy immediately after he took office and sharply stepped up by Johnson when he Americanized the Vietnam War, all kinds of imbalances, tensions, and contradictions have accumulated in the U.S. economic system. As an example, take the disproportionate growth of debt as compared to income (the figures are in billions of dollars):

	1960	1969	Increase
Personal Income	383.5	629.6	63.4%
Consumer & Mortgage Debt	197.3	388.8	97.1%

What these figures show is that on the average during the 1960s people's debts grew more than 50 percent faster than their incomes. In an atmosphere of seemingly endless boom, such imbalances don't seem to matter. But centuries of capitalist history tell us that once the boom comes to a halt, they quickly rise to the surface and often acquire a tremendously disruptive force of their own. It is true that, like the boy who cried wolf, radicals have too often cried depression in the years since the Second World War. Many, especially in the European Left, seem by now to have convinced themselves that capitalism has really changed and that there need never again be a serious economic breakdown. Predictions are out of order here, but a reminder that the wolf finally came is not.

So far we have confined attention to the domestic problems and aspects of inflation in the United States. Its international ramifications and implications are no less important.

For reasons which have already been alluded to, all monopoly capitalist economies—and nowadays the entire capitalist world, including its backward sectors, is dominated by monopolies—are inflation-prone. If the rate of inflation were approximately equal throughout the system, this would not be an important cause of international disequilibria. But of course no such equality exists, and the law of uneven development under capitalism, so much stressed by Lenin and other early Bolshevik writers, guarantees that if equality ever were achieved it would be only accidentally and momentarily. In practice rates of inflation vary widely from country to country and from time to time, with highly significant consequences for the various national entities and their dominant classes.

In the case of the United States in the last five years, prices have been rising faster than in other leading capitalist countries. This means that it has become progressively harder to sell U.S. goods abroad and easier to sell foreign goods in the American market. The result has been a reduction in the excess of merchandise exports over imports and hence an impaired ability to acquire the foreign currencies needed to carry out U.S. operations in other countries (especially military operations which, as in the case of Vietnam, can be tremendously costly in terms of foreign currencies). Since the Americanization of the Vietnam War, a robust export surplus of approximately $6 billion in 1964 largely disappeared by 1969. The result has of course been a drastic weakening of the U.S. balance-of-payments position: on an international scale the United States is now living far beyond its means. In the last few years this fact has been obscured by a number of special circumstances. For example, the long U.S. stock-market boom of the 1960s attracted billions of dollars from European speculators and investors. And when this source of strength to the U.S. balance of payments started to dry up about a year ago, U.S. banks began borrowing foreign-owned dollars on a massive scale in order to escape, at least in part, from the adverse effects on them of the Federal Reserve's increasingly restrictive domestic credit policy. But inflows of funds of this kind are no panacea: indeed, being reversible, they are potential sources of longer-run weakness rather than strength.

How is it possible that the United States can live beyond its means? The answer, in its simplest form, is that up to now the other capitalist countries have been willing to accept more and more U.S. dollars on the implicit assumption that they are a form of IOU which can eventually be cashed in. The United States, in other words, has been like a high-living rich man who is allowed by his grocer, tailor, wine merchant, etc., to run up bigger and bigger bills because they believe that sooner or later he will pay them off. The question, in the one case as in the other, is how long this can go on.

There is of course no pat answer. It all depends on the specific circumstances, and in the U.S. case the factors involved are so numerous and interconnected that precision is completely out of the question. But one thing does seem sure: the piling up of IOUs cannot go on forever. There must come a time, sooner or later, when the creditors will say "No more!" and begin to try to collect on what they already have. And that would mean a complete breakdown of the present international monetary system, with consequences perhaps even more profound and widespread than those which followed the breakdown of the international monetary system in 1931.

It is not our purpose here to speculate on the nature of these consequences but rather to point out that given the present rate of inflation in the United States, the day of reckoning is inevitably drawing closer and that it is this more than anything else which dictates to the Nixon administration a policy of inflation control.

At this point a question naturally arises: Why have the other capitalist countries been willing to accept U.S. dollar-IOUs as long as they have and in the quantities they have? Since the 1940s there have been only two years in which the United States has had a favorable balance of payments, and the cumulative amount of dollars paid out in excess of the amount taken in for the two-decade period is of the order of $35 to $40 billion. As of the end of 1968, U.S. short-term liabilities to foreigners were more than twice as great as the sum of the U.S. gold stock, foreign currency holdings, and reserve position at the International Monetary Fund. What explains this remarkable willingness of the rest of the capitalist world to go on absorbing these seemingly weaker and weaker dollars?

In general there are two sets of answers to this question. The first has to do with the role of the dollar as the reserve currency of the capitalist world and the second with the fears, which are shared by all bourgeois regimes, of what might happen if the supremacy of the dollar were seriously challenged.

A reserve currency is one which other countries treat the way they do monetary gold, i.e., they use it as backing for their own currencies and as a medium for settling their international accounts. The dollar and the pound both used to be reserve currencies, but in recent years the dollar has acquired a virtual monopoly position. When the international monetary system is working smoothly, dollars are literally "as good as gold," and indeed even better since dollars can earn interest while gold cannot. To this we have to add that as national economies grow and world trade expands, the need for monetary reserves also increases. And since, for reasons which need not detain us, the production of new gold in recent times has been incapable of meeting this need, the gap has had to be filled with dollars. The mechanism by which these dollars have been added to the capitalist world's monetary reserves has been precisely the continuing deficits in the U.S. balance of payments.

This has been a most convenient and profitable arrangement for the United States.* But it has also been useful for the rest of the capitalist world, and indeed one might even say necessary as long as none of the other currencies is able to fulfill the role of the dollar. De Gaulle often talked about dethroning the dollar, but his alternative was an unrealistic return to a pure gold standard and he obviously never had the strength to do more than talk. Up to a point therefore one can say that the capitalist world *had* to accept a steady outflow of dollars as the price of keeping its global structure intact. This is one aspect of the problem.

But "up to a point" does not mean forever or without limit. There seems to be little doubt that the outflow of dollars which has been taking place since the Americanization of the Vietnam War is much more than would be needed on a continuing basis to meet the need for increased monetary reserves. And yet the other capitalist powers continue to show a remarkable tolerance in the face of this situation. Why?

At the most basic level the reason is simple: fear of the revolutionary forces which any upheaval in the capitalist system might unleash. The ghetto uprisings in the United States from 1964 to 1968 and the May events in France in 1968 proved that these forces are there. Ever since, the international bourgeoisie has been worrying and wondering about where and when the volcano will erupt the next time. And in these circumstances there is, not surprisingly, pretty general agreement among the powers that be that it is no time to rock the boat. A story in the *New York Times* of November 18, 1969 (by Clyde Farnsworth, datelined Basel, Switzerland) casts a revealing light on what is at issue here:

The United States, at a meeting here of central bankers from ten major nations, has linked its continuing deficit in the balance of payments to the problem of black unrest in the country.

Central bankers from the United States have told their Western European and Japanese counterparts that the United States cannot accept the social cost implicit in getting rid of the balance-of-payments issue.

The most effective way to eliminate the payments deficit is

---

* For a fuller explanation, see Harry Magdoff, *The Age of Imperialism*, New York, 1969, pp. 80-100; excerpted below, pp. 213 ff.

by prescribing a recession, but the Americans argue that the first men to be laid off, according to traditional employment patterns, would be unskilled black workers. This, they say, would provoke an intolerable aggravation of racial disquiet.

The argument is not a new one, but it is unusual for it to be raised in international monetary discussions. . . .

The reaction of the Europeans and Japanese was said by the same sources to have been sympathetic. Their attitude was summed up as follows:

Since the growth of international trade depends on the healthy evolution of the American economy—the richest market in the world—little can be gained by having this economy slip into a recession torn by violence.

The American argument was advanced after Paul A. Volcker, Under Secretary of the Treasury for Monetary Affairs, disclosed that the quarter ended in September had resulted in another large deficit in the American balance of payments. . . .

The American policy remains to curb inflation by maintaining credit restraint. But, judging from the American position here, the stress is now on taking precautions to prevent any substantial increase in unemployment. The rate is now around 4 percent. . . .

Implicit in this policy is the belief, though not frequently stated openly, that a rise in unemployment would worsen black unrest.

According to this account, the European and Japanese capitalists have two reasons, one positive and one negative, for their tolerant attitude toward continuing large U.S. balance-of-payments deficits. The positive reason is that an inflationary U.S. economy is an excellent market for their exports on which, in the final analysis, their own prosperity is crucially dependent. And the negative reason is that deflation in the United States would be likely to produce dangerous political instability.

We would like to suggest a possible third reason, namely, that the capitalists of other countries are really not as opposed to U.S. military expenditures and activities—which, as noted above, underlie both inflation and balance-of-payments deficits —as they sometimes appear to be. Insofar as the purpose of the U.S. war machine is to maintain in power throughout the Third World regimes which are hospitable to capitalist trade and investment, the capitalists of other countries are co-beneficiaries of its activities. Since they do not have to bear any of the direct costs of this worldwide policing, they may well feel that the least they can do is to help indirectly by absorbing the outflow of dollars which is one of its unavoidable by-products. Furthermore, if the United States were to assume a more modest military posture, the Europeans and Japanese would probably feel it necessary to do more of their own policing. From their point of view such a development would be doubly disadvantageous. On the one hand, the Americans, with a less inflationary economy and fewer resources committed to the military effort, would be better able to compete in world markets. On the other hand, the necessity to expand their military effort would make the Europeans and Japanese less formidable competitors in the world market. In other words, the existing arrangements under which the United States undertakes to do most of the policing and to bear all the direct costs involved can hardly fail to appeal to European and Japanese capitalists as an eminently sensible one. Why jeopardize it by putting unnecessary pressure on the dollar?

There is, then, no mystery about the tolerance of the rest of the capitalist world for U.S. dollars. In part they are necessary for the functioning of an international monetary system based more and more on the dollar and less and less on gold.*

---

* The recent decline of the free-market price of gold to, and on occasion even below, the official monetary price of $35 an ounce clearly demonstrates that for the present at least the capitalists of the industrially advanced countries have decided to accept what is essentially a dollar standard. The decision was made easier for all concerned by the establishment of the system of Special Drawing Rights (SDRs) at the International Monetary Fund. These SDRs, of which $9.5 billion worth are to be created in the next three years, are in effect fiat international money and are of course being apportioned according to the time-honored capitalist principle of "To him that hath shall be given." Under the caption "Monetary system provokes ire of poor nations," *Business Week* commented as follows in its issue of October 4 (p. 111):

"While the rich industrial nations patch and prop up the international monetary system, poor nations look on with increasing bitterness.

"They see little benefit for themselves in such schemes as special drawing rights and expanded quotas in the International Monetary Fund. . . .

"This week's annual meetings of the World Bank and the IMF only reinforced the view of many delegates from poor nations that the international financial agencies are rich men's clubs.

"Their mood is distilled in a Latin American delegate's acid comment on SDRs: 'It is disgusting to see the fat nations voting themselves an extra $9 billion while they cut back on their aid to us. It is like feeding steaks to dogs in front of starving people.' "

The validity of the comment is hardly vitiated by the fact that the

And refusal to accept even more than are needed for this purpose would most likely have very disagreeable consequences for the capitalists of the industrially advanced nations. They have therefore generally refrained from pressuring the United States, preferring to leave it to successive U.S. administrations to decide for themselves when and how to tackle the inflation and balance-of-payments problems. And since the policies of the Johnson administration proved inept and ineffective, the Nixon administration on coming to office found itself faced with a situation which threatened to get out of hand.

Here we come full circle to the point where we left the domestic aspects of inflation a few pages ago. For international no less than for internal reasons, bringing inflation under control assumes increasing importance for the U.S. ruling class. But can it be done short of a real depression and a lengthy period of stagnation?

Liberals like J. K. Galbraith are wont to answer, on the basis of experience in the Second World War, that it can be done by means of a system of direct controls (price and wage fixing, allocation or rationing of scarce resources, etc.). But neither the Johnson nor the Nixon administration has ever seriously considered this course, probably mainly because both the big corporations and the trade unions are strongly opposed to controls. Another reason, which may or may not have been operative, is that controls, to be effective, require a certain amount of national unity and civic discipline, lacking which they fail of their purpose and become a bottomless source of graft and corruption. Unlike earlier wars, the Vietnam War has produced in the United States the exact opposite of national unity and civic discipline. Thus even if the government had been disposed to use controls—which it has never been—it is quite likely that the situation would have been made worse rather than better.

So we are left with the strong probability that what lies ahead is either a continuation of inflation or a depression and stagnation. Obviously, neither prospect is "acceptable" to the U.S. ruling class, so we can expect much talk about other solu-

---

delegate in question undoubtedly represented an oligarchy which specializes in feeding steaks to dogs in front of starving people.

tions and maneuvering to try to realize them. But in the final analysis what we are likely to get is, one way or the other, a profound deepening of the multiple crises which are slowly but surely weakening U.S. monopoly capitalism and sapping its ability to control its victims and retain the support of its allies.

The Long-Run Decline in Liquidity

September 1970

In most respects the current economic recession has closely resembled previous post-Second World War recessions. As usual the major immediate factor at work has been a decline in private investment, and also as usual the most volatile component of private investment has been investment in inventories. Here are the figures (in billions of dollars at annual rates) from the third quarter of 1969 (when total investment reached its peak) through the first quarter of 1970 (the latest available at the time of writing):

	Total gross private domestic investment	Change in business inventories
1969: III	143.3	10.7
1970: I	135.0	0.8
Decline	—8.3	—9.9

It thus appears that the decline in inventory accumulation actually exceeded the decline in total private investment and can therefore be pinpointed as *the* immediate cause of the recession.

It is interesting to note that in 1966-1967 a very similar decline in investment took place in an identical period of time, only on an even larger scale. Here are the comparable figures:

	Total gross private domestic investment	Change in business inventories
1966: IV	122.2	18.5
1967: II	105.1	0.5
Decline	—17.1	—18.0

180

Yet despite this very large swing in private investment, there was no recession (in the sense of a decline in the real Gross National Product*) in 1966-1967. Why?

The answer is that in 1966-1967 the escalation of the Vietnam War was in full swing and the military budget was zooming upward (from $65.6 billion in the last quarter of 1966 to $72.5 billion in the second quarter of 1967), and this had a sufficiently strong stimulating effect on the economy as a whole to allow it to weather the drastic slump in private investment. This time, in contrast, military spending has undergone a moderate decline (from $80.3 billion in the third quarter of 1969 to $78.9 billion in the first quarter of 1970) and has therefore had the effect of reinforcing the slump in private investment. Given this coincidence of a decline in private investment and a decline in military spending, the question which naturally comes to mind is why the overall slump has not been sharper. The reason is that consumer incomes and expenditures have continued to rise. This is usual in the early stage of a downturn, changes in consumption typically lagging behind changes in investment. During the current recession, however, the expected decline in consumption has been prevented by government actions, largely an increase in social security payments. Writes *Business Week* in its issue of July 25th: "Fattened by the spring increase in social security, these payments [to individuals from the government] are running at an annual rate of $77.5 billion—up $8.7 billion since January." And, we might add, up almost $10 billion from a year ago.

All this has to do with the "normal" cyclical functioning of the U.S. economy and the ways in which it is interfered with—reinforced or weakened—by state action. Nothing particularly new or unexpected seems to be involved, and it can be seen that one does not need to blame tight money for the recession or invoke fancy monetary theories to explain the recent behavior of the economy. Nor is there anything irrational

---

* Actually official figures show a decline of $400 million from the fourth quarter of 1966 to the first quarter of 1967, but in a total of about $660 billion this is statistically insignificant. From the third quarter of 1969 to the first quarter of 1970 the decline in GNP was $6.3 billion, which explains why this time it is generally admitted to be a recession.

in the view which is now widespread among economists and other observers of the business scene that the recession has, in the current jargon, "bottomed out" and that what lies ahead in the next year or so is a recovery to higher levels of GNP, with some improvement in the unemployment situation. There are, naturally enough, considerable differences of opinion about how rapid the recovery will be or how far it will go, but these are minor compared to the extent of agreement that the direction of movement from here on will be upward. That's what past experience leads us to expect, and in the absence of compelling reasons one does not lightly ignore the lessons of past experience.

And yet there are differences between the present situation and previous postwar recessions. One is that price inflation has continued more strongly throughout this recession. But this is a difference of degree rather than of kind: for example, prices continued to rise during the 1957-1958 recession, which followed a particularly vigorous investment boom. In this respect, therefore, the present recession is by no means unique. What is really new this time, however, is in the area of business failures. It is not simply that the number of failures and the amount of liabilities involved have increased: that always happens in a recession. The crux of the matter is that for the first time in the postwar period a growing number of giant corporations have been forced into bankruptcy or face the threat of bankruptcy. An editorial in the *New York Times* of July 26th under the title "Failing Companies" begins as follows:

The nation is facing a problem that it has not confronted to a comparable degree since the Great Depression: what should the Federal Government do about private enterprises that are failing?

This issue has emerged dramatically with the bankruptcy of the Penn Central Railroad, the threat to the financial solvency of the Lockheed Aircraft Corporation, and the liquidation or merger of a number of failing stock-brokerage firms.

The editorial immediately proceeds to attempt to reassure readers that the situation isn't really all that bad:

These three cases have greater differences than similarities.

Admittedly the threat to railroad companies, aircraft producers, and stockbrokers—as well as to companies in other fields—was intensified by the prolonged economic slowdown and liquidity squeeze. Although that threat is not yet over, there is reason to believe that the greater flow of money and credit to the economy will in the months ahead prevent a widening wave of business failures. The country is almost certainly not on the brink of anything resembling the universal disaster of the Great Depression of the 1930s.

The logic here is curious. On the one hand, we are said to be faced with a problem that has been nonexistent since the Great Depression, which surely suggests that long-run forces are at work. On the other hand, the only causal factor mentioned is the purely cyclical one, which is judged to be turning favorable. And finally comes the "almost certain" conclusion that we are not on the brink of another Great Depression. What the *Times* seems to want to avoid—and in this it is by no means alone among commentators on the economic scene—is any discussion of why this particular problem of business failures has arisen in an acute form now and not at any other time in the last quarter century.

To get at the explanation, we first need to have before us some facts about the debt and liquidity situation not of individual companies but of the system as a whole. It is well known that the country's debt structure was pretty thoroughly deflated during the Great Depression, and that during the Second World War both corporations and individuals were swimming in cash while supplies of many kinds of goods and services were shrinking or (as in the case of new automobiles) nonexistent. Under the circumstances, an obvious use for cash was to pay off debts. It is therefore not surprising that the U.S. economy emerged from the war in an unprecedentedly liquid condition. By way of illustration, total corporate assets (and liabilities) grew between 1941 and 1945 by 30 percent, while corporate debt increased only 2.8 percent. Individuals and noncorporate business fared even better: their debts actually declined by 2 percent during the war years, while disposable personal income was increasing by 62 percent.*

---

* The figures are all taken from *Historical Statistics of the United States, Colonial Times to 1957*, Washington, D.C., 1960, pp. 664, 139.

But this is not the way capitalism usually works. In a period of moderate prosperity, to say nothing of a real boom, both businesses and individuals incur increasing debts in order to expand, respectively, their capital and their consumption. In fact, it is precisely this borrowing to expand and spend which, apart from government action, is responsible for the general prosperity of the economy. Knowing this and taking into account the fact that the period since the Second World War has been characterized by long prosperities and brief and mild recessions, we should expect to find a more or less steady increase in private debts, not only absolutely but relatively to the physical growth of the economy as a whole. And indeed we are not disappointed. Table 1 presents figures for total private debt, Gross National Product, and the percentage of debt to GNP for selected years since the war.

TABLE 1

PRIVATE DEBT (NET)

(billion $)

	Total private debt	GNP	Debt as percent of GNP
1946	153.4	208.5	73.6
1950	276.8	284.8	97.2
1955	392.2	398.0	98.5
1960	566.1	503.7	112.4
1965	870.4	684.9	127.1
1969	1.247.3	932.1	133.8

Source: *Economic Report of the President*, February 1970, and *Survey of Current Business*, May 1970.

Before we go on to examine the corporate debt/liquidity problem, it may be useful to take note of the growing burden of debt on consumers. This may not be a large factor in the present or near-future economic situation as a whole, but the trends are very striking and certainly portend serious trouble later if not sooner. Table 2 (page 185) gives the essential data, using what seem to be conservative estimates where official figures are lacking.

One can summarize the message of Table 2 by saying

TABLE 2
CONSUMER DEBT PAYMENTS
(billion $)

	1946	1950	1955	1960	1965	1969
(1) Outstanding mortgage debt[a]	23.0	45.2	88.2	141.3	212.9	266.8
(2) Outstanding consumer credit	8.4	21.5	38.8	56.0	90.3	122.5
(3) Interest & amortization on (1)[b]	2.1	4.1	7.9	12.7	19.2	24.0
(4) Interest on (2)[c]	0.5	1.3	2.3	4.5	9.0	14.7
(5) Installment debt repaid	6.8	18.4	33.6	46.1	70.0	94.6
(6) Total consumer payment on debt (3)+(4)+(5)	9.4	23.8	43.8	63.3	98.2	133.3
(7) Disposable income	160.0	206.9	275.3	350.0	473.2	629.6
(8) Percent of debt payment to disposable income (6)÷(7)	5.9%	11.8%	15.9%	18.1%	20.8%	21.2%

Source: *Economic Indicators,* various issues.

a. On one- to four-family homes.

b. Assumed that interest and amortization together = 9 percent of outstanding debt.

c. Assumed that interest rates charged consumers averaged as follows: 1946, 1950, 1955—6 percent; 1960—8 percent; 1965—10 percent; 1969—12 percent.

that while total consumer payment on debt has increased fifteen-fold since the Second World War, consumers' disposable income has increased slightly less than fourfold. In other words, debt payments have grown nearly four times faster than the incomes from which they have to be paid. Or in still other words, whereas debt absorbed 6 cents of the average consumer's take-home dollar in 1946, today it absorbs 23 cents. No one knows exactly what the outside limit of this process of relative debt growth may be, but it is obvious that there must be a limit: after all, consumers wouldn't be consumers any more if 100 percent of their incomes went for debt payments. As the limit is approached, wherever it may be, markets for consumer goods traditionally bought on credit (including housing) will also tend to reach limits, with stagnation-producing effects on the economy as a whole. Meanwhile, it is hardly surprising to learn that mounting debts, in the words of *U.S. News and World Report* (June 22, 1970), "are threatening a financial crackup in more and more families. . . . Excessive debt is engulfing thousands of families."*

Table 3 tells why the very same words could be applied with equal truth to the plight of U.S. corporations. Here the most revealing comparison is not between total debt and income but rather between liquid resources (cash and government securities) on the one hand and short-term liabilities (debts which have to be paid off in the near future) on the other: this is the so-called liquidity ratio.

TABLE 3

LIQUIDITY RATIO: NONFINANCIAL CORPORATIONS
(billion $)

	(1) Cash and government securities	*(2)* Current liabilities	*(3)* Liquidity Ratio *(1)÷(2)* percent
1946	38.1	51.9	73.4
1951	50.7	92.6	54.8
1956	53.9	130.5	41.3
1961ᵃ	59.9	155.8	38.4
1966	64.7	254.4	25.4
1969	64.3	333.8	19.3

Source: 1946-1966: *Economic Report of the President,* February 1970; 1969: *Federal Reserve Bulletin,* June 1970.

a. The series in 1961 and later years is not strictly comparable with earlier years. Investment companies are excluded, and certain definitions and classifications are changed.

Here we see that since the war liquid assets of nonfinancial corporations increased by about 70 percent while current liabilities were zooming up by more than 540 percent, with a resulting drop in the liquidity ratio from 73.4 percent to 19.3 percent. This signalizes a truly dramatic decline in what may be

* Quoted in Labor Research Association, *Economic Notes,* July 1970, p. 5.

called the average corporation's margin of security against insolvency. An analogy may help to bring out the meaning of this development: Two individuals each have debts of $100 falling due in the near future. One can immediately lay his hands on more than $70 and therefore needs to take in only $30 to be sure of paying up on time. The other can lay his hands on only $20 and therefore must take in $80. Other things being equal, it is obvious that the second individual is much more vulnerable than the first to any change in the economic weather which might have the effect of reducing his income or his ability to borrow afresh. What has happened since the war is that the average corporation has passed from the situation of the first individual to that of the second. And this is why a recession is so much more likely to touch off a wave of bankruptcies now than at any time in the past ten or twenty years.

The reader may object that there are few if any "average corporations" and ask whether the same generalizations can be applied to the big and the small alike. Table 4, though relating only to manufacturing corporations (not, as in the case of Table 3, to all nonfinancial corporations), provides a convincing answer: the drop in the liquidity ratio has been most marked for the largest corporations (assets over $100,000,000) and least marked for the smallest (assets under $1,000,000). Hence those Wall Street jitters.

TABLE 4

LIQUIDITY RATIO: MANUFACTURING CORPORATIONS

(Cash and government securities as percent of current liabilities)

Corporations by asset size (million $)	Liquidity Ratio (percent)	
	March 31 1947	March 31 1970
All corporations	88	21
0—1	71	31
1—5	66	24
5—100	82	22
Over 100	113	19

Source: Federal Trade Commission and Securities and Exchange Commission, *Quarterly Industrial Financial Report Series for All United States Manufacturing* and *Quarterly Financial Report for Manufacturing Corporations*.

Let us turn now from the general and historical to the concrete and immediate. Against the background of statistical material which we have passed in review, the following story which appeared in the financial section of the *New York Times* of July 5th under the by-line of Jerry M. Flint takes on its full significance:

DETROIT, July 4—The wolf has again been beaten from the Chrysler Corporation's door, and this time the bankers did it.

"It was a magnificent thing," said Lynn Townsend, Chrysler chairman, gratefully as the week ended.

For 10 days the automaker was against the wall, its ability to survive in the auto and money markets questioned. A panic was under way.

Chrysler's ups and downs . . . are chronicled regularly, but the company attributes the latest crisis to the Penn Central. When the railroad subsidiary moved into reorganization under the bankruptcy laws, it sent the investors and creditors looking for potential trouble spots—and there was Chrysler. It was:

• Losing money—$29 million in the red in the first quarter.

• In debt—$673 million payable in one year for the parent company as of March 31, and $1.6 billion in short-term commercial paper outstanding for its subsidiary, the Chrysler Financial Corporation.

On June 23, Mr. Townsend tried to stop a panic. He said there would be a small profit in the second quarter and listed the manufacturer's cash and bank-credit lines to prove it was not in the same shape as Penn Central which was unable to pay its bills and payroll or deal with the commercial paper.

The next day the run began, but on the commercial paper —the I.O.U.'s—of the financial subsidiary. These 30- to 270-day notes are backed by car installment notes, and in a good day Chrysler can sell $100 million of them to keep its financing operations going.

Chrysler Financial had $600 million in bank-credit lines, too, and when it couldn't "roll" its commercial paper—sell new to pay off old—it turned to the banks, which put up hundreds of millions of dollars.

"They demonstrated that to a good credit risk, they have the ability and the will to step up to the job. They came right through with their lines of credit" and not one bank fell out, said Mr. Townsend.

On Tuesday and Wednesday Chrysler executives were in New York, and the bankers came up with $410 million in bank lines, credit pledges to lend money if needed. It was hoped that would stop the panic.

Chrysler officials and bankers say the financial unit's commercial paper is solidly backed. "But when you start a run on a bank, you run out of the liquidity at some point," said Gordon Areen, president of Chrysler Financial.

The bankers also had their own interest to protect. If Chrysler had followed Penn Central, there could have been a general panic, draining banks and bankrupting businesses. "We're going to survive whatever happens," said a Chrysler executive this week, as he listed the company's assets, "but if we can't, there are a lot of companies that are going to go down."

The anonymous executive was certainly not exaggerating. No one knows how far or fast the chain reaction resulting from an actual as distinct from a merely threatened failure of Chrysler would have gone. But there was every reason to fear the worst. "My recent conversations with financial leaders," Senator Jacob Javits told a news conference on July 27th, "have convinced me that the economy has just skirted the edges of economic disaster, and that for some days it was a matter of touch and go." (*New York Times,* July 28, 1970.) Nor is there any reason to suppose that it is necessarily all over. Writing of the railroads in its issue of July 25th, *Business Week* had the following to say:

Many railroads were large creditors of the Penn Central at the time its bankruptcy was announced. And although Judge Fulham has approved payment of railroad interline settlements due after July 1, some roads were owed as much as $2.5 million before the bankruptcy announcement was made on June 21. Whether they will get this money—and when—is still undetermined.

Interline payments are in constant motion from one railroad to another and back again. Keeping the money flowing smoothly is essential to keeping the industry operating. If road X fails to pay its bills, road Y may not be able to pay either. Even the wealthy roads can have cash problems if the Penn Central, which generates about 15 percent of total industry revenues, temporarily suspends interline payments.

What rail managements are wondering is whether Penn Central's troubles can be stopped from spreading. "If even one or two more roads go under," says John P. Fishwick, president of the Norfolk & Western, "it will have a multiplied effect on the rest of us. . . ."

Alan S. Boyd, president of the Illinois Central, points out that "liquidity is a problem throughout the whole railroad industry. The railroads are in a cash bind like anybody else." Boyd adds that he will be "very much surprised if there are not more railroads following the PC into reorganization."

The kind of liquidity or monetary crisis faced by the U.S. economy today is of course nothing new. Marx provided a classic description and diagnosis of the phenomenon more than a hundred years ago:

Such a [monetary] crisis occurs only where the ever-lengthening chain of payments, and an artificial system of settling them, has been fully developed. Whenever there is a general and extensive disturbance of this mechanism, no matter what its cause, money becomes suddenly and immediately transformed, from its merely ideal shape of money of account, into hard cash. Profane commodities can no longer replace it. The use-value of commodities becomes valueless, and their value vanishes in the presence of its own independent form. On the eve of the crisis, the bourgeois, with the self-sufficiency which springs from intoxicating prosperity, declares money to be a vain imagination. Commodities alone are money. But now the cry is everywhere: money alone is a commodity! As the hart pants after fresh water, so pants his soul after money, the only wealth.* In a crisis, the antithesis between commodities and their value-form, money, becomes heightened into an absolute contradiction. Hence, in such events, the form under which money appears is of no importance. The money famine continues, whether payments have to be made in gold or in credit money such as bank notes. (*Capital*, Kerr ed., I, 155.)

It used to be thought that monetary crises resulted from defects in the banking system. Given a powerful central bank operating under suitably flexible rules—so the argument went— it would be possible to nip the crisis in the bud. This was perhaps the most important rationale for the establishment of the Federal Reserve System just before the First World War. But the crisis of 1929 and the ensuing depression showed that the argument was fallacious: no amount of banking reform could prevent monetary crises in the face of profound economic

---

* Marx here mimics the language of the 42nd Psalm: "As the hart panteth after the water brooks, so panteth my soul after thee, O God." (King James Version.)

instability. During the 1930s attention therefore shifted away from the problem of monetary crises as such to the problem of controlling or mitigating the business cycle, the implicit assumption being that monetary crises were by then, and henceforth would be, mere by-products of severe slumps in income and employment. If the latter could be eliminated, the problem of monetary crises would, for all practical purposes, cease to exist. Since the Second World War, bourgeois economists have reached pretty general agreement, though not all by the same theoretical route, that economic fluctuations can in fact be kept within fairly narrow limits.* The logical conclusion is that, barring gross mismanagement by monetary and fiscal authorities, monetary crises are a thing of the past. It is not surprising, therefore, that they have all but disappeared from current economic literature.**

What the economists have overlooked is that whenever capitalism "solves" one contradiction it invariably creates another. It therefore never even occurred to them that "success" in controlling the business cycle would *inevitably* be accompanied by a long-run decline in liquidity and hence an increasing proneness of the economy to "old-fashioned" monetary crises. At the same time, present-day economists have forgotten what their predecessors knew very well, that panics and the debt-deflation which normally followed them were not simply recurring disasters but played a most important therapeutic role in the functioning of the capitalist economy. During the prosperity phase of the business cycle, debts always and necessarily grow faster than real production and income. This is partly owing to the fact that prices are rising and debts are based on monetary values, not on physical quantities. But it is

---

* In the United States the two main "schools" are the "Keynesians" and the "monetarists." Oversimplifying their differences, one can say that the former stress fiscal policy as the main instrument of control, while the latter give pride of place to monetary policy. They do not disagree about the controllability of economic fluctuations.

** For example, Paul Samuelson's *Economics* (5th ed., 1961), by far the most popular elementary textbook of the postwar period, contains only two or three passing references to "panics" of bygone days. Perusal of the relevant chapters reveals not even a hint that such a thing might happen in the future.

also and perhaps even more importantly caused by the proliferation of debts within the financial superstructure itself. As
paper values rise, they become the basis for more borrowing
and more spending, which in turn induce further inflation of
values, and so on. Interwoven with the process are pie-in-the-
sky expectations, increasingly frenetic speculation, and outright
swindling. What used to bring it all to an end was normally
the downturn in the underlying economy, followed by falling
prices and a more or less thorough squeeze-out of the financial
superstructure. After the havoc of the panic and the depression,
real and paper values would once again be brought into a
viable relationship and the basis would be established for the
next upswing.

What the various schools of "new economics" neglected to
ask is what would be the consequence of eliminating or greatly
mitigating the downturns. Now at last hard experience has
provided the answer: the debt structure just goes on swelling
to the point where even a relatively mild setback in the underlying economy sends tremors through the bloated financial
superstructure and threatens to bring it down like a house
of cards.

It may not happen this time. It may even be that, as
has occurred after previous postwar recessions, there will be
a small temporary improvement in corporate liquidity ratios.*
Let us assume that this is the course events will actually take
in the next year or so. Will any problems be solved? Will the
crisis be eliminated? Or merely postponed?

The answer seems obvious: there is no escape from the
corner the system has now painted itself into. If a crisis is
avoided now and even moderate prosperity is restored, the
debt/liquidity squeeze will get progressively worse and more
explosive. Sooner or later—and, speaking in historical terms,
it matters little whether it is this year or a few years from
now—the bubble will burst and the crisis will be upon us.

The more foresighted members of the financial and busi-

---

* The complete series from which Table 3 selects certain years to give
a clear picture of trends shows small increases in corporate liquidity ratios
in 1949, 1953, 1958, and 1960.

ness community seem to recognize this and are making plans accordingly. There are really only two possible alternatives. One is to let nature (i.e., capitalism) take its course in the form of a good old-fashioned panic and debt squeeze-out. The result would almost certainly be a new economic collapse of Great-Depression dimensions. It is obvious—if only because of the doubtful ability of world capitalism to survive another such episode—that the U.S. ruling class will not idly stand by. The alternative is for the state to step in with a salvage operation which would make the New Deal's not inconsiderable efforts in that direction look puny by comparison. And it is already quite obvious that this is the course which is going to be adopted.

When it became clear that the Penn Central was in deep trouble, the first impulse of the Nixon administration was to come to the rescue in the simplest way possible, i.e., by directly putting the government's credit, via the Defense Department, at the Penn Central's disposal. But politically this was too crude, especially since there was reason to believe that the Penn Central debacle was in large part due to bad management—or perhaps even worse. Representative Wright Patman of Texas, a powerful figure as chairman of the House Banking Committee and one of the few old-time populists left in U.S. public life, succeeded in scotching the Defense Department ploy, and it was then too late to devise any other means of saving the company from bankruptcy. This was followed by the near-panic on Wall Street which has been commented on above. It seems that the financial elders then put their heads together and called in Senator Javits, the senior Republican senator from New York, who doubles as a great liberal and one of the corporate elite's most faithful political henchmen. Out of this came a legislative proposal which Javits unveiled at a Washington press conference on July 27th and which may well turn out to be one of the most important in a long time. Here is the way *Business Week* (August 1) reported the development:

Companies in a bind for cash may find a friend at the federal Treasury—if they can hold out long enough.

Support is growing in Congress for legislation to provide

government guarantees for loans to cash-short but sound companies. Even Penn Central Co., which went into reorganization in June after Congress spurned its bailout plea, might get some help this time around.

The focus of attention now is a bill introduced by Senator Jacob K. Javits (R-N.Y.) to give the Treasury temporary authority to stand behind otherwise sound companies that cannot get loans on their own in a liquidity crunch. Next year, by the terms of the bill, the Treasury would recommend whether permanent machinery is needed.

Key Congressional Democrats like the idea. In fact, the chairmen of the two banking committees—Senator John Sparkman (D-Ala.) and Representative Wright Patman (D-Tex.)—are willing to skip the transitional phase and create something akin to the Depression-era Reconstruction Finance Corporation. The Patman-Sparkman approach, unveiled this week, would set up a National Development Bank to make and guarantee loans not just to business but to state and local governments.

Nothing will be done without support from the Administration, but early signs are that the White House may go along.

Javits of course disclaims any intention of bailing out private stockholders and bondholders and sanctimoniously declares that "it would be a disastrous mistake to use federal monies to keep unsound firms from failing or to substitute public for private tests of creditworthiness, or to convey the impression that the Federal Government will bail out loosely managed or speculative enterprises." But we all know what the road to hell is paved with, and much experience suggests that a capitalist state, once embarked on a salvage operation of this kind, must find it practically impossible to fix rational limits (some may even be tempted to express the heretical opinion that there is something contradictory about the concept of a sound and well-managed bankrupt company). The *New York Times,* we believe, touched much nearer to the heart of the matter when (in the editorial quoted on pp. 182-183 above, it warned of the dangers of bail-out efforts and concluded: "The United States must not slide into a highly inefficient form of collectivism under the pretense of preserving a private enterprise economy."

The collectivism in question is of course the collectivism of a class state, and whether it would be more or less inefficient than what we now have would seem to depend on the answer to the question: efficiency for what? But in any case it is hard to see what other method of tackling the debt/liquidity problem—short of inaction in the face of another Great Depression—the U.S. ruling class can adopt.

Not that a government bail-out operation—paid for, of course, out of the pockets of all taxpayers—would really solve anything. By warding off the danger of financial panic now it would help lay the basis for a bigger one some time in the future. The truth is that as long as "prosperity" depends on the intertwining of inflation and speculation, ever more pyramiding of corporate (and individual) debt will be unavoidable. The government can, and probably will, get deeper and deeper into the morass without ever finding a way out.

As a sort of footnote to the above, it may be useful to glance very briefly at one of the earliest and perhaps the most comprehensive exercise in bailing out private capital that has yet been undertaken anywhere in the capitalist world, that of Italy in the period before the Second World War.

It all started even before the First World War. According to a leading authority on the subject:

The basic idea was simplicity itself. When profits were fat, they went to small private financial groups, as the proper rewards of the capitalistic system; when losses were heavy, they were distributed among the taxpayers, as an expression of community spirit.*

Throughout the subsequent period, under bourgeois democratic and fascist governments alike, this course was maintained with remarkable constancy. Finally, when the Great Depression hit Italy, practically the whole economy faced imminent bankruptcy. Mussolini's government rose to the occasion, bailing out and taking over right and left. By the mid-1930s a state agency, the Institute for Industrial Reconstruction (IRI), owned the country's three largest commercial banks and companies employing the following percentages of the labor force in the industries listed:

---

* Ernesto Rossi, "Nationalization in Italy," in Mario Einaudi, Maurice Byé, and Ernesto Rossi, *Nationalization in France and Italy*, Ithaca, 1955, p. 194.

TABLE 5

Engineering	13.3%
Iron & steel	48.6
Shipping	48.6
Public utilities & broadcasting	38.0
Telephones	70.0
Banks	30.0

Source: *Ibid.*, p. 205.

By the end of the fascist regime, according to the same authority, Italian banking was 87 percent nationalized through IRI and various other government agencies.

The naive and untutored may exclaim, ah, but that is socialism pure and simple—and indeed many a politician in opposition has been known to hurl the damning accusation. But the Italian bourgeoisie did not cringe or retreat. Instead, like its counterpart in Germany, it proceeded to put "socialism" to its own uses. Those who seek to look ahead to the possible consequences of what is now happening in this country could do no better than ponder the following words:

In 1937 IRI was given a new, and more permanent, legal structure. Not only was IRI to continue to manage the assets which it owned, but it was also authorized to make new investments in "industrial enterprises having as principal aim the solution of national defense problems, or the attainment of national economic self-sufficiency, or the industrial and agricultural exploitation of Ethiopia." IRI had become a principal economic arm of the Fascist regime. From a mere device used to rescue the banking system, it was transformed into an instrument for furtherance of the industrial policy of the Fascist state. "Nationalization" had taken place in 1933 under the pressure of events, and with little thought given to the problems of the future. It was to be continued as a deliberate policy in ever-widening fields. After 1938 the policy of liquidating the assets of IRI gradually came to a stop. IRI slowly proceeded to invest in the industrial areas that were being developed by the Fascist policies of self-sufficiency (in cellulose, synthetic rubber, chemicals), as well as to expand the capacity of those industries that were specifically devoted to war production. Only the disastrous events of World War II were to put a stop to these plans of the Fascist dictatorship. (*Ibid.*, p. 200.)

The End of U. S. Hegemony

October 1971

Nixon's new economic policy (NEP) marks the end of one phase of postwar global capitalist history and the beginning of another. This, rather than the specific actions it initiates or envisages, is its real significance.

The first postwar phase was that of U.S. hegemony, symbolized and to a considerable extent implemented by the Bretton Woods monetary system, according to which the dollar was established along with gold as the monetary reserves of all member countries. Nixon's formal abandonment of dollar convertibility ends that phase once and for all.

Partly by design and partly by chance, the Bretton Woods system became the financial framework of U.S. hegemony over the imperialist world in the period since the Second World War—the mechanism for financing wars of counter-revolution, foreign alliances, globe-straddling military bases, and the penetration of U.S. industry and banking throughout the capitalist world. Foreign exchange rates, some of which were set more or less arbitrarily by U.S. commissions or under U.S. influence, were designed with a view to propping up and strengthening allies in the Cold War. Political and military alliances were closely interrelated with financial alliances. While the United States carried the main military and financial burdens of the postwar imperialist system, the leading capitalist nations cooperated with greater or less enthusiasm, because the network of alliance, together with U.S. military strength, helped to stabilize capitalism and to initiate a new burst of prosperity. At the same time, from the point of view of these countries, such cooperation was essential in keeping the newly independent colonial and semi-colonial countries integrated into the imperialist trade and financing system.

But such an arrangement generated inevitable strains, which in recent years have been reaching critical proportions. These strains, in the final analysis, arose from two sources: (1) the very nature of capitalist states; each one must necessarily do its utmost to protect the interests of its own capitalist class, and (2) the restraints on U.S. financial freedom, since this freedom could ultimately only be bought at the expense of other capitalist nations. Thus, while we believe that Nixon's speech marks a turning point, it should be recognized that the turbulence of the international financial system has been intensifying over a period of years, approaching closer and closer to what the physicists call a critical mass, the point at which the chain reaction starts.

Once the cohesion of the postwar financial system is torn apart, it is reasonable to expect that the cohesion of political and military alliances will also be shaken. This does not mean that the essential nature of the imperialist system changes, but what it probably does mean is that important features of its structure are much more subject to change than in the past. During the entire postwar period, centripetal and centrifugal forces have been at work: those pulling the leading capitalist countries together under U.S. hegemony, and competitive strains working to break up the system. Hitherto, the centripetal forces have been the more powerful. From now on, and increasingly as time goes by, the centrifugal forces seem likely to assume the dominant position.

It is too early to characterize the new phase which is now opening in a definitive way, but it seems reasonably certain that no country or group of countries will be able to establish a clear hegemonic position, and that an intense struggle among the major capitalist powers is opening, in the course of which various alliances and alignments will be sought, sometimes successfully and sometimes not, sometimes as a temporary expedient and sometimes for longer periods.

Domestically, too, the NEP marks a turning point—the

end of the era of illusions about the possibility of stabilizing capitalism by means of monetary and/or fiscal policies and the beginning of a new approach through which the United States will seek to "solve" its internal problems at the expense of foreigners and U.S. workers. The international and internal aspects of the NEP are of course intricately interrelated.

One of the clearest indications that we are dealing with a real turning point in capitalist history is the way Nixon's August 15th speech marks a clear break with the strategy and rhetoric of the U.S. ruling class during the preceding quarter century. Throughout that period, the United States was all for cooperation, internationalism, freer trade, mutual aid, etc. But Nixon now talks the language of hard-nosed national self-interest. Competitiveness takes the place of cooperativeness as the great virtue. And the NEP itself is a blunt rejection of negotiation in favor of a unilateral declaration of a *fait accompli*—the repudiation without prior warning, or even notice, of the whole system of money and trade created by the United States itself in the period of its maximum relative power. This procedure is a sure symptom that the United States has lost its hegemonic position, since there is no doubt that if Nixon had felt powerful enough he would have preferred to impose the new system at which Washington is aiming through a process of negotiation similar to that which established the International Monetary Fund (IMF), the General Agreement on Trade and Tariffs (GATT), etc. At the same time, and in a sense paradoxically, the U.S. ruling class seems to feel relieved to be able to throw overboard all that internationalist, liberal claptrap which its spokesmen have been mouthing so long, and to plunge into a good old orgy of national chauvinism. An article by Pierre Rinfret, head of a well known firm of financial consultants, in the *New York Times* of August 30th typifies a reaction to Nixon's speech which seems to be widespread in the upper levels of the economic and political establishments:

I praise the program. I support the program. I applaud the program. I breathe a sigh of relief. I have a sense of joy and elation. I am proud of a President who had the courage, stamina, and strength to move forward vigorously . . . .
This is the end of Marshall Plan liberalism and the beginning

of Nixon-Connally pragmatism. For the past 25 years the United States has pursued a policy of excessive liberalism in international trade and international negotiations. Whatever we offered, they took and took. They took so much and we offered so much that there was a hemorrhage in our balance of payments. That is over. We have finally recognized and acted in the belief that the United States is the most powerful economic entity in the world and that we have economic muscle. . . .

The real target of our international trade and monetary moves was Japan—not the Europeans. U.S. patience has worn thin with the onesided, lopsided, inequitable, unfair economic and monetary treatment we have received from the Japanese. The day of bowing and scraping to them is over. From now on the Japanese will have to give more than they get or suffer more counterattacks.

The fact that the New York stock market zoomed up by an unprecedented amount the day after Nixon's speech also seems to reflect a sort of national euphoria. The President was at last doing something, the eager buyers of stock seemed to be saying, but above all he was doing it to foreigners who in the folklore of the United States—as perhaps in that of all national societies—are regarded as the real source of the country's woes.

It might appear that the immediate aftermath of Nixon's initiative belies the thesis of the end of U.S. hegemony over the global capitalist system. Didn't his strong-arm measures achieve their intended purpose? Even the Japanese had to bow to the pressure and float the yen. And doesn't the 10 percent surcharge on imports give Washington an enormous reserve of bargaining power in whatever negotiations are to come?* Certainly the idea of predominant U.S. power is far from dead in official circles in this country. In a news analysis entitled "Bitterness Abroad," datelined Washington and appearing in the *New York Times* of August 23rd, Edwin L. Dale Jr. reported as follows:

---

* It turns out that the 10 percent surcharge of dutiable imports is not the only measure of protection in Nixon's package. In his speech he hinted at what was later confirmed, i.e., that the 10 percent tax investment credit would apply only to capital goods produced in the United States. Because the tax bracket of large U.S. corporations is around 50 percent, this means that foreign sellers of capital goods would in effect be put at a 20 percent price disadvantage compared to their U.S. competitors. And on top of this must be added the effects of dollar devaluation. This is protectionism with a vengeance!

What is entirely clear is that the United States in a single dramatic stroke has shown the world how powerful it still is, despite all the talk about a "weak" dollar. In breaking the link between the dollar and gold and imposing a 10 percent import tax, the United States has shown who is Gulliver and who the Lilliputians.

The Lilliputians obviously do not like it. But it is not at all evident that they can do anything about it that will hurt the United States in any significant way.

By "Lilliputians"—originally the little people found in Swift's *Gulliver's Travels*—are meant not the Nicaraguas or the Gabons but West Germany, Japan, Britain, and the other leading industrial nations.

If, as seems likely, this assessment of the situation reflects the views of Washington policy-makers, we can conclude that the Nixon administration is operating on the theory that U.S. hegemony is very far from a thing of the past. According to this way of thinking, the problem has been not loss of U.S. hegemony but a reluctance on the part of the United States to throw its weight around. Or to use the analogy introduced by Nixon in his August 15th speech: "There is no longer any need for the United States to compete with one hand tied behind her back." The implication seems clear that with both hands out in front, we'll soon see who is boss. The same idea was expressed by Pierre Rinfret in the article already cited (*New York Times*, August 30). "The night of the President's speech," Rinfret reports, "one of the most powerful men in this country told me, 'We're smart and we're competitive and we're the biggest. We're in the driver's seat and, dammit, that's where we ought to be.'"

Before accepting this simplistic position, however, we should have a closer look at the realities. It has already become a cliché in the short time since the announcement of the NEP that the dollar is overvalued, the clear implication being that this is the root of the trouble and that it can be put right by a suitable devaluation of the dollar vis-à-vis the currencies of the other advanced countries. The cheaper dollar will supposedly stimulate exports and discourage imports, and the resulting improved balance of trade will lead to a progressive elimination of the balance-of-payments deficit. When this process has gone far enough, it should be possible to negotiate a new international monetary arrangement, with all currencies at new (and now "correct") parities and the dollar once again stabilized and able to resume its role as a reserve currency, possibly sharing this role now with marks, yen, Special Drawing Rights (SDRs), etc. Where gold would fit into the new picture has perhaps not yet been thought out, but the fact that Nixon terminated the convertibility of the dollar while the U.S. gold stock was still approximately $10 billion certainly suggests that he and his advisers have by no means written off gold's monetary future. In this analysis, the heart of the matter is trade imbalances, and the key remedy is readjustment of exchange rates.

But is this really so? Is the weakness of the dollar which precipitated the crisis the result of a *trade* deficit? No. The trade deficit is a very recent phenomenon, and in any case it would be quite normal for a creditor country like the United States (i.e., a country with substantial net earnings from foreign investment) to have a long-run unfavorable balance of trade, as Britain did in the half century preceding the First World War (how else are the debtor countries supposed to be able to make the required payments?). The *balance-of-payments* deficit, on the other hand, goes back more than two decades, and it is this which has been responsible for the trouble. The truth, in other words, is that the balance-of-payments deficit has not been caused in the field of trade at all, and even now only a small part of it is attributable to the trade deficit. Somewhat oversimplifying but still not falsifying the essentials of the problem, we can say that the balance-of-payments deficit has been caused by U.S. politico-military activities abroad (propping up client governments, maintaining U.S. bases and troops, subsidizing puppet armies, waging hot wars, etc.). These activities have poured out tens of billions of dollars which have gravitated into the hands of governments and financial institutions which have no intention—and by the nature of their functions could have no intention—of spending them for goods and services produced in the United States.*

---

* In this connection it is important to understand *why* a capitalist government or central bank couldn't simply take its surplus billions and buy things from the United States for distribution to its needy citizens. Obviously such action would depress domestic markets and destroy pro-

The question is what these foreign recipients of surplus dollars do with them. A detailed answer would involve matters of extreme complexity, some of which are understood only by a relatively few financial experts and operators. From our present point of view, however, the problem is not to try to explain these technicalities but rather to avoid getting bogged down in them while at the same time illuminating the underlying forces and relationships.

The Bretton Woods monetary system was set up in such a way as to provide a use for these surplus dollars—at least reasonable amounts of them. In dealing with each other, countries are constantly buying and selling and engaging in a great variety of other international transactions (for freight, insurance, borrowings, repayment of past debts, etc.). If each country's outlays always exactly matched its receipts, there would never be any need for money to change hands: bookkeeping entries would suffice. But of course this is not the case. For every country in any given period, outlays exceed receipts or viceversa, and it is only over a succession of periods that a rough balance can be expected to be achieved. In the meantime, mutually acceptable means of payment must change hands to keep the system operating smoothly. For this purpose all countries need to maintain a reserve of such means of payment, and it is obvious that the total amount of needed reserves will increase as the volume of international trade and financial transactions grows. There are thus two basic requirements that a satisfactory international monetary system has to fulfill: it must define mutually acceptable means of payment that can be held as reserves, and it must provide a way that the overall amount of reserves needed by all countries combined can be expanded as the need grows.

How did the Bretton Woods system meet these requirements? First, by establishing gold and dollars, interchangeable

---

fitable opportunities of the capitalist class whose instruments the government and central bank necessarily are. If a socialist government, on the other hand, should come into possession of surplus billions of dollars, it would have no difficulty disposing of them in a socially useful way. We see here, as in so many other areas of socio-economic life, that capitalism's problems can be traced back to the imperatives and contradictions of the profit-making process.

at $35 an ounce, as acceptable means of payment for reserve purposes.* As for the second requirement, Bretton Woods did not make any specific provision, and it seemed to many critics at the time that the whole system was irrationally dependent on what might happen to the world's monetary gold stock. It turned out in practice, however, that this was not the case. By running a continuing deficit in its balance of payments, the United States could feed out dollars (equally acceptable with gold as reserve money) to the rest of the world.** And for a long time this device—always implicit in the Bretton Woods system but probably understood by very few of those who took part in the founding conference—seemed to work quite satisfactorily. Thus during the 1960s the world's monetary reserves increased by an average of $2 billion a year, only 10 percent of which was gold and most of the rest dollars generated by an uninterrupted U.S. balance of payments deficit.*** This increase in reserves proved to be sufficient to underpin an enormous expansion of international trade.

But this use for surplus dollars is obviously not unlimited, and beginning in 1970 the rate of outflow far exceeded the world's need for dollars as monetary reserves. During the single year 1970 the world's total monetary reserves increased by no less than $14.1 billion, nearly all of which was accounted for by a flood of dollars originating in a huge U.S. balance-of-payments deficit. (It is important to understand that once the outflow rises above a certain critical level, it opens valves which increase the rate of outflow still further. This is where Nixon's *bêtes noires*, the international monetary speculators, come into the picture. But far more significant than speculation is the prudence of the treasurers of the giant multinational corpora-

---

* Pounds sterling were also accorded a reserve role, and later on Special Drawing Rights (SDRs) at the IMF were added as a form of reserve money. From our present point of view, however, these are not important considerations.

** For a fuller explanation, as well as an analysis of the benefits accruing to the United States from this arrangement, see Harry Magdoff, *The Age of Imperialism,* pp. 80-95 and pp. 101-110.

*** These figures, and those for 1970 below, are taken from Robert Triffin, "International Reserves in 1970 and Beyond," *The Morgan Guaranty Survey,* February 1971, p. 8.

tions who are charged with managing billions of dollars: their motives are not those of speculators, but the consequences are much the same.*)

In the theory of the Bretton Woods system, there was a braking mechanism which was supposed to prevent an excessive outflow of dollars. This was based on the convertibility of the dollar into gold at the official price of $35 an ounce. Foreign central banks receiving more dollars than they wanted were supposed to be able to present them to the United States in exchange for gold, and the loss of gold would sooner or later induce the United States to adopt deflationary policies which would stem the outflow of gold. In practice, however, this mechanism was completely unworkable. The number of dollars held by foreigners long ago added up to more than the U.S. gold reserve, and it was clear to everyone that a scramble to convert dollars into gold would simply result in the suspension of convertibility. Moreover there was never any chance that U.S. economic policies would be dominated by considerations of the gold reserve. And finally, as long as U.S. global military policy remained what it was, the outflow of dollars would continue anyway. As time went by, therefore, the Bretton Woods system came increasingly to resemble a house of cards which remains standing only because no one tries to live in it.

So we return to the question of what to do with the growing pool of surplus dollars. For quite a while the usual answer was to lend them out at interest. This was the origin of the so-called Eurodollar market which in recent years has grown to enormous proportions. One of the ironies (and complexities) of the international financial system is that when central banks follow this course the result is to build up, via credit creation, still more dollar balances and thus to exacerbate the underlying problem. Finally, as the pool continues to grow, it becomes increasingly clear that the only sensible thing to do with surplus dollars is to get rid of them, i.e., to exchange them for currencies which don't have the same troubles as the dollar. When this stage is reached, the supply-and-demand relationships be-

---

* For a fuller explanation, see "How Multinational Firm Protects Its Flanks in Monetary Dealings," by Charles N. Stabler, in the *Wall Street Journal*, August 20, 1971.

tween the dollar and the currencies of the other industrialized countries is transformed, and the whole concept of fixed parities provided for in the Bretton Woods system becomes untenable. With more and more dollars being offered for marks, yen, etc., it is inevitable either that the price of these currencies should go up (and hence the dollar down) or that the central banks in question should create enough additional marks, yen, etc., to match the increasing supply of dollars coming on the foreign exchange markets. The latter course can be, and indeed has been, followed for a while, but not forever. Sooner or later the old parities have to be abandoned and the various currencies allowed to float on the sea of supply and demand. The approach of this situation has been signalled for several years now by increasingly frequent monetary "crises" which, following that of last May, were in the process of becoming the norm rather than the exception. What Nixon's speech of August 15th did was simply to acknowledge publicly that the jig was up. After 23 years the Bretton Woods system was dead.

What next? Nixon is said to be aiming at a devaluation of the dollar averaging something like 15 percent, apparently in the belief that if this could be attained the problem would be solved. We have not, however, seen any attempt at an analysis to back this up; and on the face of it, it seems highly implausible. As noted above, the favorable effect of devaluation comes through its impact on the trade balance: with dollars cheaper, exports are stimulated and imports inhibited. This cannot be an overnight process, however, and even the most optimistic projections seem to fall far short of what would be needed to produce the desired results. In the second quarter of this year, the trade deficit was running at an annual rate of $4.2 billion compared to a total balance-of-payments deficit at an annual rate of no less than $23 billion.* If we assume, what seems unlikely, that the trade deficit can be eliminated by the end of the year, there would still remain a probable huge gap in the balance of payments. (In this connection we must remember that devaluation of the dollar will *increase* the number of dollars needed to finance the overseas military

---

* The figure for the quarter was practically the same on the "net liquidity basis" ($23.4 billion) and on the "official reserve transactions basis" ($23.1 billion).

establishment and in this way will at least partially offset the gains that may be achieved in the field of trade.) And even if we make what seems to us the totally unrealistic assumption that the trade deficit turns fairly soon into a surplus and that the latter expands to, say, the $5-billion level which existed in 1965 before the decline associated with the Vietnam War began, even then there is no assurance that the balance of payments would be brought under control.

Here we must digress briefly to stress a point which seems to have been largely overlooked in the discussions and debates of the past few weeks. The prevalence of multinational corporations in the U.S. economy has introduced a relatively new factor into the determination of the balance of trade which may make it considerably less sensitive than it has been in the past to changes in the rate of exchange between dollars and other currencies. Many companies which used to be large exporters now produce abroad much or all of what they sell abroad; and many have even taken to producing abroad (in their foreign subsidiaries) products or components of products which they import into the United States for sale in the domestic market. While no reliable quantitative estimates exist, there is no reason to doubt that relationships of this kind can have a serious adverse effect on the balance of trade and at the same time put roadblocks in the way of attempts to improve the balance of trade through manipulation of exchange rates.

We conclude that the outlook for the U.S. balance of payments, despite all the fanfare accompanying Nixon's supposedly decisive moves, is at best very uncertain and at worst very dark.* Under these circumstances it is hardly surprising

---

* One sometimes meets the argument that in an international regime of free-floating currencies, balance-of-payments problems cease to exist. This is not so much wrong as it is highly misleading. What needs to be understood is that the same forces which manifest themselves in balance-of-payments deficits and surpluses in a regime of fixed parities show up in the form of currency depreciations and appreciations in a regime of floating exchange rates. The U.S. balance-of-payments deficit could in theory always be eliminated by a sufficient depreciation of the dollar against other currencies. But the United States—or for that matter any other industrialized country—could not acquiesce in a progressive deterioration in the value of its currency. And the kind of remedial policies called for are similar whether the problem takes the form of a growing balance-of-payments deficit or a steadily depreciating dollar.

that Treasury Secretary Connally, reputed to be the main architect of Nixon's NEP, has been voicing demands on the United States' "free world" allies which go far beyond mere currency realignments. In a May 28th speech to the Munich conference of the American Bankers Association—which, with the benefit of hindsight, we can now see to have been a good deal more important than it seemed at the time—Connally spoke as follows:

> Inflation has contributed to the prolongation of our balance-of-payments deficit. But it is far from the only factor.
>
> Specifically, we today spend nearly 9 percent of our gross national product on defense—nearly five billion dollars of that overseas, much of it in Western Europe and Japan. Financing a military shield is part of the burden of leadership; the responsibilities cannot and should not be cast off. But 25 years after World War II legitimate questions arise over how the cost of these responsibilities should be allocated among the free-world allies who benefit from that shield. The nations of Western Europe and Japan are again strong and vigorous, and their capacities to contribute have vastly increased.
>
> I find it an impressive fact, and a depressing fact, that the persistent underlying balance-of-payments deficit which causes such concern is more than covered, year in and year out, by our net military expenditures abroad, over and above amounts received from foreign military purchases in the United States.
>
> A second area where action is plainly overdue lies in trading arrangements. The comfortable assumption that the United States should—in the broader political interests of the free world—be willing to bear disproportionate economic costs does not fit the facts of today.
>
> I do not for a moment call into question the worth of a self-confident, cohesive Common Market, a strong Japan, and a progressing Canada to the peace and prosperity of the free-world community.
>
> The question is only—but the "only" is important—whether these nations, now more than amply supplied with reserves as well as with productive power, should not now be called upon for fresh initiative in opening their markets to the products of others. (*U.S. News & World Report,* June 14, pp. 52-53.)

What Connally seems to be saying is that the United States expects the countries of Western Europe, Japan, and Canada not only to revalue their currencies upward but also to relieve the United States of a large part of its self-imposed burden of policing the world and to change their trade and investment policies in a way to favor not their own capitalists but on the contrary their most dangerous rivals, the capitalists of the United States.

Such demands might have been realistic 25 years ago, when the other countries needed U.S. help as a matter of sheer survival. But why should they knuckle under now when the shoe is on the other foot and it is the United States that needs *their* help? Isn't the Nixon administration talking the language of hegemony at a time when the objective basis of hegemony has disappeared?

And if it turns out that U.S. hegemony cannot be restored, what is the alternative? In as complicated a situation as this, specific prophecies are of course impossible. But there is no mystery about the general direction events may take. *Business Week*, for example, after noting what it called "widespread anger at the U.S. for letting the dollar get so overvalued," proceeded as follows:

> Indeed, tempers are running high throughout the international monetary system. The spirit of cooperation that pulled the system through crisis after crisis in the late 1960s is badly frayed today. [This "spirit of cooperation" is essentially a euphemism for "acceptance of U.S. hegemony."] And the longer the present turmoil lasts, the greater the peril that nations will simply take off on their own—erecting more capital controls and more trade barriers. "What worries me most," says a Swiss economist "is that there will be no action of any kind. We would then move into a generalized float—and that will be chaos."
>
> Ironically, the most hopeful element in the whole picture is the memory that central bankers still have of the 1930s, when monetary cooperation disintegrated, the world moved into a generalized float, and there was chaos. No government official anywhere wants that to happen again. (*Business Week*, August 21, p. 27.)

It may well be true that no government official wants such a situation. But what government officials want is one thing, and what is possible in the global anarchy of capitalist production and finance is something entirely different. "If," warned the London *Financial Times* on August 23rd, "there were to be prolonged deadlock on the monetary front, the danger of a trade war would grow with every day that passed." Now almost a month later, with the deadlock on the monetary front showing no signs of easing, the warning takes on ever greater relevance.

Turning now to the domestic aspect of Nixon's NEP, we can be much briefer. To begin with, we may take note of the completion of Richard Nixon's economic odyssey. He started out as a great champion of free markets and swallowed whole the Friedmanite monetary nonsense which was supposed to provide a painless method of dealing with the twin problems of stagnation and inflation. When this showed no signs of working, Nixon suddenly proclaimed himself a Keynesian and plumped for salvation through fiscal policy. And when this too—or rather this in conjunction with continuing monetary expansionism—produced a disagreeable combination of supposedly incompatible phenomena, more inflation and more unemployment, he suddenly emerges as a protagonist of what he once considered anathema, direct controls over wages and prices. As a display of unprincipled opportunism, it would be hard to cite a more virtuoso performance. (At the same time it must be admitted that in this field unprincipled opportunism is a considerably less unattractive quality than stubborn adherence to worn-out dogmas. The discredited economists, whether Friedmanite or Keynesian, have absolutely no reason to adopt a holier-than-thou attitude: they have no more understanding than Nixon of the way monopoly capitalism really works, and a greater vested interest in defending their ignorance.)

Will the 90-day freeze on prices and wages succeed? In the strictly limited sense of slowing down the rise during the freeze period, it doubtless will. But this is of no great importance since the troubles of the U.S. economy are in no sense 90-day problems. The question is what comes after the freeze.

Even a month after the anouncement of the freeze it is clear that the Nixon administration still has no definite plans. But obviously it has a tiger by the tail and can't simply let go. It must attempt to devise and operate some sort of continuing incomes policy. But here past experience, in other countries no less than in the United States, is anything but encouraging. Writing from Washington in the *Financial Times* of September

1, Paul Lewis reported that

it is frequently argued here that as the administration could not enforce an effective price and wages freeze during the Second World War when it had an army of bureaucrats for the job and patriotism was high, it has little chance of doing so in the divided and embittered climate of present-day America and when it is pledged to reduce, not to increase, the civil service.

There is of course no answer to this argument; and, so far as we know, no one has even tried to concoct one. Nixon's dilemma is typical of the "damned if you do and damned if you don't" variety. Without a new version of the wartime Office of Price Administration (OPA), whatever incomes policy he may adopt will certainly turn into a fiasco.* And with a new OPA it will turn into a bureaucratic nightmare and a bottomless pit of cheating and corruption, ending in a fiasco as well.

In practice what is likely to happen is that the whole thing will be more or less rapidly transformed into some sort of machinery for compulsory regulation of wages (much easier to monitor and enforce than price controls) based on alleged productivity criteria. This is what the U.S. bourgeoisie has really been hankering after for a long time, and the crisis atmosphere which will be generated by the end of the freeze can be expected to provide a golden opportunity to turn wishes into reality.

There should be no mistaking the fact, however, that this would be a perilous course for U.S. capitalism to embark upon. The reason is that it would unavoidably put the whole question of income distribution, now presumably determined by eternal and ineluctable laws of economics, into the very center of the political stage. It is hard to see how this could fail to initiate a

---

* No one has pointed out the reasons for this more clearly than Nixon himself. Here is the opening paragraph of an article by Leonard Silk on the Op.-Ed. page of the *New York Times* of August 23rd: "Shortly after he assumed the Presidency, Mr. Nixon said, 'I want to emphasize that we believe it is possible to control inflation without increasing unemployment in, certainly, any substantial way.' And he added that he would not try to accomplish this feat by urging labor leaders or businessmen to restrain their wage and price decisions, because 'much as these men might personally want to do what is in the best interests of the nation, they have to be guided by the interests of the organizations they represent.'" No Marxist could put the point more succinctly or lucidly.

process of politicizing the U.S. working class to a far greater degree than ever before, increasingly transferring the class struggle from the strictly economic sphere (bargaining table and picket line) to the political sphere where weapons and tactics, and in the long run strategy and goals as well, are necessarily very different.

The rest of Nixon's domestic package—providing tax incentives for more investment (at a time when 25 percent or more of existing capacity is idle), relying on increased production of automobiles as the mainstay of recovery (at a time when every high-school student knows that what the country needs is fewer, not more, automobiles), reducing government spending and employment (at a time when all sorts of needed public services are starved of resources)—all of this is a typical potpourri of reactionary, antisocial measures which rely for whatever efficacy they may have on short-run responses and trickle-down effects. In reality, however, there is not much reason to expect any great stimulus to the economy as a whole.

We are forced to conclude that the whole new economic policy—foreign and domestic—is essentially irrelevant to what is really wrong with U.S. society today: the mad expansionism of monopoly capitalism on a global scale and its growing inability to satisfy the essential needs of its own people for peace, work, food and shelter, and human dignity, at home. What Nixon's NEP presages, therefore, is not a period of peace and prosperity such as he likes to prate about, but rather a period of unprecedentedly intense imperialist and class struggles and more and deeper crises.

The Age of Imperialism:
The Financial Network

1969

The Dollar as the World Currency: New York as the World Banker

The late Professor Schumpeter, if memory serves, once remarked that the money market is the headquarters of the capitalist system. It was undoubtedly in this sense that the United States assumption of leadership of the capitalist world coincided with New York City's becoming the undisputed center of international finance, and the United States dollar's becoming the international currency of the capitalist world.

The previous center of the world money market was The City—a square mile in London containing the Bank of England, the gold market, the international insurance market, leading commodity exchanges, and the head offices of the major banks. It was backed up by the conquest of the seas, the world's largest merchant marine fleet, the world's largest colonial empire, and the domination of international trade. In arguing against the romantic notion still held by some in England about restoring its old glory, the Oxford economist, Dr. Thomas Balogh, reminds us that

the rise of London to the center of an international economy was based on Britain's *mercantile supremacy* as an Imperial Power and her *industrial leadership* as an initiator of mechanized mass production. It was this double superiority which enabled London to become the world center for short- and long-term finance, and added further cumulative gains. The play of the Gold Standard became a source of profit and actively contributed to maintaining

This article by Harry Magdoff is excerpted from his *The Age of Imperialism*, New York, 1969, pp. 80-93, 101-113.

the British balance of payments.[1]

The financial advantage England achieved through this process still gives sustenance to England even after it has descended to the rank of a secondary power. In 1966 Lord Comer, the Governor of the Bank of England, testified to this in the following terms:

> I think we have to recognize the extent to which the British standard of living is dependent today, as it has been throughout this century, on our invisible earnings, particularly on our investment income from overseas. The figures speak for themselves. The origin of our overseas investments, which served as our financial mainstay in two world wars, and which provide the foreign exchange we need so badly today, lies of course in our history.[2]

It has taken quite a bit of time for the United States, despite its overwhelming productive strength, to break through Britain's preferred position as the world center of finance. And, significantly, the opportunities for accomplishing this were always associated with war. At first it was the Boer War:

> With England financially and economically burdened by the Boer War, a number of nations including England herself began turning to American bankers for funds. However, the cessation of the war in 1902 and the United States financial panic of 1903, interrupted this trend and dashed some premature hopes of New York's replacing London as the world's financial center.[3]

The financial pressures of the First World War opened the door much wider for a transfer of the financial center. The Allied Powers needed financing first for the arms race and then for the war itself, and much of it was found in New York. The factors underlying the drift in power from Europe to the United States were carefully evaluated by Thomas W. Lamont, the most articulate member of the firm of J. P. Morgan & Co. In an article in the July 1915 *Annals* of the American Academy of Political and Social Science, he identified the elements of the change brought about by the first year of the war and which could become increasingly important, depending on how long the war was to run: (1) "Many of our manufacturers and merchants have been doing wonderful business in articles relating to the war"; (2) the increase in war business contributed to a "prodigious export trade balance"; (3) the good export trade balance enabled buying back United States securities held by foreign investors; (4) the repurchase of these securities helped to eliminate the drain of foreign exchange that had been going to pay interest and dividends to foreigners; (5) the resulting transformation from debtor to creditor status enabled the United States to lend to foreign nations on a large scale, and thus to become a major recipient, rather than a payer, of interest and dividends.[4] But while all this was moving in the direction of a transfer of the financial center, Lamont guessed quite soberly that such changes do not come overnight:

Many people seem to believe that New York is to supersede London as the money center of the world. In order to become the money center we must of course become the trade center of the world. That is certainly a possibility. Is it a probability? Only time can show. But my guess would be that, although subsequent to the war this country is bound to be more important financially than ever before, it will be many years before America, even with her wonderful resources, energy, and success, will become the financial center of the world. Such a shifting cannot be brought about quickly, for of course to become the money center of the world we must, as I have said, become the trade center; and up to date our exports to regions other than Great Britain and Europe have been comparatively limited in amount. We must cultivate and build up new markets for our manufacturers and merchants, and all that is a matter of time.[5]

This cool and deliberate analytical ability did not interfere with Lamont's grander vision, based on deep faith that finance capital will go on forever:

When that terrible, blood-red fog of war burns away we shall see finance still standing firm. We shall see the spectacle of the business men of all nations paying to one another their just debts. We shall see the German merchant keeping his word sacred to the English; and the French to the Turk. We shall see finance standing ready to develop new enterprises; to find money to till new fields; to help rebuild a broken and wreck-strewn world; to set the fires of industry blazing brightly again and lighting up the earth with the triumphs of peace.[6]

The Bolshevik repudiation of the Tsarist debts must surely have shaken this credo. Now, finance was needed to hold back the tide of Communism. Still, the postwar reconstruction needs of a prostrate Europe did have an effect: they brought United

States finance into the international arena with full force. On top of this, the flight of capital from Europe to this country in the 20's and 30's strengthened United States finance, because this flight occasioned an unusual accumulation of gold in the United States. The changing tides were summarized by William Woodruff, a historian of Europe's international role:

> While there was little recognition in the immediate post-First World War years of the essential change that had taken place, the war had undermined Europe's position as the financial center of the world; and without adequate finance trade could not prosper. The Bank of England even tried to resume its nineteenth-century role as the controlling agency in the international capital market, and took the initiative in arranging reconstruction loans when the war ended. Long-term lending by Britain, France, and, to a lesser extent, by Belgium, the Netherlands, and Switzerland was renewed. Sweden also emerged as a creditor country. . . . But only the United States possessed the financial resources needed in the postwar period. As that country assumed some of the responsibilities of the world's greatest creditor nation there began to flow from America to Europe a succession of loans and gifts (charity and business have been inextricably linked) which is without parallel, and which has continued until the present day.[7]

Actually, some Marxist scholars did recognize in the early postwar years what was impending. E. Preobrazhensky, for example, underscored in 1924 the essential nature of the new phenomenon on the world financial scene in classic, historic-perspective fashion:

> It is interesting to recall that currency dictatorship has usually belonged, in the course of history, to that country which played the dominating role at any given moment in world trade and world economy. In the period when Phoenician and Greek trade was dominant in the Mediterranean Sea a very great role was played by the Greek and Phoenician talent. The florin ruled in the period when Italian merchant capital dominated the Mediterranean. The mercantile role of Spain brought the piastre to the forefront of inter-currency relations. Holland ruled not only with its fleet, its cloth, and its trade generally, but also with the gulden. As the center of gravity in world economy and trade passed to the "ruler of the waves," the British pound's role advanced to the forefront. Finally, America's economic domination of the world has led to the domination of the dollar.[8]

As is not too uncommon with analysts who take the long

view, Preobrazhensky was a bit premature. The influence of the dollar, it is true, was on the rise: the result of the large increase in the export of capital from the United States and the appearance of the dollar for the first time as a reserve currency and a vehicle for international transactions. Before the First World War, other nations kept, in addition to gold, mainly British sterling (plus lesser amounts of French, Swiss, and Dutch currency) as a reserve against balance-of-payments fluctuations. The war changed that: the dollar joined sterling as a major reserve currency—but still only in a position junior to the British pound. It took still another world war, the devastation in Europe and Asia, and the financial bankruptcy of the other leading industrial powers to set the stage for the United States to take over the financial as well as military and political supremacy of the capitalist world:

> Like England in its heyday, when it was the major center of world trade and finance and sterling was the key currency, the United States in turn emerged from the Second World War as the world's financial center and its currency as the most important medium of exchange.[9]

The change in the world position of the dollar since the war is quite clearly evident in the comparison of the holdings of gold versus dollars as reserves by foreign governments and their central banks (see Table 1 on the following page).

Thus, it can be seen, the dollar though accepted as an international currency before the Second World War was still a relatively small proportion of the gold reserves of central banks. Since the end of the war, however, it has assumed a major and growing significance.

To understand the import of this development, we should first review what is meant by the dollar as a reserve currency. Money enters into the commerce of nations as payment for goods and services transferred from one country to another. When a United States manufacturer sells a refrigerator to a customer in Brazil he is paid in cruzeiros. The cruzeiro represents in effect an IOU on Brazilian goods and services: it is only useful for buying in Brazil. If, however, the United States manufacturer has nothing to buy in Brazil, he will want only United States dollars. For he can use only United States dollars

TABLE 1
GOLD AND DOLLAR HOLDINGS BY FOREIGN COUNTRIES[a]

At end of	Gold (in billions	Dollar Assets [b] of dollars)	Dollar Assets as a percent of gold
1938	$11.0	$0.5	5
1950	11.5	3.4	30
1955	14.4	7.0	49
1967	26.9	15.7	58

(a) Excludes reserves held by Communist countries. Also, excludes holdings of the International Monetary Fund.

(b) United States liquid liabilities to official institutions of foreign countries (central banks and government departments). The data prior to 1967 do not include holdings by foreign governments of U.S. government bonds and notes. These instruments were then a quite small item in the dollar assets of foreign governments. The resulting statistical discrepancy is not significant enough to affect the validity of the trend shown.

Source: *Federal Reserve Bulletin,* September 1940, December 1951, December 1956, June 1968.

to pay for the labor, raw materials and other costs of making the refrigerator, and to reap his profit. But to get paid in dollars there must be another United States businessman who needs cruzeiros. If there is such a businessman who needs cruzeiros, there can then be an exchange of cruzeiros for dollars. Obviously, only such United States businessmen will need cruzeiros as wish to buy Brazilian goods for sale in the United States (or services which are sold to United States nationals).

In the trade between nations such transactions are multiplied many times over, so that the individual needs of the importer and the exporter are accumulated through the banking system and worked out in the overall balance of international payments between nations. If the total value of exports equals the total value of imports, there is no problem about there being, for example, too many unwanted cruzeiros.[10]

However, if the exports and imports do not balance, then some means of acceptable payment has to be found by the country that has bought more than it has sold. The universally accepted means of payment, of course, is gold. Gold is the universal solvent—one that has been established over centuries, not for mythical reasons but because gold has the virtues required of a repository of value and of a generally acceptable means of payment in international exchange between "free" markets.

In recent times there have been two main exceptions to the use of gold as an international monetary reserve: the British pound and the United States dollar. This means that other countries were willing, or compelled by force of circumstances, to maintain these currencies in addition to, or as a substitute for, gold.

For the normal course of international commerce each nation must keep reserves of an acceptable means of payment, if only to smooth out the customary recurrent imbalances between exports and imports. Moreover, a country's reserve of international means of payment is the final recourse for settling bills when there is an excess of imports over exports (other than temporary adjustments funded by investments and loans by foreigners). In the final analysis, the size of a country's reserves influences the limit of how far a country can go in economic development, if its economic development depends on imports of capital goods and raw materials.

The size and viability of the reserves of international means of payments are clearly of vital import to a nation's economic well-being. When these reserves are in the form of gold, there is no present or potential restraint to the use of the reserves in any fashion a government desires. This is so because gold as a commodity has value, and is universally accepted as a means of payment.

However, when reserves consist of another nation's currency then there is a real or potential restraint. For a national currency, in the final analysis, is only good as an IOU for goods and services produced by the country issuing the currency. As long as the dollar is considered "as good as gold" by international traders and bankers, the dollar acts as a vehicle for the exchange of some 110 distinct currencies. Traders shift from one currency to another through dollars. In fact, the concept of the "as good as gold" dollar has been embodied in the very structure of the International Monetary Fund (IMF). Article IV of the treaty that established the IMF provides: "The par value of the currency of each member shall be expressed in terms of gold as a common denominator or in terms of the United States dollar of the weight and fineness in effect on July 1, 1944."

It is clear that this equating of the dollar with gold sets up a relationship of dependency of all capitalist nations on the United States. The degree of dependency will vary in accordance with the relative strength of the various capitalist nations. The reliance on the United States dollar means that in the final analysis—and this becomes painfully apparent on the brink of crisis—the holders of the United States IOU's can use them only to purchase United States goods at United States prices (assuming, of course, that the United States keeps its faith when it itself is faced with special difficulties).

As long as the leading trading nations accept the United States dollar as international money, and foreign businessmen and governments are willing to keep their reserves in United States banks, the dollar can act as a substitute for gold. This implicitly assumes that there is no end to the power and strength of the United States, and that foreign businessmen and bankers will be forever "patriots" of the United States dollar. But the underlying reality of business life is that financial ties based on interdependence can only be temporary. They last as long as there is immediate or near-term advantage—either in the form of better profits or security of one's capital. When the boat rocks, it is each man for himself. The fact that the financial power of the United States is not limitless is clearly evident in the strains already produced in domestic and international finance merely by adding the costs of the war in Vietnam on top of the costs involved in trying to hold on to United States political and military dominance throughout the capitalist world.

The key thing to understand here is the potential restraint: —the continuous danger of restraint—imposed by this involvement of the capitalist world with the dollar. The world role of the dollar has become one of the main instruments of control which the United States attempts to exercise over the capitalist world. On the one hand, the dollar as world currency is possible because of the economic and military strength of the United States. On the other hand, the very fact that the dollar has evolved as *the* international currency supplies the United States with the means to finance its activities directed towards controlling the world environment and enhancing its economic and military strength.

A sense of this role can be gathered by the way Secretary of the Treasury Henry H. Fowler moved to get the industrialized allies of this country to fall into line as this country approached an international monetary crisis in the spring of 1967. Heading a news report, "Monetary Threat Voiced by Fowler," the *New York Times* quoted him as saying:

I continue to find it necessary and relevant to emphasize to my colleagues from other countries that the way in which this nation handles its balance of payments problem depends in large measure on the cooperation it receives from other countries in the process, and upon the way in which other important financial nations act in dealing with their own domestic and international monetary problems.

I find it also necessary to emphasize that this cooperation is not a matter of helping the United States deal with its problem, but a matter of enabling the United States to deal with its problem without undermining the international monetary system, subjecting that system, by unilateral action, to radical and undesirable change, or withdrawing from commitments involving the security and development of others.[11]

Secretary Fowler's implied threat consists of two parts: (1) that the United States can by unilateral action undermine the international monetary system and thus pull the house down; and (2) the United States needs this international monetary system to carry on military action, military assistance, and economic aid—the ingredients of the United States program to preserve the imperialist world as constructed today.

Currency Blocs as Instruments of Control

In the normal course of events, the nature of the restraint imposed by the use of foreign currencies is not readily apparent: the operations of such a system are too closely interwoven with the accepted, ordinary, and taken-for-granted course of economic affairs. The uses to which such monetary arrangements can be put become crystal clear, however, when one examines their use as instruments of control by metropolitan centers over their colonies or in times of economic crisis and war.[12]

For example, one of the early measures taken by Britain, as the world depression of the 30's set in, was the development of a "sterling area" in which the members of the British Commonwealth and Empire (except Canada) participated. Included eventually were other countries which were either within the British sphere of influence or found such a defensive arrangement to their advantage. The purpose was to protect the trade of the empire and its temporary trading allies in the stiff competition of the depression onslaught. For this purpose, the "sterling area" arrangement included three features: (1) its members held sterling currency for all or part of their monetary reserve; (2) in the main, their foreign trade payments were made in sterling; and (3) the group aimed to keep their currencies stable in relation to sterling rather than to the dollar.[13]

The control potentials implicit in the use of a particular currency as a reserve became even clearer during the Second World War, when Britain was able to directly dominate the international activity of its empire through the use of Payments Agreements:

> During the war Britain, seeking to live as much on credit as possible and not to engage her manpower at home on making exports merely to pay her way—save for exports urgently required to sustain the economies of countries which were furnishing her or her allies with supplies—entered into agreements, known as Payments Agreements, with most countries, whereby sterling, accruing to them by the sale to her of goods or by the provision to her of services for her forces overseas or in any other way, was to be held by them in Special Accounts and was only usable for discharge of liabilities to the sterling area.[14]

Actually, Britain went even further by requiring that the dollar earnings of the members of the Commonwealth be spent only with the metropolitan center's consent. Sir Dennis Robertson's caustic comment on how this dollar pool functioned is much to the point:

> It meant that each country as a country agreed to hand over its surplus dollar earnings to Mother in exchange for sterling, and to go to Mother when it wanted extra dollars to spend. Naturally, the degree of confidence with which it exercised or presented claims on the dollar pool depended partly on its political status: the little black children who were often the best earners could be smacked on the head if they showed too great a propensity to spend dollars, while the grown-up white daughters, who were often pretty extravagant, could only be quietly reasoned with.[15]

The Payments Agreements generated during the war became weapons for getting Britain back on its feet: by setting up conditions as part of the price the colonies paid for their independence. To this day, sterling performs a reserve function for much of the sterling area, and acts as a medium for maintaining established trade relations against the erosion introduced by the competition of the United States and other countries. France, too, still uses the franc as the trading and reserve medium for many of the present or former French overseas territories.

But it is not only in times of austerity or when there is an established colonial tie that the reserve currency role acts as a lever for influence and control. Along with the United States take-over of the military responsibility of the capitalist nations in the Pacific, the economic influence over even British Commonwealth nations in that area also grows. What is happening in Australia is a useful illustration. As the flow of United States capital to Australia rises (almost half of Australia's capital inflow now comes from the United States) and trade with the United States swells, the policy issue confronting Australia is whether or not to shift from the sterling to the dollar sphere of influence, and accordingly to decide which currency to use for reserve purposes. An *Economist* (London) report comments:

The proportion of the reserves held [by Australia] in sterling has now slumped to 60 percent, from 80 percent as recently as 1960 and from all of 94 percent at the beginning of the 1950's.

Top Australians, who make the decisions about these matters, are absolutely firm about asserting Australia's loyalty to the sterling area. But public discussion about the merits of staying with sterling is no longer thought treasonable, and there has been some debate about it this year in the Australian financial press. One widely held unofficial view is that Australia might secure privileged access to the American capital market, like Canada and Japan, if it switched to the American dollar bloc. Another view is that it might be worth staying with sterling—if Britain manages to get into the Common Market.

Given the big swing that has already taken place in Australian trade and overseas borrowing it is hardly surprising that the dollar content of Australia's reserves has risen twelve-fold over the past 17 years and three-fold since 1960.[16]

The Devaluation Road

The economic advantage accruing to a country by its involvement in international banking and the use of its currency as a reserve currency is also revealed in the different roads of adjustment taken by the leading industrial powers and the economically dependent nations when imbalances crop up in international payments transactions.

Normally when a country faces a deficit in its international account—i.e., when it has to pay out more than it receives—it has recourse either to its reserves of gold and foreign currency or to borrowing from foreign bankers (or government institutions). Once these means are exhausted, a deficit country must face an internal adjustment process which reduces itself mainly to a reduction of purchases from abroad. To a lesser extent the problem is attacked by trying to expand exports— lesser because a country can more easily control imports than expand exports, especially when increasing exports often means trying to get more sales in the very moribund markets which helped create the imbalance in the first place.

Reduction in imports can sometimes be achieved by higher tariffs or by direct controls. This itself can induce a slump owing to the impact of a reduction in the import of raw materials and intermediate products. A more effective technique for a "free enterprise" economy is to take measures that will more directly induce a slump, as, for example, lowering wages to reduce consumption or restricting credit to damp down production. An economic decline will cut the demand for imports and help remove the deficit.

In most cases a persistent and severe deficit ultimately induces devaluation. Countries are inclined to take this measure only as a last resort because of the enormous dislocations usually induced thereby. Devaluation brings about a rigorously enforced adjustment through the market place: it raises the prices of imported goods, thus forcing a reduction in consumption, especially by those social classes with low incomes; it reduces the prices of exports in foreign markets, thus putting exported goods in a more competitive position.

It is especially noteworthy, in the context of the present discussion, that recourse to either severe internal adjustments or devaluation is a common feature of the economically and financially dependent nations and is much less frequent in the centers of financial power. This was so even in what economists consider the heyday of a smoothly working international system. The gold standard of the 19th century was supposed to have been an ideal market mechanism for keeping international finance on an even keel. But automatic mechanisms are more often the product of the abstractions and models created by the thought processes of economists than a representation of reality. The fact is that the so-called automatic gold standard operated through the channels of the international money market centers. The adjustments called for by the gold standard were made through the credit operations of the international bankers and the international transfers of capital made by these bankers. It is little wonder then that these operations worked to induce exchange-rate stability in the advanced countries and instability in the countries of the "periphery." In a summary analysis of the gold standard mechanism, the first two observations made by Professor Robert Triffin are:

(1) The nineteenth-century monetary mechanism succeeded, to a unique degree, in preserving exchange-rate stability—and freedom from quantitative trade and exchange restrictions—over a large part of the world.

(2) *The success, however, was limited to the more advanced countries which formed the core of the system*, and to those closely linked to them by political, as well as economic and financial ties. The exchange rates of other currencies—particularly in Latin America—fluctuated widely, and depreciated enormously, over the period. The contrast between the "core" countries and those of the "periphery" can be largely explained by the *cyclical pattern of capital movements and terms of trade, which contributed to stability in the first group, and to instability in the second.*[17] (Emphasis added.)

The point is that the main banking centers had the power and the mechanisms made available by this power to smooth out deficit problems, in contrast with the dependent countries in the capitalist world system, where financial discipline was imposed by the undiluted pressures of the market. In another context, Triffin observes:

The second factor which explains the successful functioning

of nineteenth century convertibility lies in the fact that the emergence of *major* imbalance was *prevented ex ante* by the institutional monetary and banking framework of the times, rather than *corrected ex post* by large price and income adjustments. In spite of the greater flexibility of prices and costs in the nineteenth century, I doubt very much whether a 20 or 30 percent reduction in wages, if called for to restore equilibrium in the balance of payments, would have been tolerated then any more than it would be today. The fact is that the ability of the system to correct such major maladjustments through internal price and income adaptations was rarely put to a test in the major Western countries which constituted the core of the system. Whenever it was put to such a test—as it repeatedly was in most Latin American countries— the correction was uniformly brought about by currency devaluation. . . .[18]

Financial Centers Create Their Own Money

The focal point of the network of economic relations between the great industrial powers and between these powers and the rest of the imperialist world is found in the concentrated financial power of the international money markets. As remarked earlier, the headquarters of the capitalist system is the money market. The financial power exercised through the banks and other institutions of the money market enables the industrialized nations to fend off or alleviate balance-of-payments difficulties; it is also the power which, directly or indirectly, keeps the underdeveloped countries in line as the raw materials suppliers. This does not happen as a plot or conspiracy; it results from the normal and self-defense behavior of capital.

The source of financial power, in its crudest form, is the ability to create and use money as a means of exchange and a means of payment. The creation of money used to pay for investments and to make loans arises in two banking activities: (a) the conversion of inactive into active funds, and (b) the creation of credit. The creation of money through the extension of credit (or the printing of money) is at the heart of modern banking.[19] The Brazilian bank and the Chilean bank are able to do this too. But who, outside of Brazil, other than importers of Brazilian products, wants cruzeiros? And who outside Chile, other than importers of Chilean products, wants escudos? The predicament for such countries is that they have too much of their own currency and not enough foreign currency.

Quite the reverse is the situation with respect to the diversified and large world traders in desired manufactured goods. Their money is useful internationally for several reasons: (1) It can be used for the settlement of debts, even between other foreign countries. In normal circumstances, Belgian money can be converted into French, French into British, British into United States, etc. (2) These countries produce a multitude of products wanted by the underdeveloped countries and by other industrial nations. In other words, their IOU's are usable. (3) Through colonial and sphere-of-influence arrangements, the underdeveloped countries are typically lined up in special trading channels with one or more of the major nations. Because of these trading blocs, former French territories will be able to settle balance-of-payments deficits with French francs, because a good part, if not all, of their debt outstanding is to French firms. The same is true for the spheres-of-influence of British and other financial centers.

These, then, are the reasons why the ability to create money (or, expand the money supply) by the leading industrial and financial powers is of use not only to their domestic economy but to their international economic relations as well. Because of this ability, they can (1) finance a deficit they themselves may have with a satellite nation, and (2) extend loans to satellite nations when the latter have deficits, and in the process keep them close to mother's skirts. Moreover, they can frequently ward off impending deficits in their own balance-of-payments with the rest of the world. This is done by internal credit controls, changes in interest rates, and other maneuvers by which, for example, needed capital (foreign currency or gold) can be attracted for a time from another financial center (the money market of another industrial and financial power).

The technical ins and outs of these operations cannot be spelled out here. Suffice it to say that it is through this very financial power, and the banking mechanisms through which this power is exercised, that the advanced capitalist nations are able to cope with balance-of-payments fluctuations without drastic damage to their economy; indeed, under proper conditions, they are valuable instruments for economic growth and development.

Naturally, there are limits to the creation of credit for domestic and international operations, limits that are rooted in the nature of the underlying productive capacity and the uses to which this capacity is put. When these limits are reached, whether as a result of war or preparation for war or too rapid accumulation of capital, or trying to bite off more than the country can digest, crises of various degrees set in. But even these crises are of a different order than those of the satellites. For the latter, the issue is one of survival as a dependency of a metropolitan center, under which the ruling elite can remain in power. For the metropolitan centers, the issue posed by financial crises is usually how to jockey for position with respect to other financial centers and how to maintain their existing empires: for example, Britain striving from one devaluation to another to maintain the sterling bloc, its worldwide military and naval bases, and the remnants of colonial relationships.

The Case of United States Finance

The most extravagant and unparalleled use of financial power for control over other parts of the world is that exercised by the United States since the Second World War. In every year since 1950, with the exception of a single year during the Suez Crisis, the United States balance-of-payments has been in deficit. Three main points should be fully and clearly understood in considering this persistent deficit.

(1) The deficit has been created and maintained only as part and parcel of the United States role as organizer and leader of the imperialist system. This can be seen by a quick survey of the 1967 balance-of-payments, as shown in Table 2 on the next page, the 1967 pattern being similar to that of the entire preceding era of deficits.

The facts are as simple as they can be. The deficit is used to finance:

• Military expenditures—for the war in Vietnam and to maintain air, naval, and infantry forces over a large section of the globe. (This does not, of course, include all such expendi-

TABLE 2
U.S. BALANCE OF PAYMENTS SUMMARY: 1967
(billions of $)

Purpose	*Money Received From Abroad*	*Money Going Abroad*
Balance on exports and imports of goods and services	+ $7.9	
Private and Government remittances [a]		− $1.2
Military expenditures, net		− 3.1
Military assistance and economic aid		− 4.0
Private capital investment		− 3.5
Total	+ $7.9	− $11.8

(a) Gifts sent abroad by United States nationals; payments by the government to individuals abroad, such as social security payments to persons living abroad.

Source: *Survey of Current Business,* June 1968.

tures, only that part which results in transferring dollars abroad.)

• Military assistance and economic aid: the instruments used for exercising United States control over other nations.

• Investment by United States industry and finance in foreign countries.

(2) The deficit is financed by the expansion of the supply of United States dollars via the credit created by the government and by banks. Professor James Tobin, former member of the President's Council of Economic Advisors, testified in 1963 before a Congressional committee as follows:

Under the reserve currency system properly functioning, the initial beneficiary of an increase in the supply of international money is obviously the reserve currency itself. It is pleasant to have a mint or printing press in one's backyard, and the gold exchange standard gave us, no less than South Africa, this privilege. We were able to run deficits in our balance of payments for 10 years because our IOU's were generally acceptable as money.[20]

(3) We can finance the deficit over so long a period because the United States is the world banker and the rest of the capitalist world has been willing (though chafing at the bit, lately) to hold dollars as a reserve asset.

The case was clearly summarized by the then Secretary of the Treasury C. Douglas Dillon, when asked by Senator Javits what benefits the United States obtains from being the world's banker. Mr. Dillon declared that

we have a very real benefit in that we have been allowed to finance our deficits through increased foreign holdings of dollars. If we had not been a reserve currency, if we had not been a world banker, this would not have happened. It would have been the same situation as other countries face; as soon as we got into deficit we would have had to balance our accounts one way or another even though it meant restricting imports, as Canada had to do last year, or cutting back our military expenditures much more drastically than our security would warrant. . . . I would say that is the chief area of benefit although there is one other very important one and that is that somebody had to be the world banker and provide this extra international liquidity. It has been the United States, which is proper, because we are the most powerful financial country and we had the most powerful currency.[21]

The former Under Secretary of the Treasury for Monetary Affairs adds another reason for the cooperation of other countries, in addition to the financial power of the United States:

Moreover, the political stability and enormous economic and military strength of the United States have also increased the desirability of keeping balances here rather than in any other country in the world.[22]

Of course, any other country in the world that tried handling as big a deficit as that of the United States for even a few years, let alone 18 years, would be in for a major depression along with a drastic reduction in the country's living standards. But then no other country would incur such deficits for such noble purposes.

Witness the exchange between Senator Proxmire and Under Secretary of the Treasury Roosa at a Congressional hearing:

Senator Proxmire. If we had no domestic considerations, if we were not also burdened with world leadership as the world banker, the classic, ideal and still effective way to bring about balance in our international payments would be an austerity program, I presume.

Secretary Roosa. Yes.

Senator Proxmire. In other words, a program that would be deflationary?

Secretary Roosa. Yes.

Senator Proxmire. Drive our prices down so that we can sell abroad, drive our wages down, reduce federal spending sharply?

Secretary Roosa. Yes.

Senator Proxmire. Increase taxes, hike interest rates, and so forth?

Secretary Roosa. Yes.

Senator Proxmire. Obviously we can do none of these things because that would be disastrous domestically and that would also contribute to an international depression?

Secretary Roosa. Yes.[23]

This exchange followed upon Under Secretary Roosa's presentation in a formal statement, which summarizes the case in more orderly fashion. If we had not been a world banker, he said,

we might have been forced long ago to cut down our imports (perhaps through deflation of our economy), reduce materially our foreign investments, income from which make a substantial contribution to our current balance of payments, and curtail, perhaps sharply, our military and economic assistance to our friends and allies. Had we taken these steps, our customers abroad would have sharply reduced their purchases in this country and we would now be confronted with discriminatory policies against the dollar in most countries of the world. Instead of the rapid growth of world trade, we would have witnessed stagnation that would have been harmful to our own prosperity and to that of the whole free world.[24]

Here then is the synthesis of today's imperialist network of international relations. The United States as leader has the economic power to invade the industry and markets of its chief trading partners and politico-military allies. It has the resources to maintain a dominant world military position. It can carry on foreign aid, invest in and lend to the underdeveloped countries, thus tying them closer to the United States through the resulting financial dependency of these countries. All of this, plus the maintenance of prosperity and fending off depressions, is made feasible because of the position of the United States as the world banker and of the dollar as the world reserve currency. And it can be the world banker and supply the reserve currency, because of the cooperation its military and economic strength commands among the other industrialized nations.

And, necessarily, within the United States this is accompanied by "an inexorable entanglement of private business with foreign policy."[25]

The cooperation of the other industrial nations is not the fruit of pure wisdom. It came at a time when these countries had little choice. Roosa's comment on this is noteworthy:

> The dollar reached its pre-eminent position, of course, during and immediately following World War II when there was in reality no other currency available to play a world role and when so much of our governmental assistance was made available in freely usable dollars. By the time some of the European countries achieved convertibility and large surpluses, the dollar was deeply entrenched in the usages of trade and payments throughout the world. . . . And so long as the American economy remains committed to principles of market freedom, there will be American banks and other financial institutions here eagerly seeking to perform the banking functions identified with the dollar's role as the vehicle currency. From that role, in my view, we cannot in practice withdraw, short of a revolutionary change in our entire economic structure.[26]

The central bankers of the other imperialist centers are as well aware as Mr. Roosa, now a partner of Brown Brothers Harriman and Company, of the "revolutionary" implications to the United States economic structure and consequently to the rest of the capitalist world of a basic departure from the present international monetary system. What is at stake here is not mere adjustments in the credit mechanism of the International Monetary Fund—the kind of monetary reforms now being introduced and considered—but the central issue of the dollar as the international currency. At the same time, the partners of the United States in this monetary system have their own necks to protect and their own competitive interests to pursue. The source of fear of the central bankers of other nations is traceable to the ordinary common sense of international banking, and is simply summarized in the data shown in Table 3.

What this table shows is the simultaneous movement in opposite directions of gold reserves and dollar obligations to foreigners: the rapid decline of United States gold reserves and accumulation of dollar holdings by foreigners. At the end of May 1968, the liquid dollar assets held by foreigners were almost three times the gold held by the United States. In case of a "run on the bank"—if all foreigners who own dollars should over a short period ask the United States to make good on its paper IOU's, the United States would be some $20 billion short of the universally acceptable means of payment, gold.

The magnitude of the difference between gold reserves and dollar obligations to foreigners is an important indicator of the financial limits of U.S. external activities. That such limits exist was made more apparent as the United States balance-of-payments deficits kept mounting from year to year, despite the opposition of other money centers: the arrogance

TABLE 3

U.S. GOLD RESERVES VS. DOLLAR LIABILITIES TO FOREIGNERS
(billions of $)

End of	Gold Reserves of the United States	Dollar Assets Held by Foreigners [a]
1955	21.8	11.7
1960	17.8	18.7
May 1968	10.7	31.5

(a) The 1960 and 1968 data are liquid liabilities of the United States to other governments and to foreign banks and other foreign institutions and businessmen. The 1955 data are short-term liabilities and do not include United States government bonds held by foreigners. This lack of comparability does not negate the point made here; a comparable figure for 1955 would probably be somewhat higher than $11.7 billion, but not by more than 10 percent. Note that the data on dollar holdings are considerably in excess of those shown in Table 1. The latter include only dollar holdings of foreign governments and their central banks. The data shown here are the total liquid dollar obligations to foreigners, including banks, other financial institutions and businessmen.

Source: United States Bureau of the Census, *Statistical Abstract 1966,* Washington, D.C., 1967, and *Federal Reserve Bulletin,* August 1968.

of United States foreign military and economic operations was matched by the arrogance of its international financial practice. Shaken from time to time by gold and currency speculators on European exchanges, the United States continues its financial practices, with increasing limitations, by relying ultimately on the voluntary and involuntary cooperation of the central bankers of other nations.

Most of the nations in the imperialist network have no alternative: as creditors of the United States government and banks they must submit to being members of what is virtually the dollar bloc. The more independent metropolitan centers, however, do have some options. Almost half of the dollar obligations to foreigners are concentrated in six nations: Britain, Japan, France, West Germany, Italy, and Switzerland. They therefore have the weapons with which to pressure the United States. Nevertheless, under present circumstances, their options are limited. Their interests are aligned with the United States to the extent that United States military and economic power is used to secure the imperialist system and push back, if possible, the borders of the non-imperialist world. At the same time they are worried about their own skin and the competitive threat of United States business and finance. Hence, the jockeying for power that does take place operates within the limits of present international monetary arrangements. It is important always to keep in mind that at the heart of the conflicts of international finance is a struggle over *power*. This was well pointed out by Eugene A. Birnbaum, senior economist for Standard Oil Company (New Jersey):

> We may ask why, after a hundred years of internal monetary conferences, men still have not resolved their differences. The answer lies in one word—*power*. That is what one hundred years of international monetary conferences have been about. The 22nd meeting of the International Monetary Fund held at Rio, where a new facility for creating international liquidity was recommended, is no exception to this general rule.[27]

Maneuvers over reforms in the international money system are only one form of the power struggle. The tensions within the centers of imperialist power show up in many ways. Within the dominant business circles of the other industrial powers are groups whose immediate business interests are tied up with those of the United States, while others see their profit opportunities shrinking in the face of United States expansion. Both as a self-defense measure against United States expansion and because of the inner dynamics of their own economies, foreign business firms and banks are engaging in their own outward expansion via export of capital, international banking, and the use of economic and military aid by their governments in underdeveloped nations.

At work are three main vectors: (1) centripetal forces binding the main financial centers with the United States for the preservation of the imperialist network; (2) centrifugal forces, stimulated by profit competition, seeking special advantages as weak spots in United States operations show up; and (3) "vertical cohesion," with each imperialist center trying to consolidate the economic and financial ties with their colonial and sphere-of-influence areas.

NOTES

1. Thomas Balogh, *Unequal Partners,* Oxford, England, 1963, Vol. II, p. 25.
2. Lord Comer, Speech at Guildhall, Bank of England *Quarterly Bulletin,* March 1966, pp. 51-52.
3. T. M. Farley, *The "Edge Act" and United States International Banking and Finance,* New York, Brown Brothers & Harriman & Co., May 1962, p. 5.
4. Thomas W. Lamont, "The Effect of the War on America's Financial Position," in The American Academy of Political and Social Science, *The Annals,* July 1915, pp. 106-112.
5. *Ibid.,* pp. 108-109.
6. *Ibid.,* p. 112.
7. William Woodruff, *Impact of Western Man, A Study of Europe's Role in the World Economy 1750-1960,* London, 1966, p. 277.
8. E. Preobrazhensky, *The New Economics,* Oxford, England, 1965, p. 155. This book merits more attention by students. For the subject discussed here, see the entire section, pp. 150-160.
9. Henry G. Aubrey, *The Dollar in World Affairs, An Essay in International Financial Policy,* New York, 1964, p. 109.
10. In this simplified explanation, we are ignoring capital movements. While the balance of payments problem cannot be properly analyzed without taking capital movements into account, the main issues can be explained for the present purpose by referring merely to the balance of goods and services.
11. *New York Times,* March 18, 1967.
12. For a description of the British practice in keeping control over its colonies, both before and after independence, as applied to Ghana, see Bob Fitch and Mary Oppenheimer, *Ghana: End of an Illusion,* New York, Monthly Review Press, 1966, pp. 42-47. For a more general treatment applied to African nations, before and after independence, see Thomas Balogh, *The Economics of Poverty,* London, 1966, Chapter 2, "The Mechanism of Neo-Imperialism."
13. R. F. Harrod, *The Pound Sterling,* Princeton Essays in International

Finance, No. 13, Princeton, February 1952, p. 9.

14. R. F. Harrod, *International Economics,* Cambridge, England, 1957, pp. 99-100.

15. Sir Dennis Robertson, *Britain in the World Economy,* London, 1954, p. 39, as quoted in Fitch and Oppenheimer, *op. cit.,* p. 46. A significant sidelight on this question became manifest when the United States, the richest and most powerful country, insisted on the elimination of the trade competition involved in the "sterling area" and the "dollar pool" as a condition for giving financial aid to war devastated Britain. Article 7 of the Financial Agreement Between the Government of the United States and the United Kingdom, December 6, 1945, reads: "The Government of the United Kingdom will complete arrangements as early as practicable and in any case not later than one year after the effective date of this Agreement . . . under which . . . the sterling receipts from current transactions of all sterling area countries . . . will be freely available for current transactions in any currency area without discrimination; with the result that any discrimination arising from the so-called sterling area dollar pool will be entirely removed and that each member of the sterling area will have its current sterling and dollar receipts at its free disposition for current transactions anywhere." (The Agreement is reprinted as an appendix to Richard N. Gardner, *Sterling-Dollar Diplomacy,* Oxford, England, 1956.)

16. *The Economist,* October 7, 1967, p. 89.

17. Robert Triffin, *The Evolution of the International Monetary System: Historical Reappraisal and Future Perspectives,* Princeton Studies in International Finance, No. 12, Princeton, 1964, p. 9.

18. Robert Triffin, *Gold and the Dollar Crisis,* New Haven, 1961, p. 27.

19. This is not the place to undertake an explanation of the technical aspects of credit and money expansion. The interested reader should consult a standard textbook on money and credit. An elementary introduction to this subject may be found in Peter L. Bernstein, *Primer on Money, Banking, and Gold,* New York, 1965.

20. Joint Economic Committee of the Congress of the United States, *Hearings on The Monetary System: Functioning and Possible Reform,* Washington, D.C., 1963, Part 3, p. 551.

21. Joint Economic Committee of the Congress of the United States, *Hearings on the United States Balance of Payments,* Washington, D.C., 1963, Part I, pp. 83-84. The reference that "somebody had to be the world's banker" has a familiar ring. Yet the way Secretary Dillon phrases his comments is an interesting euphemism. Apparently he cannot think of a capitalist world without some form of imperialist domination or of an economic order without capitalism.

22. Robert V. Roosa, *Monetary Reform for the World Economy,* New York, 1965, p. 9.

23. Same as footnote 21, p. 135.

24. *Ibid.,* p. 147.

25. From a report published under the auspices of the Council of Foreign Relations, Henry G. Aubrey, *op. cit.,* p. 15.

26. Robert V. Roosa, *op. cit.,* pp. 23-24.

27. Eugene A. Birnbaum, *Gold and the International Monetary System: An Orderly Reform,* Princeton Essays in International Finance No.

66, Princeton, April 1968, p. 2. Mr. Birnbaum does make an exception to this generalization—the Bretton Woods conference. However, in the light of subsequent history, one can question whether the facade of internationalist spirit at this conference did not cover up a real power struggle.

For an analysis of some of the underlying issues in the struggles over the international monetary system, see "Weak Reeds and Class Enemies" and "Gold, Dollars, and Empire," above, pp. 149-157 and 158-166; and the following articles in the December 1966 issue of *Monthly Review*: David Michaels, "The Growing Financial Crisis in the Capitalistic World"; Jacob Morris, "The Balance of Payments Crises."

The analysis of this question made by Paul M. Sweezy and Leo Huberman ("Weak Reeds and Class Enemies" mentioned above) stimulated a critical reply by Professor Charles P. Kindleberger, of M.I.T.; and a special Princeton Essay on International Finance (No. 61, August 1967, *The Politics of International Money and World Language*) was devoted to this reply. His argument is concerned with demonstrating that the international status of the dollar ("The dollar is the world unit of account—the standard in which foreign exchange reserves, agricultural prices in the Common Market, contributions to the United Nations budget, and a host of other international monetary units are measured." p. 2) is needed for efficiency. "My reason for wanting to keep the dollar-exchange standard is efficiency." (p. 4) Efficiency for what? This the good professor sees purely in terms of the efficiency of capital transfer and of carrying on existing trade relations. To be sure, the dollar-exchange system is a truly efficient device—especially for mobilizing the resources of the world capital markets to finance the war of devastation against the people of Vietnam.

Modern Reader Paperbacks